SIKHS IN LATIN AMERICA

SIKHS IN LATIN AMERICA

Travels among the Sikh Diaspora

SWARN SINGH KAHLON

A SIKH GLOBAL VILLAGE INITIATIVE
CHANDIGARH

MANOHAR
2012

First published 2012

ISBN 978-81-7304-938-5

Published by
Ajay Kumar Jain *for*
Manohar Publishers & Distributors
4753/23 Ansari Road, Daryaganj
New Delhi 110 002

Typeset by
Kohli Print
Delhi 110 051

Printed at
Salasar Imaging Systems
Delhi 110 035

Contents

Preface

The book is an account of the Latin American Sikh communities based on travels undertaken by the author over a period of two years. Essentially, it is the effort of a corporate executive who found it a very enriching experience to meet Sikh migrants during his travels. As he talked to and listened to the varied experiences of many old and young and recent Sikh migrants in various locations, he felt it worth sharing with a wider audience. The narrative retains both the flavour of a travelogue as well field study covering a large number of interviews. The book has no pretensions of being scholarly but rather is an attempt to draw attention of serious scholars and researchers for further detailed investigation into these subjects.

My only claim to originality is to introduce Latin America as part of the Sikh diaspora and worthy of further study. In

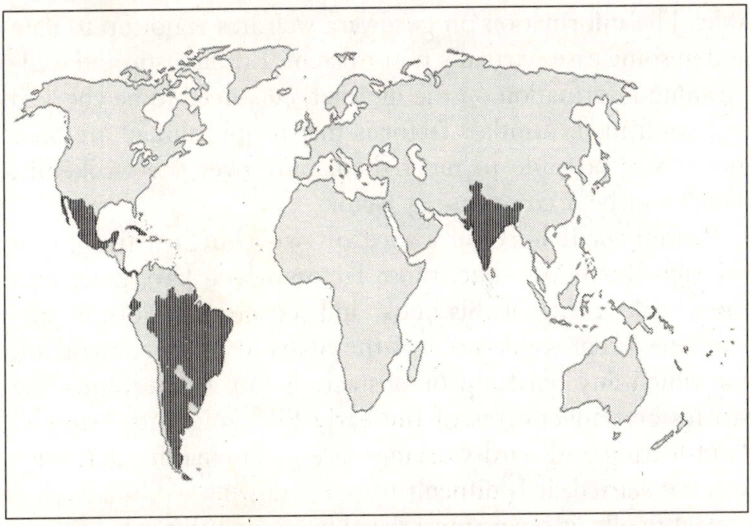

Figure 1: India to Latin America—Countries visited by the author.

any study of Sikh diaspora, Latin America has been grossly neglected. I have made a beginning, though I am also aware that I have only been able to scratch the surface and hence my observations are only an introduction and need detailed further studies by others with more time and resources.

As such, this study fills a gap within the Sikh diasporic studies. There are many other such gaps. Interest in Sikh migration to Europe has thrown up considerable research in recent years, but it still needs extension to East European countries. Similarly, while the Far East has received considerable attention from scholars, the Pacific Islands, and South and West African countries have been largely left out.

My travels, though expensive, have been worth the while as I met some interesting people belonging to the Sikh diaspora. The love and affection showered on me by them was overwhelming. Some immigrants were initially reluctant to meet me, especially those belonging to the second and third generation but it also included a few from the first generation too. To locate a Sikh in these far-flung lands took considerable efforts and resources. Their contacts are not easily available. The information on gurdwara websites is not up to date and in some cases virtually non-existent. Enthusiastic and well-meaning information on the internet, etc., need to be checked and confirmed. Another factor is that people abroad are busy and it was possible to meet them only over the weekends, which can be a constraining factor.

Readers will become aware of two things while going through this book—one, those factors which have gone into the actual writing of this book, and second and more important, the irrepressible urge of the Sikhs to improve their lot, for which any hardship or obstacle is not a deterrent. The stories and adventures of the early Sikh migrants—simple, God-fearing and hard working—are so fascinating that once you get started, it is difficult to put it down.

And finally, it seems most frivolous to mention my own experience of the various irritants and complexities involved with regard to ticketing, visas, high cost of travel, etc. This in spite of the fact that the present-day traveller like me is equipped with credit cards, laptop, mobile phone, and friends and relatives in several countries overseas. If I, or my family, in spite of the fact of having prior contacts in countries to be visited and with wide and varied experience of overseas travel of 50–60 times, did not find it easy how the migrants of that era must have managed. I would urge readers to imagine the uncertainties and anxieties ahead for the migrant of that era, and focus on the difficulties, challenges and possible humiliations they must have faced. Imagine, some of them walked thousands of kilometres in difficult terrain, where the only guide for direction to their destination was a railway track, say from Bolivia to Argentina (consult a map or go to Google Earth to fully understand the dimension of the venture), crossing borders, and that too at times surreptitiously to avoid border check-posts, in their strange Indian garments along with a turban. Oh, my brave hearts—I salute you! As I write it makes me cry. This study is to honour all these people who are my heroes!

INTERNATIONAL CONFERENCES ATTENDED

In my endeavour to highlight the role of Latin American Sikhs as part of the worldwide Sikh diaspora, I was previleged to attend several international conferences where in some cases I presented my findings in progress. I am grateful to organisers of these seminars, which included the following. *Sikhs in Multicultural Southeast Asia*, an international conference held at Institute of Southeast Asian Studies, Singapore, May 2008; *Sikhism in Global Context*, an international conference held at University of California, Riverside, December 2008; *What's Happening to Sikh Ethno-nationalism*? held by the University of Birmingham, May 2009; Punjab Research Group's joint Seminar with Punjabi University, Patiala, December 2009; *Sikholars Conference* held at Stanford University, February 2010; *Migration, Mobility and Multiple Affiliations: Punjabis in Trans-*

national World, an international conference held at Centre for Development Studies, Trivandrum, Kerala, March 2010, *Sikhs in Europe*, workshop held at University of Lund, June 2010. In addition I participated in three workshops at Centre for Research in Rural and Industrial Development, Chandigarh during 2008–9 all connected with migration from Punjab to overseas countries.

In preparing this manuscript, I am indebted to several people. In learning about the Sikh diaspora, I have gained many insights from talks with several scholars working in this field. I am particularly grateful to Dr Darshan S. Tatla for many suggestions and his dedicated hard work in improving the contents of this book. Above all, I remain grateful to all the people I met and interviewed during my travels. They all deserve my heartfelt thanks.

505, Sector 18-B SWARN SINGH KAHLON
Chandigarh website: www.sikhglobalvillage.com
March 2011 e-mail: swarnsk@gmail.com

Introduction

This book breaks fresh ground in completing the Sikh diaspora map. While the focus of most scholastic works has been to study those countries to which the Sikhs have migrated in significant numbers, there is limited interest in countries where the Sikhs are present in relatively small numbers. The significance of such a study goes beyond completing the diaspora map. The dynamics of such communities with small numbers is different from that prevalent in countries where there is a large number of Sikh migrants. Assimilation and marriage to locals of the country of their settlement is more prevalent and has led to (especially among the second and subsequent generations) even forgetting their connection to their forefathers' homeland, except perhaps as a matter of curiosity.

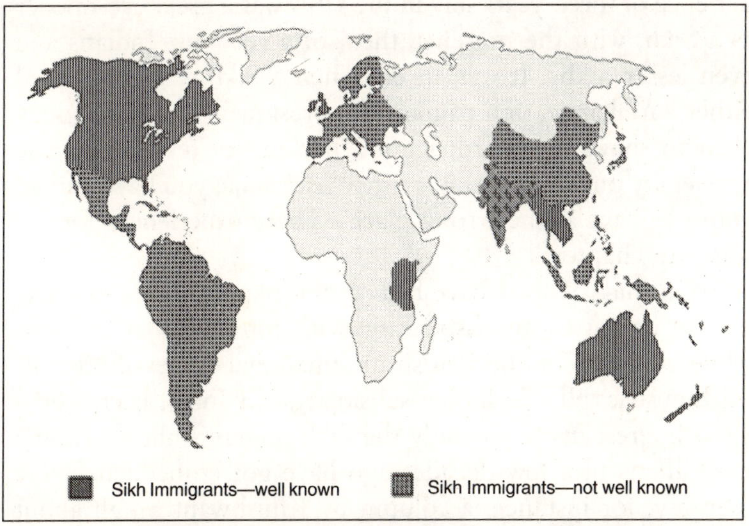

Figure 2: Sikh Diaspora Map highlighting countries needing study (a) Sikh Immigration–well known (b) Sikh immigration not well known.

In most Latin American countries, many Singhs of the third generation and some even of the second generation do not know the significance of their 'Singh' surname. A study of such migrants raises entirely different issues in terms of social, cultural, religious, historical aspects and motivations which have been ignored so far in the study of the Sikh diaspora. More effort is needed in this hitherto unexplored area. Such a study might not attract interest and financial resources because of the numbers being not significant. But in order to comprehensively cover the Sikh diaspora the importance of such a study cannot be ignored. It is hoped that this study would generate an interest, an awareness and more importantly, create a genuine challenge for scholars to undertake more detailed studies in this area.

BACKGROUND OF THE STUDY

I have been globetrotting since the late 1950s when I went to the USA for higher studies and work experience. My first experience of three-years stay in the USA was a great eye-opener as a Sikh, with the presence then, of a very few Indians and even lesser Sikhs. It was an era when a Sikh was considered either a Maharaja, or a pauper who presumably had no money even to shave his beard. I got a parking ticket once at the University on which it was written 'Maharaja, you have parked your elephant at the wrong place'. These experiences form a separate chapter.

From mid-1960s, I have had several opportunities to travel abroad owing to my association with international business while working for the British multinational Imperial Chemical Industries PLC's, Indian subsidiary, ICI India. It created a great interest in me to study the Sikh migrants abroad. Some news items of a few decades ago have got embedded in my memory; for instance, a column by Khushwant Singh about his visit to Fiji where he encountered a Sikh customs officer who, as a welcome gesture, handed over to him a few dollars, a precious commodity for Indians those days.

An article in the *Times of India* mentions that one of its correspondents visiting Mexico to study the Indian Sikh farmers there was advised to meet a certain ranch owner, Senor Sanchos. It turned out that Sanchos was none other than a flowing white-bearded Sucha Singh. When greeted by the correspondent with a 'Sat Siri Akal', the old man's eyes had filled with tears as he mentioned later that he had not heard this greeting for a long time. Soon thereafter drives in his clean shaven son with a blonde in a convertible. The contrast was startling.

Several other experiences, detailed later in the article published in the *Indian Express*, New York edition, provided further impetus in pursuing this subject. Some personal experiences too added to the interest in the subject. On landing in New York City as a student, in the autumn of 1958, an American cab driver greeted me with 'Sat Siri Akal'. He was a veteran of Second World War from Kolkata. Again late at night once, in the early 1970s on landing in Hamburg, my wife and I were helped in a desperate situation of being without a hotel booking at the height of the tourist season by a Middle Eastern gentleman. He even carried our heavy bags (Indians love to travel with large suitcases) just because one of his friends was a Sikh. The turban has its pluses and minuses. My family's international connections are wide ranging—son Gurtaj is married to Mila, an European; daughter Mini Maninder has settled in the USA with husband, Raj Patel who is a British (now American) Indian author, and my wife Livleen's passion is rivers and mountains which criss-cross national boundaries.

With such experiences, a curiosity grew in me to know more about these migrants. It became a sort of hobby—expensive but very rewarding and exciting. Now I travel frequently to study the Sikh diaspora. I visited Argentina, Bolivia and Brazil in the mid-2005 and Belize, Mexico, Cuba, Panama and Ecuador in 2006. More visits are planned in an effort to fill the gaps in the study of Sikh migration covering hitherto ignored countries of Sikh settlements. Some of the countries which fascinate me for further study are the Pacific Islands, and western and eastern Europe including Iceland, and Greenland which I am told, have some Sikh immigrants.

EARLY EFFORTS

Before homing onto the present area of study, I had travelled extensively to meet Sikh scholars in the UK (Shinder Thandi, Eleanor Nesbitt), the USA (Pashaura Singh, Arthur Helweg, Arvinder Pal Mandair) and Singapore (Bhajan Singh) and others. It was very tempting to research Sikhs in these countries as immigrants were comparatively easily available for being interviewed. There was abundant availability of contacts, sources of information, data, and references for detailed investigation of various aspects of the diaspora. Churning out another book on the success stories of Sikh immigrants (probably also an attractive proposition financially), was not much of a challenge. So my canvas had to be wider and different. And infinitely more interesting as it involved visiting some exotic locations.

My earlier visits abroad were helpful in deciding as to what to focus upon. As a result of those travels, I wrote an article coining a phrase 'Sikh Global Village' (published in the *Indian Express*, New York City, 1998). It would be relevant to quote from the same as it was the beginning of my involvement with the Sikh diaspora and entry into a totally new field of endeavour, viz., writing.

THE SIKH GLOBAL VILLAGE

At the crowded airport of Rio de Janeiro, Gurtaj was making his way towards the exit, excited by the prospect of spending a few days in the most happening capital in the Southern world. It was hard not to notice him. A young guy wearing a turban and a thick beard was not a common sight in Brazil. He was accepting the glances with a smile, but got worried when a man ran to him with a mobile phone in his outstretched hand, requesting him to speak to his friend. His friend was a Sikh living in Brazil and he hadn't spoken to a fellow Sikh for years. In another story, a Sikh student in the US in the late fifties was stunned by the outburst of joy he provoked in an unknown man who stopped him in the street and invited him home for dinner. Several years back in Iraq, another Sikh had loaned to this man some money, without even asking him his address. The distinctive turban and beard sets apart a Sikh as a symbol of Indian identity. At any airport where the Indians have to change flights, watch how an old Gujarati lady with little knowledge of English heads towards a Sikh for help and guidance as they are sure that he, being an Indian, would be helpful.

Other stories about these somehow mysterious beturbaned people take us many years back. A man, probably the first Sikh immigrant in Japan, arrived there from Basra via Moscow and Vladivostok by train with no knowledge of Russian or Japanese languages, with meager resources and not knowing what will happen next. In a more contemporary story, an Indian American took his students to Norway only to discover that the northernmost lighthouse was being run by a Punjabi, probably a Sikh. Then there is the saga of the Sikhs in Argentina. In the provinces of Salta, Tucuman, and Santa Fe, there are approximately 1000 people of Indian origin. According to documents, the earliest Indian migrants are reported to have come to Argentina around 1908 and did not go back. Their children and grandchildren are now almost totally integrated in the local community. Several of them speak only Spanish, but others have retained their Indian links, speak Punjabi and visit India. In a town called Rosario de la Frontera, they have built a small gurdwara-cum-community center. One has also heard legends about the generosity of the Sikh Immigrants in Fiji from an article by Khushwant Singh or about these who migrated to Mexico or the Pacific Islands. These settlements look so exotic now, but imagine the difficulties these earlier immigrants must have faced. In the old days for a Punjabi to go to Bombay was almost an expedition, what to talk of going overseas!

This kind of stories and historical facts excited my imagination to write about Sikh immigrants and their families. How did they adapt? What do they tell their children about their distant homeland? Are they happy and what have they achieved? Hoping that my study will grow into a book on Sikh immigrants, I am searching for compatriots who recognize themselves in these stories or have more amazing ones to tell. I am particularly interested in Sikh immigration in far off places such as the Pacific Islands, Africa, South America, etc. Starting from the roots, I would like to draw the Sikhs family tree spread throughout the world.

EARLY SIKH IMMIGRANTS

The early Sikh immigrants are heroes in more ways than one. As one tries to go back to the time when they were leaving their villages more than hundred years ago, one has more questions than answers. One is unable to fathom how and from where they got information way back in the end of the nineteenth century (with no newspapers, maps, radio, and travel guide books) about the existence of some of the countries they migrated to. How did they get to know which countries were more prosperous and thereby to be targeted as the preferred destination? One is intrigued as to how they got information on routes, shipping schedules, fares, etc., or what clothes and other things to pack and carry. They had probably no knowledge whether Punjabi food would be available in the country they were migrating to. Could they have imagined a life without their '*saag*, *roti* and *lassi*'. They had no proficiency in foreign languages—not even working knowledge of English. They would have had little money when they left and whatever they had was in Indian rupees. There were no Foreign Exchange kiosks or Wells Fargo outlets in Doaba in the late nineteenth century or for that matter in early twentieth century.

How did they bid farewell to their loved ones because they did not have a clue as to where they were heading for or whether they would ever return. Theirs was a journey into the unknown. The only reassuring spirit they carried with them was '*Chardi Kala*' and '*Jo Bole So Nihal—Sat Siri Akal*'.

Would they ever hear these words again or would they be humming these only to themselves, all alone in those far off lands? Had they even seen a map leave alone known the distances involved and the ramifications of where they were heading for? How could they allow their son, father or husband to go to a place about which one knew next to nothing? The more one thinks about these things the more one wonders about these brave souls. It may appear as all mundane today but each aspect small or big must have loomed very large—in fact, forbidding and fearsome at the time—considering that most of them would not have ventured beyond a few miles from their village in Punjab. For them to decide to go to the other side of the globe, to say Argentina in the Southern hemisphere, where even the seasons are topsy-turvy, must have required enormous courage.

GLOBALIZATION, TRANSNATIONALISM AND CONTEMPORARY TRAVEL WOES

Travel might have become easy today, but for Indians it is rather the other way around. No matter what the country is, there are many hurdles to clear for them. At times smaller the country, more the fuss. The embassies are suspicious of a prospective tourist to a not-on-the-Indian-tourist circuit destination. South America falls in this category. Once, annoyed by an Embassy's repeated questioning regarding purpose of my visit, I perforce had to say, 'To spend money!' Visa was immediately issued. It is embarrassing and somewhat demeaning to establish financial credibility and to make the Consulates believe that you are not going to settle down in their country. In some cases issue of visa takes 6–8 weeks, as tourist visas are to be cleared by their governments' Home Ministry first. Each country wants to see a confirmed air ticket and hotel booking. So planning a trip involving a number of countries can be nightmarish in terms of time and effort, not to mention money. Some countries require day-to-day travel plan. To get itineraries worked out, considering all these problems combined with the not-so-experienced travel agents in India for such out-of-routine destinations, adds to the traveller's woes. Business visas are faster and easier to get—I had hitherto travelled on business where the sponsor's invitation was available and I had faced no such problems. I had assumed that a tourist visa would be easier to get as most countries want to promote tourism. May be this is the downside for Indians due to illegal migration. Only a few embassies were generous and welcoming. Bolivia does not have a Consulate in India and the visa had to be obtained from Argentina. The out of the way help of the Bolivian Consulate is detailed later under 'Travel Nuggets'. Poor people and poor countries are more welcoming. Is there a moral in this story? Despite all these irritants, it was well worth the effort but is not recommended for the fainthearted.

The illegal migration of Sikhs (and other communities also now indulge) has had its adverse impact on Sikhs wanting to travel abroad on business or otherwise. I am sure this is true even for the genuine immigrant. I wonder how recent migrants (*kabootars*) get visas whereas I found the process to be cumbersome and annoying, despite having long-term visas for the UK and the USA, a sound financial position, and a passport (till now 23rd) showing numerous visas stamped on it.

As it turns out, my study relates to Singhs in general rather than being confined to Sikhs, whichever way one may wish to define a Sikh. There is a genuine problem as to how to define a Sikh. I have taken a broader, all-encompassing view. Turban wearing Sikhs are a rarity, especially in countries where their total number is small. Visits to these countries provide a different viewpoint from the Sikh settlers in countries/locales where there is a relatively larger concentration of Sikhs. There are issues pertaining to Sikhs and Sikhi which get thrown up in such visits.

APPROACH AND COVERAGE

I should emphasize, the book is more of a travelogue than a scholarly monograph. However, both field studies and research are the basic tools used. The geographical coverage of field studies is far more extensive as compared to other diaspora studies. Interviews with the various persons met are given in detail so that the reader gets a varied and broad idea of the history of migration of the Sikhs to these places. How and why the Sikhs migrated, the issues and problems they faced, and how they adapted to a new society especially when the locale is far away from their homeland, in this case, the Punjab and where their numbers are limited. In addition the financial challenges faced especially by the first generation immigrants, their efforts to keep linkages with Sikhi and Punjab even when married locally generally to Catholic wives, are also discussed. I have drawn my conclusions but it is more appropriate to take these as mere observations. Each interview and case study has some common elements. On the other hand, almost every interview provides some new aspect, which to a researcher or discerning reader, would provide a different dimension to the diaspora issues. When these observations are considered in totality, they help to form a broader profile of the diaspora.

Time was a major constraint in my travels. But looking back, I feel satisfied that I could cover such a broad geographic area in a short time, including a few indulgences in touristic forays. I have given the names of villages in Punjab where the interviewee migrants came from, to make it easier for readers or researchers to follow up.

The chapters on country profiles form the core of the book. I have also included notes from my travel diary, which I must admit was not written daily. More interestingly, I have included a few travel nuggets which might be useful. Some of these might ring a familiar note for the readers who are frequent travellers. These incidents are the small little things of which the memories of travel are made of, good or bad; annoying or pleasant.

In order to put the Sikh migration in broader perspective, I have also included some observations on Indian migration. This is to help readers to better understand how and where Sikh migration fits in. Following the same logic, it was considered desirable to summarize the total Sikh migration scenario, so that readers get a better perspective of Sikh migration to Latin America. A chapter 'Sikh in the USA 50 Years Ago' is included to provide a contrast to the present scenario.

This book also provides a brief outline of each Latin American country along with some excerpts from Government of India's High Power Committee's Report on the Indian diaspora to provide a broad canvas.

Some issues affecting and concerning Sikh immigrants directly or indirectly, have also been included. Some of these aspects constantly impinge on the Sikh psyche, at least on mine. The attitude towards these issues of the Sikh diaspora in turn influences the Sikhs in India.

It was considered relevant to discuss 'who is a Sikh?' and the issue of Sikh identity. Other topics which are analysed are the role of gurdwaras, turban and other Sikh symbols and finally the Punjab-centricity of the Sikh community. The study also touches upon economic, cultural and political aspects which affect the Sikhs. These are not extensive expositions but an essential reminder of major concerns.

While reading about Indian migration scene, and during overseas travel as well, I have noticed many commonalities amongst immigrants from various communities and parts of India. There are, however, some broader differences also. I thought it would be interesting to briefly cover various subdiasporas of India purely as a matter of general interest. The comments are observational taken from internet searches and are included just to give a flavour of the relative features.

At the end of this book there are details of the methodology I have followed in obtaining data and information on Latin

American Sikhs. I have also included there relevant news-clippings and some photographs including passport transparencies. Photographs speak more than words. It is useful to remind that the British Library in London, India Office Section, is indeed a treasure house of such documents which future researchers might want to examine. I have included some rare information discovered from this library which otherwise would not have given the full story of Sikh migration to Brazil.

This study also briefly covers the Ghadar movement, as it is not appreciated that although the movement was started in the USA, it had its supporters amongst the Latin American Sikhs too. This can be gleaned through the writings of 'Ghadari Babas' who provide a few written records of this connection as seen in Bilga (2004).

The present study embraces twentieth-century migration along with references on late nineteenth-century sojourners. As such this study gives far more historical information on early Indian migration than the Government of India's High Level Committee has provided. A possible reason is that the Indian Embassies have information based on who walks into the Embassy. I have noticed very little intellectual curiosity amongst the dipolomatic staff to get out of their offices to do field study and meet those PIO's who do not seek any favours from the Embassy. At a recent get-together in Chandigarh, I met our country's ex-Ambassador to Argentina (early 2000s) who informed me 'there are no Sikhs in Argentina'. When I asked him, 'well, who then constructed the gurdwara in Rosario', the Ambassador quietly moved away. He did not know about my study. There is apathy and disinterest amongst many if not most staff, particularly in dealing with Sikh diaspora and matters concerning them. Of course, as in most cases, there are exceptions too. The current Ambassador to Argentina, R. Vishwanathan shows keen interest and enthusiasm about Indian and Sikh immigrants.

The subject of illegal migration has become a major issue

both for the Sikhs in India as well in countries where these *kabootars* fly to. This issue has its supporters and detractors. So far as South American countries are concerned, it seems they are basically in transit to find legal or not-so-legal routes to USA and Canada; the two countries continue to be the El Dorado of their dreams. In their desperate pursuit of getting a 'green card', many of these adventurers chart out sad stories. Unfortunately even some Punjabi girls have entered into this venture without realizing the attendant risks or maybe despite the risks.

CHAPTER 1

Sikhs on the Move: From Punjab to Latin America

Satguru teri ot;
Khan nu de rotiyan;
Te kharchan nu de note;
Waheguru sab da bhalaa kare;
Par shuru sade ton kare.[1]

INTRODUCTION

Sikhs are as though they have been bitten by the travel bug. In a way, travel can almost be considered as part of their religious tradition, with the result that Sikhs are presently settled all over the globe. As a joke goes, Armstrong allegedly met a Sikh taxi driver when he landed on the moon. Indeed it is difficult to explain why Sikhs have been settling abroad in such large numbers for well over a century now. Is it in their blood? Sociologists have long grappled with the possible explanations for the Sikh youth's attraction, or indeed, one should say obsession, to migrate abroad. The following couplet aptly describes the current mood of the Punjabi youth.[2]

Punjab is our nation
Girls are our meditation
Drinking is our profession
Everyday is our celebration
To hell with education—
Canada is our destination.

SIKHS ON THE MOVE

Giving a chronological narrative of the Sikh emigration is a difficult task. McLeod in his article, 'First Forty Years of Sikh

Migration', asks four interesting questions about Sikh migration. First, have we identified all the destinations to which Sikh migrants travelled to late in the nineteenth century or early in the twentieth century? Second, have we accurately identified (or at least plausibly deduced) the first arrival of Sikhs in any particular country? Third, what routes were established? And fourth, what numbers were involved? This short introduction provides a summary of the Sikhs abroad thus setting the scene for meeting the Sikhs in Latin America which is the subject of this book.

Interviews conducted, quotes gathered from the internet, newspaper clippings and case studies give some answers to the questions posed by late McLeod, at least for some of the South American countries. Having thus, as it were, followed our travellers to their various destinations, we immediately encounter yet another range of questions. What problems did these people encounter, and if so how did they deal with them? What kind of employment did they typically seek? What kind of reception did they receive, and how did they cope with hostility, whenever they encountered it?

SIKH MIGRATION: A BACKGROUND HISTORY

The founder of Sikh faith, Guru Nanak (1469–1539), was a prolific traveller of his times not only within the Indian subcontinent but also beyond to the Middle Eastern countries. The ninth and tenth gurus also spent considerable time away from the Punjab from where the new religion Sikhism had originated. Soon after the death of the last Sikh guru in 1708 in southern India and the passing on of the *Gur Gaddi* to the holy book, *Sri Guru Granth Sahib*, Sikhs were still persecuted by the Mughals and Afghan raiders from the north-west. The kingdom of the Sikh ruler, Maharaja Ranjit Singh (1799–1839), with its capital in Lahore, unfortunately ended soon after his death. The Second Anglo–Sikh War of 1849 ended the short chapter of Sikh glory with the annexation of Punjab by the British. It was under the British that Punjab saw a large migration of Sikh peasants both within and outside India. Some early emigrants were prominent Sikhs who were deported or imprisoned abroad by the British administrators who had opposed their rule in Punjab, e.g. Maharaj Singh was exiled to Singapore in 1849; Prince Dalip Singh was exiled to England in 1854 and the Namdhari chief Baba Ram Singh to Myanmar in 1872.[3]

The British administration also launched several economic policies which led to social mobility and migration. Starting in the 1880s, 'Canal Colonies' were developed diverting river water to barren lands of the western districts of Punjab. Peasants from eastern and central districts were encouraged to settle in these newly irrigated tracts of land in the 'bars', leading to considerable migration across the districts. Another spurt for migration came through the new recruitment policies for British Indian armies as a result of reorganization of the Indian army after the Mutiny. As the British Empire was expanding into many corners of the world, there was a great demand for security forces in the far-flung British colonies. Sikhs so recruited to the army immediately followed the flag especially as they had no inhibition in crossing the 'seas', unlike many of their Hindu brethren. Thus starting from the 1880s, Sikh regiments took part in action in China and Hong Kong and many of them remained there as they found new opportunities.

The British encouraged the Sikhs to join the army and as policemen, watchmen or for other security duties to support the local British administration. This was the beginning of their migration abroad in significant numbers, especially to Malaya, Thailand, the Philippines, Hong Kong and China. Once settled there in sufficient numbers, many enterprising Sikhs who had retired at a comparatively young age ventured out to further British outposts of Australia, New Zealand and Fiji, while the more ambitious among them headed for the gold mines of California and to British Columbia where the Pacific Rail was expanding its route.

From the beginning of the twentieth century, the Sikhs preferred to migrate to North America but were not allowed to do so due to restrictions imposed by these countries. Both Canada and America placed racial barriers for Asian immigrants, and many Sikhs were deported back to India on flimsy grounds from Vancouver and San Francisco ports. Some of these Sikhs ended up in Latin America, especially in Mexico and Argentina, as will be discussed later.

PUNJABI MIGRATION IN THE CONTEXT OF INDIAN AND WORLD MIGRATION

Before discussing the motivation behind Sikhs leaving the land of their birth, the migration process from Punjab should be seen in the context of Indian and indeed world migration trends. Only then one can see how Punjabi migration is not a radical departure from many other migrant groups of today. True, Sikhs' first option was to take the legal route but in the early part of the twentieth century owing to racially motivated barriers, it meant taking the alternative option of sometimes perilous, and in other cases illegal and certainly more expensive routes. In the contemporary period this has meant buying the offers made by the 'people smugglers'. Yet others claim sanctuary seeking refuge from persecution. But in majority of the cases, the impetus is the same—a desire to improve their economic lot.

On a global level, more than ever before, people are crossing borders and embarking on what are sometimes long and dangerous journeys in search of a better life. Indeed, as someone suggested, 'If water is a force of nature, then migration is a force of history'. Examining the global migration trend of the last 100 years, say from mid-nineteenth to mid-twentieth century, Adam McKeown of Columbia University observes,[4]

> There were three major migration destinations during mid 19th century to mid 20th century i.e. 1846–1940 period to (a) Americas, 55–58 million migrants mainly from Europe with about 10 % of migrants from India, China, Japan and Africa (b) South East Asia, Indian Ocean

Rim, 48–52 million mainly from India and Southern China and (c) Manchuria, Siberia, Central Asia and Japan, 46–51 million from North East Asia and Russia. Migrants to category (b) countries comprised of 29 million Indians and 19 million Chinese.

Global migrations have caused a significant shift in the distribution of the world's population. All three destinations experienced massive population expansion, with growth rates twice the world population as a whole. In comparison, growth rates in the sending regions were lower than world population growth, and less than half of those in the receiving regions. Taken together, the three main destination regions accounted for 10 per cent of the world's population in 1850 and 24 per cent in 1950.

Drawing attention to barriers being resurrected by some Western countries such as the USA and the UK in the light of terrorist threats from Muslim radicals, the *Economist* (3 January 2008) of London underlined the continuity of global migration trends as an autonomous force in the world:

> Despite a growing backlash, the boom in migration has been mostly good for both [the] sending and [the] recipient countries. . . . Politicians in rich countries may tinker with migration policies. They will certainly, under public pressure, put extra resources and energy into building more fences and walls to keep people out. And by making a connection between immigration and terrorism, they may cause their societies to become more heavily policed. But the basic forces driving migration are unlikely to ebb. Most migrants move for economic reasons, many in search of jobs, and some to be united with relatives. Most appear to be doing so legally.
>
> The number of illegal migrants is by definition hard to ascertain, but likely to be smaller than the legal sort. The illegal immigrants also go for economic reasons, and they probably make up the bulk of people seen floating on rafts in the Mediterranean or scrabbling over the fence from Mexico to America. . . . Lastly, there are refugees and asylum-seekers, strictly defined as those escaping persecution but often including anybody forced to flee, for example from a war. Many go through legal channels, applying for refugee status and then asylum. But others join illegal migrants in trying to reach host countries by raft or by jumping over a fence. Genuine refugees may have no alternative.

Putting numbers in perspective, it alerts that the number of migrants in the world today, both legal and illegal, is nearly 200 million merely 3 % of the world's population. Moreover, migration as a strategy by the world's poor has proved to yield results, making their lives a little better. Just like 60 million Europeans of nineteenth and early twentieth century who uprooted themselves to the New World to double their incomes, today for those who move from a poor country to a rich one can expect to see their income increase fivefold or more. Thus as long as such differentials persist, the world migration draw will continue.

INDIAN MIGRATION

Over the centuries, India has received migrants from various parts of the world and has absorbed them as if instinctively. This has equipped them to easily adapt to different foreign cultures and ethnicities. The story of the Indian diaspora starts way back in the nineteenth century. It was mainly in response to the demand for cheap labour that arose immediately after slavery was abolished in Britain through an act of parliament on 1 August 1834. The economic situation in India for agriculture and other labour was dismal. The first phase of migrants comprised mainly indenture labour known as *kangani* and *maistry* migrants from south India, eastern UP and Bihar. It was soon followed by migration on free will of Sikhs to several countries and Gujaratis mainly to Africa.

Migration to East Asia was mainly of labourers from south India to the Malaya rubber plantations, followed by a small number of Sikhs as security guards and policemen to Hong Kong. In Fiji it was mainly Indian indentured labour followed by Punjabi and Gujarati migrants. Indentured labour from south India, Bihar and eastern UP were also sent to Mauritius, South Africa, the Caribbean, Surinam and Guyana.

Analysing Indians' movement abroad geographically, emigration to the west coasts of Canada and the USA was first by the Sikhs. Major migrations to the First World countries began after the Second World War, especially with the removal of restrictions on Indian immigration to the USA in the 1960s.

A Sikh, Jagjit Singh played an active role in getting the Luce-Cellar Bill passed in 1946 when Truman was the US President, which gave citizenship rights to the Indian immigrants. This made it possible the election to the US Congress of Dalip Singh Saund from California.

Another outflow of India's semi-skilled and skilled labour took place in the wake of the oil boom in West Asia and the Gulf in the 1970s. However, this was on a contractual basis rather than a permanent one. Also in the 1970s, many Indian immigrants got displaced in Africa (especially under Idi Amin in Uganda) and they became what has been termed as 'twice migrants', mainly to the UK, Europe and Canada. Over the last decade or more, Indian IT professionals migrated first to the USA and then to Europe and now even to China and Japan. Amongst the IT migrants, south Indians are the most dominant.

Indian migration to western Europe is largely a phenomenon of the twentieth century. Two-thirds of the Indian community in the European Union (EU) is to be found in the UK. The presence of Indians in the UK is primarily a result of the interaction between the British Raj and India. The expulsion of Indians in Uganda and problems in Kenya, etc., led to more migration to the UK. The second largest presence of Indians in western Europe is in Holland, which is primarily because of the migration of Indians from Surinam. There is also a significant presence of Indians in Portugal, Germany and France. Of late Italy is becoming an important destination for the Sikhs.

INDIAN DIASPORA: SIZE AND CONSTITUENTS

The Indian diaspora is estimated (2000–01) to be around 20 million, spread across 110 countries. In a major initiative, the Government of India set up a High Level Committee on the Indian Diaspora in September 2000 under the chairmanship of L.M. Singhvi, the Committee Report came out with a detailed study of the Indian diaspora.[5] A table prepared by the

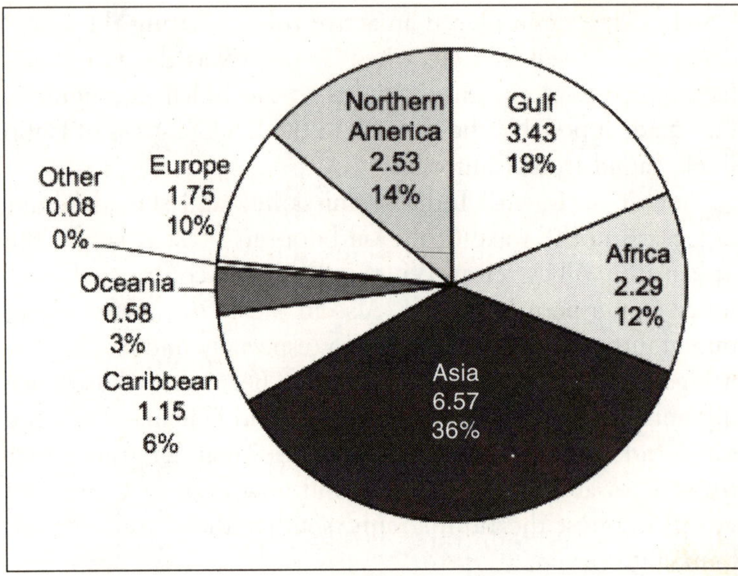

Note: Numbers are estimates in millions.
Source: *Emigration, Immigration, and Diaspora Relations in India* by Daniel Naujoks. Table based on High Level Committee Report on the Indian Diaspora, 2002.

Figure 3: Indian migration: Geographic spread

Committee which provides the size of the Indian diaspora in each country is given in Appendix 10.

After Second World War and especially post-Independence there was a fresh wave of migrants—professionals, artisans, traders and factory workers to First World countries like the USA, Canada, UK and Australasia in search of better opportunities. There was also some outflow of entrepreneurs, shopowners, and self-employed businessmen too.

Diasporic communities exist on the basis of their linguistic or regional identities such as Punjabis, Gujaratis, Sindhis, Tamils, Malayalees, Bengalis, Biharis and Telugus. A rough estimate of the size of the Indian diaspora split into its various constituent diaspora based on the High Level Committee Report is given below:

TABLE 1: VARIOUS DIASPORAS OF INDIAN ORIGIN

(*in millions*)

Tamil	5
Gujarati	3
Punjabi (Sikh)	3 (2)
Bihar & East UP	3
Telugu, Kannada, Malayalee	4
Sindhi	0.5
Others	2

Source: Author's estimates based on HLC Report.

While there are some broad similarities amongst all Indian migrants, there are some interesting differences which distinguish them from one another. While economic betterment was a common goal, the approach to migration was somewhat different for each community of India. Let us dwell on these special aspects of each Indian diaspora.

I have divided the Indian diaspora into Punjabi, Tamil, Gujarati, Sindhi, Malayalee, and Bengali for the sake of convenience. However, other important constituents such as those from the northern states of Bihar and UP give rise to some difficulty in classification. For instance to call it Bihari diaspora would not be fair to the migrants from eastern UP. Punjab, UP and Bihar are landlocked states and had thus less interaction or exposure to foreigners, who would touch the Indian ports first. International trade is a great motivator for foreign contacts and travel. Punjab, however, had an exposure to foreigners of another type—Afghan and Mughal raiders and marauders through the western route of the Khyber Pass across Afghanistan.

The nostalgia for India amongst its diaspora has to be seen to be believed, especially amongst the first generation migrants. This is despite what I found written on the back of a truck in India.

Sau mein ek sau ek baiman, fir bhi mera Bharat mahaan

Out of hundred, hundred and one people are dishonest;
still my India is the greatest.

And on the other hand, the urge to stay in India by some is reflected in the following poem.

You will be delighted to know my Charlie dear
How happily I live in my country here
Polluted air, impure water and adulterated food
Always keep me in a jovial mood.
Spurious drugs and contraband brew.
Add to my life a years few.
I am single but I am never alone
My companions are the idlers of my zone!
There are un-starred hotels and dhabas on wheels
From them I get much lunch and spicy meals
I don't have to go to a departmental store
Hawkers deliver everything at my door
I enjoy full freedom, no check, no bar
Can I have such liberty in your land afar?
My decision may appear to you a little odd
India is India, I don't want to live abroad

THE GUJARATI DIASPORA

The popular image of a Gujarati as a born businessman who will travel to any place in pursuit of profit is well attested by the fact that Gujaratis are in fact settled in many continents of the world. They exhibit enormous adaptability, energy and unbounded enthusiasm for material progress without sacrificing their identity or essential simplicity. Gujaratis, like many other communities in India, were internally divided by caste and religion, but were bound together by the common ties of language and orientation towards business opportunities. It was these two commonalities which was utilized to build their economic fortunes in the new lands. Gujaratis have been especially active in the service industry—retailing, hospitality (hotels and motels), as well as in light engineering and Information Technology.

The population of Gujarat is about 60 million and the estimated size of the Gujarati diaspora is 3 million plus. Currently, the largest segment of this diaspora is in the United States (one in five Indian Americans is of Gujarati origin). Not surprisingly, Americans refer to them as 'Potels'—Patel owners of hotels and motels!

From my personal observation, Gujaratis may be categorized as 'cautious immigrants'—followers but not pioneer settlers into new territories. As traditional traders, shopkeepers, middlemen and later, industrialists, none forced them to go abroad, nor recruited them as indentured labourers unlike other Indian migrants. The early Gujarati migrants followed closely on the heels of the indentured labour to South Africa, and later to British East Africa comprising Kenya, Uganda and Tanzania and then to Fiji. At its height, Gujaratis in Africa were estimated at 1.2 million. 'Dukawalla' was the name given to Gujarati retail shopkeepers in these countries.

During the 1970s African nationalist policies led to an exodus of Gujaratis from Uganda and later from Kenya, to the UK while some headed for Canada and the USA. Other countries containing a Gujarati diaspora are Myanmar, Malaysia, Hong Kong, Australia and New Zealand. The European diamond industry especially in Belgium has a significant presence of Gujaratis from Palanpur. Panama in South America also has a significant presence of Muslim Gujaratis—a group usually overlooked while referring to overseas Gujaratis. In recent times, the role played by Gujarati [Hindu] diaspora in the Muslim riots in 2002 and its vociferous support for VHP has been well debated. On the cultural level, Gujaratis have contributed, in parallel to Punjabi 'Bhangra' their 'Dandya Ras' and 'Garba' dances.

Total population of Gujaratis in the world is given in Table 2:

TABLE 2: TOTAL GUJARATI POPULATION

Gujarat	55 million
Other Indian states	5 million
Overseas Gujaratis	4 million
Total population	64 million

Source: CB Patel, *Gujarat Samachar* (Gujarati) and *Asian Voice* (English) in UK.

Table 3 gives the geographical location of the Gujarati diaspora.

TABLE 3: GEOGRAPHICAL LOCATION OF GUJARATI DIASPORA

North America:	USA 1 million, Canada, 1,50,000
Europe:	UK 7,50,000, France 52,000, Portugal 35,000
Middle East:	UAE 2,00,000, Muscat 50,000
Africa:	South Africa 1,10,000, Uganda 80,000, Kenya 70,000, Tanzania 65,000, Zambia 22,000
Far East:	Malaysia 1,10,000, Mauritius 22,000, Fiji 30,000, the Maldives 22,000
Australia:	2,50,000, New Zealand 22,000
Caribbean:	35,000

Source: Sahoo (2006).

There are also small pockets of Gujarati communities in many other countries including China, Japan, Singapore, Philippines, Indonesia, Seychelles, Madagascar, Kuwait, Iran, Saudi Arabia, Lebanon, Egypt, Sudan, Ethiopia, Mexico, South America, Guyana, Brazil, Gibraltar, Spain, North Africa and Italy.

THE BENGALI DIASPORA

Bengalis are proud thinkers who were often mocked by the British administration as 'timid babus'. They justly claim 'What Bengalis think today, others would think tomorrow'. However, regarding migration, they have shown much less enthusiasm—certainly they have not been in the forefront of it. I hasten to add, however, that Bengali migration within India, especially to Punjab, was considerable, e.g. the Brahmo Samaj in Lahore was largely their creation. As teachers, doctors, lawyers and other such professions Bengalis have migrated to other parts of India and one can find a sizeable number of them in different states.

One reason for the absence of Bengalis from Indian emigration scene was because 'crossing of seas' was considered taboo in the Hindu religious tradition. The website http://bangla pedia.com gives an account how this taboo gradually melted during the mid-nineteenth century when famines almost forced some of them to flee Bengal. As Europeans set up trading posts in various parts of Bengal in the sixteenth and seventeenth centuries where, poorer Bengalis were recruited as domestic servants, field workers, and sailors. Women employed as ayahs by the colonial 'nawabs' were taken with them to Britain on their return. According to the British census of 1801, Britain had about 50,000 ayahs and servants, many of these ayahs had even borne children from their masters! Many shipping companies recruited Bengalis as *laskars* (sailors), some of whom later settled overseas.

Bengali professionals, however, started migrating during the post-1947 period, prominent among them being the Nobel Laureate Amartya Sen and writer, Bharati Mukherjee, both of whom settled in the United States. However, it is from East Bengal, now known as Bangladesh that Bengalis have spread out globally, outnumbering Bengalis from Indian Bengal. Almost half a million Bangladeshis are now settled in Britain and other countries of Europe.

THE TAMIL DIASPORA

Tamils form a large chunk of the Indian diaspora with a long history of migration. The early settlement pattern of Tamils can be traced back to the indentured system of labour in the early nineteenth century. Tamil labourers were taken to work in sugar cane plantations in Mauritius, Jamaica, Trinidad and Tobago in the Caribbean, Guyana and Surinam in South America, plantations in South Africa, rubber estates in Malay States; coffee and tea estates in Sri Lanka, and to coal mines in New Caledonia off Australia in the Pacific Ocean. The Tamil diaspora include Tamils of Sri Lanka too.

In *History of Tamil Diaspora*, V. Sivasupramaniam [murugan.org/research/sivasupramaniam.htm] estimates (including Sri Lankan Tamils which can be as high as 90 per cent say in Canada) that amongst the Western countries, they are numbering about 300,000 each in Britain, USA and Canada and 30,000 in Australia. In Indonesia, he estimates the number to be 50,000, Tamils were first brought here by the Dutch around 1830. As the conditions were not conducive, many returned to India in the 1940s. However, about 2,000 to 10,000 remained in northern Sumatra with the largest concentration of Tamils in that region. In other countries of South-East Asia, Singapore has about 2,00,000 Tamils where it forms the third largest community after the Chinese and Muslims. Malaysia has a Tamil community of over a million where they came as indentured labourers. Besides, there is also the Chettiar community from Chettinadu working largely as moneylenders and wholesalers. Fiji had a Tamil population of over 1,10,000 since the 1880s but now numbers about 80,000 out of an Indian population of 3,50,000 there. Guadaloupe and Martinique in the French West Indies had 20,000 and 15,000 Tamils respectively. The migration was mainly between 1853 and 1883. Guyana had a large number of Tamils in their plantations since 1838. Trinidad and Tobago had Tamils since 1840 where there was a place known as 'Madras Settlement' near the airport.

Myanmar (Burma) had a large Tamil population of nearly 2,00,000 but after the Second World War it came down heavily. Vietnam has a small minority of about 3,000 Tamils settled in Ho Chi Minh City. Cambodia has nearly 1,000 Tamils, China 5,000 and Thailand 10,000.

Mauritius has a Tamil population of 1,15,000; the first immigrants arrived there around 1727 to work in the sugar cane plantations. Reunion has Tamil settlements which started as far back as 1848. There are presently about 1,20,000 Tamils there. Seychelles has a history of about 230 years of Tamil traders coming from Pondicherry for the timber trade.

In South Africa, Tamil migration began in 1860 as indentured labour. Today there are more than 2,50,000 Tamils spread over several cities. In the Gulf countries too there is a sizeable number of Tamil workers—in Bahrain 7,000, Qatar 4,000, and UAE 10,000. Saudi Arabia and Kuwait also have a substantial number of Tamil labourers.

In Europe, majority of the Tamils are from Sri Lanka. Britain's Tamil population is 3,00,000, France 60,000, Germany 50,000, Italy 25,000, Switzerland 40,000, Netherlands 20,000, Norway 10,000, Sweden 2,000, and Denmark 7,000.

This is to be considered against a base population in India of about 61 million with 5 million in Sri Lanka. Tamil had the advantage of the French connection because of Pondicherry. Tamils initially went as labourers but many of them over a period of time graduated to being employed in the private sector and the government. A number of traders, mainly Chettiars excelled in South-East Asia.

THE SINDHI DIASPORA

This is perhaps the most interesting diaspora of Indian origin. During the Partition of 1947, most of them left Sind but a few stayed back. Thus there is a significant Sindhi Hindu population in the Sindh province of Pakistan estimated at over 2 million as per Pakistan's 1998 census. In India, there were 2.57 million Sindhi Hindus as per the 2001 census. They have settled all over India but more so in Maharashtra, Gujarat, Rajasthan and Madhya Pradesh.

Sindhis post-1947 can be considered by any definition as a true diaspora who lost their homeland. It is Hindu Sindhis who are scattered globally trading in textiles and clothes, curios and handicrafts imported from Mumbai. Historically they settled in major ports, e.g. Hong Kong, Manila, Singapore, Jakarta, Kobe, Port Said/Alexandria, Canary Islands, Malta, Panama, and even Santiago in Chile. They literally followed the ships and catered to travellers' needs.

The Sindhi migrated in two phases; the first phase began in the second half of the nineteenth century, generally termed as 'Sindworkies'. The opening of the Suez Canal in 1871 provided a major impetus for Sindhis to open businesses in Egypt and the Mediterranean region. Sindhi firms expanded their network in far off places like Panama and Australia. Their growth followed the expansion of the British Empire. A second wave of Sindhis moved to South-East Asia as far as Japan, which became an important sourcing port for textiles, thus substituting Sind and Mumbai as their main suppliers. The second phase opened after the 1947 upheaval. More of Hindu Sindhis followed the earlier settlers. However, Sindhis in the Far East had suffered huge losses during the Second World War and had to virtually rebuild their businesses. To this were added many refugees from Sind in the wake of the Partition of India. In a yet another thrust of fortunes, during the oil boom of 1970s, Sindhis started establishing colonies specially in Nigeria and other African countries such as Ghana, Sierra Leone, and Liberia. There is also good number of Sindhis in the tourism industry in the Canary Islands.

Sindhis, no longer nurturing any association with a single territory, show remarkable adaptability in various lands. They are present in almost all countries; the numbers estimate Hong Kong 9,500, Manila 4,000 and Jakarta Indonesia including Sumatra 4,000. North America has about 8,000 Sindhi families. Sindhis are basically urban metropolitan city dwellers.

It is worth mentioning that many Sindhis follow the teachings of *Sri Guru Granth Sahib*. Their presence in different parts of the world made passage of Sikhs to some of these locales easier. It is Sindhis who took the holy Sikh book *Guru Granth* with them to these countries and built gurdwaras within their homes and otherwise. This can be seen in Bangkok and some parts of the Philippines too.

OTHER INDIAN DIASPORAS: TELUGUS AND MALAYALEES

As part of Indian emigration, people from Andhra Pradesh too settled in many British colonies. According to Sahoo (2006: 80), Malaysia, Singapore and Fiji have a considerable number of Telugus (3,00,000, 2,000, 50,000 respectively). In addition some 1,00,000 Telugus live in the US, while Canada has a much larger community at 3,50,000. Other countries with Telugu population include the UK, South Africa, Mauritius and, more recently, Australia and New Zealand. A well-known spiritual export from Andhra Pradesh is Satya Sai Baba, with 1,000 centres located in over 100 countries resulting in many philanthropic projects in those countries.

Another notable Indian diaspora is the Malayalam-speaking community of Kerala numbering 31 million according to the 2001 census of India. Starting in the 1970s, these men and some women also went to the Middle East as construction workers, nurses and nannies. However, as the Middle Eastern countries do not allow permanent settlement, these workers remain temporary sojourners, hence the label 'diaspora' might not be applicable to them. An estimate of Malayalees in the Middle East is given in Table 4.

TABLE 4: MALAYALEE POPULATION IN THE MIDDLE EAST

UAE	7,73,000
Saudi Arabia	4,43,000
Kuwait	1,35,000
Oman	1,34,000
Qatar	94,000
Bahrain	58,000

However, some Malayalees have also settled in Western and Far Eastern countries and figures relating to them: USA 1,06,000; UK 26,000; Canada 11,000; Malaysia 11,000; Singapore 8,000; Australia 3,000; and New Zealand 2,000.

THE SIKH DIASPORA

The first significant figure to note is the size of the Sikh diaspora in comparison to its home population. Sikhs form nearly 10 per cent of the Indian diaspora as a whole as also of its Sikh population in India. We know Sikhs form just 2 per cent of the Indian population. Another distinguishing character of the Sikh diaspora is its contrast with the rest of the overseas Indian population is a free migration as against overwhelming indentured form of labour migration of the majority of Indians. It is only in the last 60 years or so that other communities from India especially from south India and Gujarat have migrated in comparatively larger numbers. It is also worth noting that Sikhs were pioneer migrants in several countries such as North and South America, Hong Kong, China, and along with Muslim Punjabis and Pathans, to Australia and New Zealand.

In many countries, at least till 1947, Sikhs formed a large proportion of the total Indian immigrant population. This was especially true of Canada, UK, California, in the US and most of the South American countries except perhaps Panama and Chile. Of all the countries of settlement, Sikhs in Canada have been gaining in numbers as also through social and political importance. Ironically the Sikhs in percentage terms are declining in India, and increasing in Canada where they are likely to reach the same percentage of Canadian population as in India at about 2 per cent in the not too distant future.

Factors in Punjabi Migration

It has already been emphasized how the Punjabi migration abroad differed from Indian migration in being 'free labour' except to build railways in East Africa when they were (mostly Punjabi Muslims and Sikhs) hired under contract somewhat similar to indenture. One of the major impetus for the Sikhs to migrate was economic betterment. Indeed, the first wave of migration from Punjab were to other parts of India particularly to metropolitan cities such as Mumbai and Kolkata and in the post-1947 period to industrial towns such as Jamshedpur. Migration of Sikhs to other parts of India is a subject which needs a detailed study.

In their book, *The Sikh Diaspora*, Barrier and Dusenbery (1989) have described Sikh migration in a comprehensive manner. They observe how Jat Sikhs were loathe to associate themselves with labour contractors and valued autonomy and dignity, thus preferring free migration. Family resources were pooled to finance the trip abroad of one of the family's members. This was followed by a cycle of chain migration involving relatives and village-mates. Most migrants belonged to the peasant community and sending a son abroad was usually adopted as a family strategy as an alternative to reduction of status at home because of land fragmentation and generally low farm incomes. The objective was enhancement of social worth, *izzat*, through additional land purchase, construction of 'pukka' houses, and ability to marry off their daughters. Majority of the migrants were single men or young married men travelling without their wives, undertaking the trip with another kin or village-mate. A successful emigrant was one who worked hard, remitted the bulk of his earnings, and eventually returned to his native village. An eminent phrase at the time was: *kamao pardes, khao desh* (earn abroad, live out in native place).

A Brief History of Punjabi Emigration

As noted in the introduction, a single-most important factor in taking Sikhs abroad was the 'army connection'. This became the operative factor after the Indian Mutiny of 1857, when the Indian army was reorganized. Sikhs were categorized as a 'martial race' to be recruited in separate regiments. As soldiers in these new regiments, they were taken abroad to expand the British empire in other parts of the world. Thus began a large exodus of Sikhs from 1870s onwards. This Sikh migration consisted of soldiers who could retire after 15 years of service who would then settle in places they had seen in their active years of service. Their relatives and friends would often follow them to such overseas destinations.

The Far East

Assisted by the British administrators, certain destinations in the Far East became popular among Sikh settlers. These at first included a few states of Malaya, to which were added Myanmar, Thailand and China later. For both Hong Kong and Malaya, Sikhs were recruited especially from Punjab by the English administrators. Earlier regiments of Sikh pioneers had been sent to action in China.

In the Far East where the first round of migration took place, there were job opportunities as policemen, watchmen, agriculture workers or as small-time peddlers, retailers and traders. The British encouraged Sikhs to migrate to Malaya States (present Malaysia & Singapore) and Hong Kong as policeman and security guards. When the Sikhs in Hong Kong and Shanghai saw the Chinese migrating to the USA and Canada, it prompted them to follow suit. As a part of the Jubilee celebrations of Queen Victoria, a contingent of Sikh soldiers visited British Columbia and some of these soldiers on retirement sailed for Pacific States, in the first decade of the twentieth century.

Thus, in the period from 1880 to 1920, one can trace an ever-changing series of destinations for Sikh emigrants as country after country, after accepting an initial batch of Sikhs for a few years, would close its doors to further immigration. While many did return, others delayed their return too long and found themselves unable or unwilling to go back home.

By 1920s, most of the preferred Sikh countries of destination had erected legal barriers to further South Asian immigration, although legal migration continued to Fiji until 1930 and to Malaysia until 1953.

Thus for example, many Sikhs arrived in Australia in advance of a ban on non-white immigration enacted in 1901; another five thousand reached Canada between 1904 and 1910 before the continuous journey clause was enacted by the Canadian government. New Zealand acquired the bulk of its few hundred Punjabi immigrants in the year preceding the immigration ban of 1920.

ONWARDS TO THE PACIFIC STATES

As news began to circulate of even greater opportunities to be had in Australia, Canada, or the United States, hundreds of Sikhs started arriving there. The Canadian government decided to curtail this influx with a series of laws, which were aimed at limiting the entry of South Asians into the country and restricting the political rights of those already in the country. The Punjabi community had hitherto been an important loyal force for the British Empire and the community had expected, equal welcome and rights from the British and Commonwealth governments as extended to British and white immigrants. The restrictive laws fed a growing discontent, protests and anti-colonial sentiments within the community.

Faced with increasingly difficult situations, the community began organizing itself into political groups. A large number of Punjabis also moved to the United States, where also they encountered similar political and social problems. The Ghadar Party, initially the Pacific Coast Hindustan Association, was formed in 1913 in the United States, with Sohan Singh Bhakna as its president. The members of the party were Indian immigrants, largely from Punjab. Some of the members were students at the University of California at Berkeley including Har Dayal, who became a driving force later in India's freedom struggle.

The genesis of the Ghadar movement lay with the non-support of the British Indian government for the losses incurred by Indian, mostly Sikh immigrants who suffered financial hardships as a result of riots against them in the USA and Canada. The Japanese and Chinese governments supported the cause of their nationals in a similar act of hooliganism against their citizens by taking up the matter strongly with the host governments. The Ghadar Party as it came to be known, quickly gained support from Indian expatriates, especially in the United States, Canada and Asia.

Arising from the voyage of the *Komagata Maru* in 1914 to Vancouver, which blatantly reflected the Canadian racist anti-Indian immigration laws, several thousand Indian residents in the USA sold their business and homes, ready to drive the British out from India. In San Francisco, the remaining Ghadar activists were put on trial in the 'Hindu German Conspiracy' case in 1917.

Some other Destinations

In contrast to the Jat-dominated migration to the Pacific Rim, early Sikh migration to East Africa was dominated by the Ramgarhias (artisans) who were recruited to build the Ugandan Railway (*c.* 1897–1901). In Britain, the earliest migrants were the Bhatra Sikhs, a small social group with the traditional occupation of peddling. They secured an economic foothold in some outlying cities of England and Scotland by the early 1920s. However, depression and the Second World War was not conducive to further Sikh migration. Although illegal immigration continued during the period, most countries with immigration restriction actually lost their Sikh population by the 1940s. Many migrants returned to the village during the lean years of depression, others had returned for political reasons as members of Ghadar Party, later in the 1940s some as fighters for Indian independence. Sikhs were prominent in the fight for justice and freedom struggle for an independent India despite enjoying British patronage in many spheres.

Post-1947 Migration

In the aftermath of the Second World War and India's Independence, some of those countries which had previously erected barriers to Asian immigration began to lower them. Since the late 1940s Sikh immigration once again became a significant worldwide phenomenon. The social dislocation brought about by Partition of India was another factor in the immediate post-Independence era. More recently, the social consequences due to lack of economic development in Punjab and the political turmoil of 1980s, have served to further stimulate migration. As with the earlier period of migration, the variable immigration policies in preferred destinations have continued to determine the type of Sikh migration and where they will settle.

The USA, Canada, and the UK—in that order—constitute preferred, prestigious countries for migration at present. Other European countries as well as Australia, New Zealand and countries of the Persian Gulf have also experienced growth in their Sikh populations. Part of this current movement is a reflection of the better opportunities in the free economy centres. Given the earlier patterns of settlement and the continued effects of chain migration, relatively uneducated direct migrants from rural Punjab continue to constitute a significant part of the flow.

The bulk of Sikh migration to the UK took place during the 1950s and early 1960s when the British economy was in full recovery. Just when British immigration requirements began to tighten in the mid-1960s, Canadian and American policies became more favourable towards potential Sikh immigrants, as country quotas gave way to qualification-based policies. In contrast to the situation in Canada, where, at least for a brief period in the early 1970s, the policy allowed unskilled workers relatively easy access, the liberalization of immigration laws in the United States in the mid-1960s removed national quotas but did not open the door to unskilled labourers. While the agricultural communities in California have continued to absorb additional rural, working class Sikh immigrants through processes of sponsorship and family re-unification, the bulk of the new independent immigration has come from Sikh professionals. As a result of the efforts of one such recent Sikh Immigrant, Yogi Bhajan, several thousand North Americans and many in South America and some in Europe have converted to Sikhism since the early 1970s.

Besides there are quite a few Sikhs in the Netherlands, Germany, Denmark, France, Spain and some East European countries, e.g. Poland. Italy has now a large Sikh immigrant population. Many people smuggling rings have come up with international links and people pay lakhs of rupees to move out by any means. European countries are popular for such adventurous immigrants.

An aspect of Sikh migration is that it comprised mainly of Jat (rural) Sikhs who had to go through adjustments one of the foreign land and the other of city/urban living.

Illegal Punjabi Immigrants

Historically there have always been a high share of illegal immigrants from among Punjab especially in North American countries which had introduced restrictions from the first decade of the twentieth century. While such racial legislature was dismantled in the 1940s, the Punjabis by then had developed a culture of migration far exceeding those who could legally qualify to enter particular countries. By the 1990s, even more competitive ethos of migration abroad gripped the rural Sikhs especially to Canada, leading to a high demand for overseas opportunities.

Catering to such high demand, there is a new industry of travel agents in contemporary Punjab who have acquired specialized skills in taking Punjabis out to various locations through legal and illegal channels. Newspapers carry news of smuggling of Punjabis to various European locations. There have been numerous marriage scandals involving brides and bridegrooms from the UK or Canada arranging 'convenient' or fake marriages.

While the US, Canada and the UK are the most preferred destinations of the Sikh migrants, Australia and New Zealand have been added to the dream list. Just below the scale are European destinations such as Italy, Greece and Spain, indeed any country that promises a better life and would accept Punjabis legally or otherwise. A dead man's passport, if it has the right visa, is a precious document to be turned into gold with a changed photo. It is a serious subject but in true Punjabi style, a verse sent by e-mail by Arvinder Singh Garcha from UK captures the ethos:

I cross ocean, poor and broke.
Take bus, see employment folk.

Nice man treat me good in there.
Say I need to see welfare.

Welfare say, 'You come no more, we send cash right to your door.'
Welfare cheques—they make you wealthy! NHS—it keep you healthy!
By and by, I get plenty money.
Thanks to you, you British dummy!

Write to friends in motherland.
Tell them 'come fast as you can'.

They come in turbans and Ford trucks,
And buy big house with welfare bucks!

They come here, we live together.
More welfare cheques, it gets better!

Fourteen families, they moving in,
but neighbour's patience wearing thin.
Finally, British guy moves away.
Now I buy his house, then I say,
'Find more immigrants for house to rent.'
And in the yard I put a tent.
Everything is very good,
and soon we own the neighbourhood.

We have hobby, it's called breeding.
Welfare pay for baby feeding.
Kids need dentist?
Wives need pills?
We get free! We got no bills!

British crazy! They work all year, to keep the welfare running here.
We think UK damn good place.

Too darn good for British race!
If they no like us, they can scram.
Got lots of room in Afghanistan!

As a result of the 'culture of migration' there are a whole set of social issues and vocabulary surrounding would-be migrants. Known in popular parlance as *kabootars* (pigeons) the Punjabi youth has been sold on exaggerated stories of 'golden valleys' abroad. As a result, they set out on expensive voyages. Incidents such as the Malta boat tragedy, frozen-to-death stowaway in airplane's landing gear, shooting at border crossings, suffocation inside cargo containers, and many such horrendous incidences have not proved sufficient deterrents.

Largely due to Canadian laws of immigration where family connections count towards permanent settlement, there are now several hundred Punjabi brides who have been abandoned by their husbands after arranging 'convenient' marriages charging fees. During my travels I came across a few of them and I was amazed at the extent to which Punjabis can go to migrate. Some such cases in Belize and Ecuador in Latin America are discussed in the respective country profiles.

Sikh Diaspora: Country-wise Location, Numbers, Earliest Arrivals and Gurdwaras

Although it is difficult to get exact figures of the size of the Sikh diaspora, some close approximation is possible for many countries. There are several figures in relevant literatures though none can assure us of the accuracy or authenticity of such data. A broader internet survey and statement of the NRI Department in Punjab estimates the Sikh Diaspora as 10 per cent of the Sikh global population of about 20 million but there is no basis or evidence for the figures quoted.

Then there is the additional issue of the number of 'illegal immigrants'. Except for Canada and UK, where Sikhs are recognized as part of the Census category, no other country explicitly enumerates Sikhs. Many countries such as USA, Australia, New Zealand, and several European countries collect data within the broad category of 'India origin'. But there is no reliable way to ascertain the proportion of Sikhs from this Indian category. In each country there are micro level data usually on religion also but Sikh scholarly studies of diasporic communities have not advanced that far to analyse those. For example, in Indonesia, Sikhs as a religious group are not recognized but they have to declare some religion for getting the national ID cards.

In earlier times, the situation was even worse. In many countries they were known as 'Bengalee', as say in Malaysia, or 'Hindoos' in the US and other South American countries.

Tables 5 and 6 provide the best estimates possible of the Sikh Diaspora. Table 5 contain a set of data provided by Tatla in his book *The Sikh Diaspora* which is often quoted in many publications. Table 6 is derived from the internet. The latter can be considered as somewhat amateurish but nevertheless useful guide compiled with the efforts of ordinary Sikhs who take considerable interest and show enthusiasm but subject to some 'reasonable' exaggeration.

In order to get a better understanding of the history of Sikh migration, an effort is being made for the first time to chart out the earliest known Sikh migration to various countries in Table 7. In Table 8, a further attempt is being made to chart out the first gurdwaras set up by the Sikhs in various countries and broader geographic areas.

TABLE 5: SIKH DIASPORA: LOCATION AND NUMBERS

Country	Period	Population
COLONIAL PERIOD (1860–1947)		
Americas		
Argentina	1950s	500–1,000
Mexico	1930	1,000–1,500
Canada	1905–13	7,500–10,000
USA	1905–13	7,500–10,000
	1920–47	3,000
East Africa		
Kenya/Uganda	1885–1950	5,000
Tanzania	1880–1920	750
Europe		
UK	1930–47	1,500
Far East		
Australia	1890–1910	150–2,500
Fiji	1890–1910	200–500
Hong Kong	1900–40	10,000–50,000
Malaya States	1865–40	30,000–35,000
New Zealand	1890–10	200–382
Philippines	1910–30	4,000–2,500
Thailand	1920–40	2,500–5,000
Indonesia	1880–40	3,000–6,000
Middle East		
Afghanistan	1900–30	2,000–2,500
POST-COLONIAL PERIOD (1947–90)		
Americas		
Canada	1960–90	1,47,440
USA	1960–90	1,25,000
Europe		
United Kingdom	1960–90	4,00,000–5,00,000
Germany	1960–80	2,500
Far East		
Australia	1950–70	2,500
New Zealand	1950–80	2,500
Singapore	1940–50	32,000
Middle East		
Abu Dhabi	1970–80	7,500-10,000
Iraq	1970–80	5,000-7,500

Source: Tatla, *Sikh Diaspora:* 1999: p. 42.

TABLE 6: GLOBAL SIKH POPULATION: CURRENT ESTIMATES

Country	Estimates	Country	Estimates
Afghanistan	2,000	Mauritius	37,700
Australia	26,429	Mexico	8,000
Austria	2,794	Nepal	5,890
Belgium	10,000	Netherlands	12,000
Brunei	1,000	New Zealand	9,507
Burma/Myanmar	70,000	Niger	3,000
Canada	4,15,000	Norway	5,000
China PRC incl. HK	7,500	Pakistan	26,000
Cypress	400	Philippines	20,000
Denmark	700	Poland	700
Fiji	4,676	Portugal	9,000
France	10,000–12,000	Russia	5,000
Germany	40,000	Singapore	15,000
Greece	1,000	South Africa	4,000
Iceland	100	South Korea	2,000
India	215,00,000	Spain	1,000
Iran	6,000	Sweden	1,500
Ireland	1,200	Switzerland	500
Italy	70,000	Tanzania	14,000
Japan	2,000	Thailand	70,000
Kazakhstan	800	Uganda	5,000
Kuwait	20,000	United Kingdom	7,50,000
Lebanon	3,000	United States	5,00,000
Malawi	3,000	Zambia	3,000
Malaysia	1,00,000		

Source: Wikipedia: Sikhism by country, accessed April 2010.

TABLE 7: GLOBAL SIKH MIGRATION:
EARLIEST ARRIVALS

Country	Year of migration	Comments and Source
Hong Kong	1841	Sikh soldiers at Captain Elliot's flag raising
Singapore and Malaya	1849	Baba Maharaj Singh—sent as prisoner to Singapore (Tatla, 1999).
China–Shanghai	1850s	Opium War, Sikhs recruited in Shanghai Police 1884 (Sarabjit Singh Gill blog)
UK	1854	Maharajah Dalip Singh (*Lady Login's Recollections*, n.d.)
Myanmar	1872	Baba Ram Singh—Namdhari head extradited
Indonesia	1880s	Sumatra, *Indian Communities in Southeast Asia* (Sandhu & Mani, 1993)
Thailand	1884	'*Indian Diaspora—A Comparative Study of Punjabis and Gorakhpuris in Thailand*' (Gupta)
Europe	1886	Prince Dalip Singh (Campbell), 2000
East Europe	1887	Prince Dalip Singh—Moscow (Campbell), 2000
Fiji	1890	*The Sikhs in Fiji* (Singh, n.d.)
Australia	1890s	Ram Singh—Hew McLeod email to S.S. Kahlon
New Zealand	1890s	*Punjabis in New Zealand* (McLeod, 1986)
South America	1890s	Argentina: Ram Singh (McLeod); Brazil—1912, Panama—1904, Canal construction. (S.S. Kahlon)
East Africa	1890s	Indians in East Africa (Gregory, 1972)
USA	Late 1890s	Sibia website (also Leonard, 1995)
Canada	1897	'Patterns of Sikh Migration to Canada, 1900–1960' (Johnston, 1988) www.wikipedia.com
Afghanistan	Late 18th c.	*Hukamnamas* of various Gurus—*The Story of Valiant Sikhs* (2004)
Philippines	1902	www.sikhspectrum.com (M.S. Ahluwalia, *The Indian Ghadar Movement*, Issue no. 24, May 2006).
Japan	1920s	*Sikh Diaspora in Japan* (Masako Azuma, unpublished thesis)
Iran	1920s	www.sikhnet.com (Bik S. Dhillon)
Gulf States	1970s	Large scale migration due to oil revenue

Courtesy: Darshan Singh Tatla.

TABLE 8: EARLIEST (FIRST) OVERSEAS GURDWARAS: COUNTRIES AND BROADER GEOGRAPHIC AREAS

Date	Name
1897	Myanmar, Yangon—Foundation stone laid
1898	East Africa—Kenya, Singh Sabha Gurdwara, Kilindini, Mombasa
1899	Malaysia, The Wadda Gurdwara, Penang
1890s	Shanghai (Ka Kin Cheuk)
1901	Hong Kong—Khalsa Diwan Sikh Temple
1907	Vancouver (Abbotsford Gurdwara, BC 1912, proper building)
1911	UK, Shepherds Bush
1912	Sikh Temple, Stockton, California
1912	Singapore, Central Sikh Temple
1913	Thailand, Bangkok rented wooden house Phahurat and Chakraphet Rd. (Chiang Mai—*c.* 1908, Gurdwara at 134 Charoenrat Road)
1920	Scotland, Glasgow
1922	Fiji, Samabula, Suva
1925	Indonesia, Sikh Temple, Tg. Priok
1941	Iran, Teheran
1966	Japan, Kobe
1968	Australia, Woolgoolga (McLeod)
1977	New Zealand, TaRapa, North of Hamilton (McLeod)
1970s	Continental Western Europe, Germany—Frankfurt/Main (Goel 2002b)
1980s	Latin America, Bolivia
2010s	East Europe (Poland 2004)
2010s	Gulf Countries (Likely Dubai 2010s)

Note: In many places, the prayers and gatherings started in individual homes where the devout Sikh had taken the trouble to take the holy book (almost a project and not an easy document, e.g. Bible, Quran or *Bhagawad Gita*, which can be carried in the hand bag) kept the *Sri Guru Granth Sahib*, followed by setting up of gurdwaras in rented premises which were later on either bought over and expanded or moved to entirely new places. Above dates should be taken as indicative—sometimes there was a substanitial time gap between laying the foundation to the actual inauguration. In certain other countries such as Russia and Gulf countries, permission for setting up a religious worship place is difficult or almost impossible and requires it to be declared as a Sikh society rather than a gurdwara.

SOUTH AMERICA

There are only a few references to Latin America as far a Sikh global migration is concerned. Among a few odd entries are Bhagat Singh Bilga's account of his life as a Ghadarite in Argentina where he found many ex-Ghadarites.[6] Similarly there is reference to Teja Singh Sutantar's visit to some Latin American countries as reported by Williamson, a spy working for the Government of India.[7] *Prima facie*, it would appear there was a fair bit presence of Indian Sikh immigrants in South America between the two world wars. Some of them were supporters of the Ghadar movement. Many of these activists had gone there to avoid being harassed or arrested by American authorities.

On the Indian migration to Latin America, the Government of India's High Level Committee (HLC) had little to say regarding the Sikh constituents of Indian settlers. As this book contends, Sikhs form a large proportion of the total Indian population in this continent. The HLC, unfortunately, neither highlights the presence of Sikhs nor acknowledges the real difficulties faced by Sikh settlers in various countries. The Report of HLC says:

> Our purpose has been to pay our tribute to the relentless spirit of the 'Overseas Indian' who has ventured forth to remote corners of the world in search of adventure or profit, whatever the impediments or challenges he or she has had to encounter. There are relatively few PIOs and NRIs in most of these countries. But their achievements in what may sometimes have been hostile or unwelcome milieu must command our respect and admiration. A comparative table has been included (in a later chapter). The chart shows at a glance, the comparative presence of the Indian community in the many countries of Central and South America.

More recently there have been many converts to Sikhism as the followers of Yogi Bhajan's 3 HO in some Latin American countries. I met some of these Sikhs in various countries and my interaction with them will be discussed later.

The Sikhs have thus been on the move from Punjab both within and outside India. Although the above is a somewhat broad picture, it brings out the fact that Sikh migration has been far more widespread than other Indian communities despite the fact that Punjab is a land locked area far away from the Indian sea ports.

This chapter sets the scene for discussing the continent of Latin America which has a sparse population of Sikh communities. But their small numbers indeed bring out some unique features of Punjabi migration especially the persistence and resilience of Sikhs to settle abroad in the face of several odds. Indeed, the more challenging the destination, the better for the Sikhs' sense of achievement in settling there, as some of the narratives in this book will testify.

NOTES

1. Sikh/Punjabi humour or pragmatism, from Khushwant Singh's column in *Tribune*, sent by J.P. Singh Kaka of Bhopal, from lines written on the rear side of a Punjab autorickshaw.
2. From Khushwant Singh's *Tribune* column contributed by a reader, Naveen Laiker.
3. J.S. Grewal (1988).
4. Adam McKeown, 'Global Migration, 1846–1940', *Journal of World History*, June 2004.
5. Report of the High Level Committee on the Indian Diaspora, Indian Council of World Affairs, New Delhi, 2001.
6. See Bhagat Singh Bilga (1989), '*Unfole Varke*'.
7. *Ghadar Directory* issued by the Government of India, 1934.

CHAPTER 2

Travels Among the Latin American Sikhs

General Observations, Gurdwara, Impact of Migration, Travel Diary and Nuggets

WHAT IS LATIN AMERICA?

There are several definitions of Latin America. A common understanding is that Latin America includes territories in the Americas where Spanish or Portuguese language prevails: Mexico, most of Central America, South America, and (in the Caribbean) Cuba, the Dominican Republic, and Puerto Rico. Sometimes, especially in the United States, Latin America is understood to be all of America south of the US. In this study countries such as Belize, Guyana, French Guyana, Surinam, Costa Rica, Guatemala, El Salvador and Nicaragua have been included but not the Caribbean countires.

Brazil is by far the largest country of Latin America, both in area and population with Portuguese as its language while other Latin American countries have Spanish as their language. Argentina, Chile, Costa Rica, Mexico, Uruguay and Brazil are relatively more prosperous. The Latin American G7 is composed of Argentina, Brazil, Chile, Colombia, Mexico, Peru and Venezuela. The largest economies of the region are Brazil, Mexico, and Argentina. Population-wise, the largest countries are Brazil, Mexico, Colombia, and Argentina. Land area-wise Brazil covers almost half of the total area followed by Argentina at one-sixth of total area.

GOVERNMENT OF INDIA: SINGHVI HIGH LEVEL COMMITTEE REPORT

The above report under the chapter 'Other Countries of Central and South America' has the following to say:

Most of the countries covered in this chapter fall outside the Caribbean region. The French West Indies and Jamaica may be notable exceptions, as well as one or two of the smaller members of CARICOM. We have added brief sketches here about many of the countries of Central and South (or Latin) America, where there is even a small Indian presence. In doing so, our purpose has been to pay our tribute to the relentless spirit of the 'Overseas Indian' who has ventured forth to remote corners of the world in search of adventure or profit, whatever the impediments or challenges he or she has had to encounter. There are relatively few PIOs and NRIs in most of these countries. But their achievements in what may sometimes have been hostile or unwelcome milieu must command our respect and admiration. A comparative table has been included below to show, at a glance, the comparative presence of the Indian community in the many countries of Central and South America.

TABLE 9: HLC REPORT: PIOs, NRIs AND STATELESS PERSONS IN SOUTH AND CENTRAL AMERICA

Country	Population	PIOs	NRIs	% of the Population
Argentina	36,600,000	1,200	400	Insignificant
Barbados	260,000	2,100	100	0.81
Belize	250,000	50	NA	Insignificant
Brazil	169,000,000	1,500	400	Insignificant
Chile	15,650,000	Few	650	Insignificant
Colombia	42,000,000	1	19	Insignificant
Costa Rica	3,600,000	1	15	Insignificant
Ecuador	12,000,000	Nil	5	Insignificant
Guatemala	11,500,000	22	NA	Insignificant
Guyana	775,000	395,250	100	51.01
Jamaica	2,600,000	60,000	1,500	2.36
Mexico	99,580,000	400	NA	Insignificant
Panama	2,800,000	211	1953	Insignificant
Peru	25,200,000	5–10	135	Insignificant
St. Lucia	156,260	250	NA	Insignificant
Surinam	438,026	153,306	150	35.00
Trinidad & Tobago	1,282,000	500,000	600	39.04
Venezuela	24,000,000	400	280	Insignificant

Source: High Level Committee Report.

From this study point of view, the most important country visited by me was Argentina. This country therefore has been covered in more detail. I had also an opportunity to interview several returnees from Argentina and Bolivia. My first visit was to Argentina and I was very excited about it. I spent more days there than in any other country in Latin America. I had also more contacts in Argentina because I could get the help of an Argentinean researcher, Lia Rodriguez De La Vega, whose area of study was with respect to some societal aspects of Indian immigrants. Apart from this, an AIESEC exchange student in Chandigarh on her return to Buenos Aires had run a reconnaissance mission for me before my visit. A senior officer, Tarsem Singh at the Indian Embassy was also of great help. It is interesting to note that hardly any immigrant moved out of Argentina in favour of another Latin American country. The flow was always into Argentina except in some cases when the migrant returned to Punjab. From my own personal experience, it would appear there is something about Argentina which makes it more attractive—the warmth and affection of the people was overwhelming. There was a certain chemistry, probably because of my turban, which was very exciting to the young Argentineans, especially the ladies who are married locally but whose fathers or grandfathers were Sikhs and who were proud to be a Singh. There was a certain joy that came out after meeting them. If I could feel this during my short stay, may be the early immigrants also felt the same way which helped them dig in roots in this country. Panama is another country which is more interesting from the viewpoint of this study.

Before detailing out the country-wise reports beginning with the next chapter, some observations and comments might be appropriate. The emphasis in country writeups is based on interviews. Although these might appear repetitive but each person's saga is unique in some ways. The interviews bring out, sometimes tangentially, certain features which are worth noting. I leave it to the readers to weave his or her own narrative from the various voices that emerge. These interviews should also be handy for future researchers, as a base to build upon.

The country profiles start with an introduction which highlights features of that country's Sikh immigration. This is followed by the country profile with respect to its history, geography, culture, etc. This is the touristy bit and is drawn from the book, *Lonely Planet Travel Guide*, which the author used during his travels. I have included comments on each country by the Government of India's HLC on Indian Diaspora. The reader thus gets a feel of the total Indian scenario so as to place the Sikh migration in context. The High Level Committee has, in general terms, not delved into any details of the Sikh diaspora. It suggests how a minority can get overshadowed by the majority. This is followed by some interesting or special aspect of the Sikh diaspora in that country. Case studies and interviews follow thereafter. I have quoted from newspaper clippings, books and journals where available.

But why did some of the Sikhs choose to go to South America? As pointed out earlier, there were problems in settling in Canada and USA. Latin American governments were not as hostile as other White dominated countries. In fact, some countries such as Brazil, were positively seeking immigration of Indian farmers. But distance and lack of regular sailings from India were deterrents. Language was another disadvantage. Most follow up immigration, as is often the case, was through family or friends or village mates. It is stated by several immigrants that Argentina was more attractive than any other South American country because of its climate being similar to Punjab, especially in the North-West, where most of the Sikhs ultimately settled. The quality of farm land was considered similar to Punjab. Even though good farming conditions may have been the initial attraction, many immigrants are now into non-farming professions. But the lure of land is the biggest magnet for a 'Jat' and seems also to be the case for the early Sikh migrants.

An interesting pattern particularly in Latin American countries had been that many of them did not settle down straight away in one country except for in Panama and Argentina. Argentina in the earlier twentieth century was a prosperous country and was referred to as the Europe of South America. Panama was another potential workplace for migrants because of English-speaking Americans, not that many of the Sikhs were proficient in English.

Another feature of the Sikh settlers has been their non-active involvement in supporting a separate Sikh homeland. The 1980s developments in India and Operation Blue Star and murder of innocent Sikhs in Delhi and other parts of India have, after the assassination of Indian Prime Minister, Indira Gandhi, no doubt, hurt the sentiments of Sikh immigrants. But it is not to be surmised that Sikh immigrants are not in sync with what happens in Punjab and India. Their involvement in the Ghadar movement in the early decades of the twentieth century stands testimony to their India orientation.

GURDWARA

As the Sikh community became sizeable anywhere, a gurdwara was set up which helped them to keep in touch with each other. For the migrants, the gurdwara was also the first contact point to get to know others. In most of the countries, initially the *Sri Guru Granth Sahib* was brought by an individual and kept at his house which became the gathering point on Sundays and other holidays. The Sindhi migrants were also prominent in bringing the *Sri Guru Granth Sahib* to their homes.

The community develops more cohesiveness and closeness with the setting up of a gurdwara. The Argentina gurdwara is one such example (see its country profile). One hears of many stories from immigrants where the gurdwara played a significant role in their migration. Many of them stayed in gurdwaras in Kolkata and Singapore for months on end in some cases, before they could get a ship to their destination.

Initially the first gurdwara set up in Stockton, USA (true elsewhere also), was the meeting point in the afternoons for all Indians including Hindus and even Muslims. In Teheran (Iran) all community functions of Indians were held at the local gurdwara or Khalsa School attached to the gurdwara. When I went there as part of a business delegation sponsored by the Government of India, the meeting was held in the gurdwara premises, sometimes referred to by the cab drivers of Teheran as 'Sikh Masjid'.

Gurdwaras in Latin American countries were built only in the 1980s or even later. Sikhs migrating to North America, UK, Africa or East Asia were faster in setting up gurdwaras. May be this is one reason why *Sikhi* has almost disappeared in Latin America. There is some revival in setting up of gurdwaras there but it might be a case of too little too late.

In an article published in the *Sikh Review*, titled 'Gurdwara: Its Concept and Role', Dr Ujaagar Singh Bajwa, says:

> The gurdwara is set up primarily to serve all mankind. The multifarious role assigned to it is not a historical accident but assigned directly by the Gurus. The gurdwara during Guru Nanak Sahib's time was a full-fledged commune where, besides Path, Kirtan, and Katha, lodging, and boarding of itinerants was considered an integral part. The Guru toiled along with his disciples for tilling the land. The Guru thus demonstrated the dignity of work and worship aiming at the well-being of the people, both material and spiritual.
>
> The gurdwara is not only a place of worship but a training ground of social service, public deliberation and other kinds of practical religion as well. The leaders of the Gurdwara Reform movement in the first quarter of last century made a declaration that they will properly utilize their income and property so that Sikhism will be propagated to every nook and corner of the world. Every Sikh will be educated. Technical and industrial schools shall be opened, and unemployment shall be eradicated. Evils like drinking, litigation, etc., shall be rooted out.
>
> Managers of the present-day gurdwara should see that these multifaceted roles assigned to these institutions are properly and adequately played by them. To a Sikh, the gurdwara is the symbol of everything he stands for—his faith, love, and courage. Talking of gurdwaras in

the West, Bajwa adds: 'Let us examine the role of gurdwara today, especially in the Western world. It seems that the nature and the role of this institution have been severely mauled. It still performs some of the mundane and routine functions but has failed to perform many other essentials. It has become a place these days where congregations do meet to celebrate Gurpurabs and birthdays, commemorate deaths, and the rituals of wedding-related activities.' At the end of each service, Guru Ka Langar is served. It has also become a place of social gathering. These are acceptable functions. Unfortunately, these are the only functions a gurdwara is currently performing. Gurdwara is a place to visit from where should come solace and comfort to our minds and souls. This should not be a place for theatrics and show business, nor should it be used for amusement only. The internecine fights over the control of gurdwaras particularly abroad needs to be condemned by all Sikhs.

In another book titled, *Perspectives on Sikhism*, by Prithipal Singh Kapoor and Dharam Singh (2001), the authors describe the overseas scene in the USA beautifully:

During the past four decades immigrant Sikhs have built over 100 gurdwaras in this country. These gurdwaras, worth several million dollars, are ostensibly dedicated towards the preservation and transmission of the Sikh heritage. But they are primarily directed towards one purpose: to capture or recreate the sights, sounds and smells of home in Punjab.

The immigrants who built the gurdwaras and affiliated institutions are now nearing the end of their life's work. In not too distant future, their progeny will inherit these gurdwaras. For the new generation of Sikhs the home is here, the sights, sounds and smells are different. The activities in gurdwaras, whether social, political or religious, are not always in pace with their needs and expectations. This is clearly seen by the dwindling interest and attendance in gurdwaras by young Sikhs. Will young Sikhs want these institutions as presently constituted and what will they do with them once they inherit them? Many of these gurdwara buildings once housed churches and with decreasing commitment by new generations of Christians, many churches were sold. With dwindling interest and diminishing participation by the next generation of Sikhs, will some gurdwaras meet a similar fate?

IMPACT OF LARGE MIGRATION

The present Sikh diaspora is a dynamic force, subject to significant secondary migration between (and within) countries and still growing through continued migrations from Punjab, and natural increase. Further, recent events suggest that Sikhs diaspora has come to play an increasingly important role in the affairs of the Sikh Panth. The Sikh diaspora are no more considered marginal nor is their behaviour insignificant to action in the main social arena of Punjab. Marriage networks are now transnational; news of praiseworthy or blameworthy behaviour in the diaspora affects group *izzat* (honour or prestige), worldwide. Regional, caste, and sectarian differences, long salient to Sikh society in Punjab, are replicated in the diaspora, while new bases of differentiation of persons within the Sikh Panth are created. The Sikhs with higher education, particularly in the USA, Canada and England, have raised the levels of study of Sikhism through well-researched writings, translations of the *Guru Granth Sahib*, seminars, political patronage and cultural activities. In Canada a few have risen to become ministers and members of parliament. In short, the Sikh diaspora are an important and integral part of a worldwide Sikh society.

There is a fear amongst the Sikhs of Hindu domination but there is a second threat which faces the Sikhs which is due to migration in large numbers. The difficulty the Sikhs living outside India are facing in balancing their religious practices with the expectations of modern-day life is very real. It is sometimes natural for those Sikhs who associate closely with other cultures to avoid including practices in their lives that are not acceptable to Sikhism. It is likewise difficult for them when living outside the Sikh community to rigorously adhere to practices required by Sikhism. It is these changes in lifestyle that threaten Sikhism and have created differences of opinion among Sikhs. Such differences of opinion have divided the Sikh community and have occasionally led to violence among them.

The NRIs exercise an influence far greater than their numbers especially for the youth for whom they are role models. Any trend of Sikhs in overseas gets exaggerated importance in Punjab. Out of all the Indian communities with possibly the exception of Sindhis, Sikh migration numbers in percentage of total community strength are the largest. This issue thus is more unique to the Sikhs. This by itself is a vast subject requiring detailed study but some of the factors that get talked about are mentioned here. These are more pronounced in countries and places where Sikh population is significant. So in that sense they are less relevant to Latin America.

1. Effect on Sikh religious organizations, viz., SGPC. There is talk of nominating representatives from overseas to SGPC to be able to better understand the global issues as increasingly more Sikhs are settling abroad.
2. Sikh converts such as Yogi Bhajan's 3HO followers.
3. Translation of holy books including *SGGS* into foreign languages such as Spanish.
4. Issue of Sikh symbols especially the turban has become more acute in foreign lands. Other issues are of carrying the *kirpan* and wearing helmet both for two wheeler driving and as industrial workers. Identity card and passports without the turban is mandatory in some countries.
5. There are over hundred gurdwaras in North America alone, wherein during the last couple of decades over 20 have witnessed violence and legal suits pertaining to elections. Gurdwaras have wound up in the local civil and criminal courts, with high legal fees that come out of the meagre resources of an immigrant community.
6. The Sikh world in India appears split into Jats, non-Jats and Ramdasia. Sikh migrants have brought over such labels in the new settlements too. It is quite customary for groups in gurdwara elections to be defined along such divisions. Panama, on the other hand, has jumped far ahead by having a Sindhi as its President.

7. Despite the fact that most Sikh migrants have found a permanent home outside India, support for the idea for Khalistan remains. The causes for this ideological support are varied. Many of the post-1984 Sikh migrants have lived through the torment in India. Their bitterness is not without reason. Even more supportive of the idea of a Sikh homeland are some of the young people in the Sikh diaspora who have otherwise little emotional attachment to Punjab. They, however, identify with a society in which raising one's voice for justice is not a crime. They cannot see why, after 25 years following the killing of thousands of Sikhs in November 1984, arrests, trials and conviction of the guilty have not been made. They do not understand how a government could treat its own people so callously.
8. The continuation of social and cultural baggage, e.g. arranged marriages with its attendant stress on dowry, and preferential treatment of boys against girls. Of the major religions of the world none is clearer that Sikhism on gender issues, sexism, racism and casteism. Yet, it is in these matters that Sikhs show a yawning gulf between principle and practice. The young people raised away from Punjabi culture question these actions of their elders.

TRAVEL DIARY

I thought it might be useful to give my travel diary in a summary form as it describes some aspects of travel as a tourist and a researcher. Under 'Travel Nuggets' I have highlighted some travails, both funny and serious, which an Indian traveller would face. Some of the incidences look trivial in retrospect but did not seem so at the time. Each individual person's travel experiences are unique but it might be useful to share experiences.

First Trip: 16 August–6 September 2005

16 August 2005: At San Francisco Airport, there were a few hiccups encountered while checking my luggage to Buenos

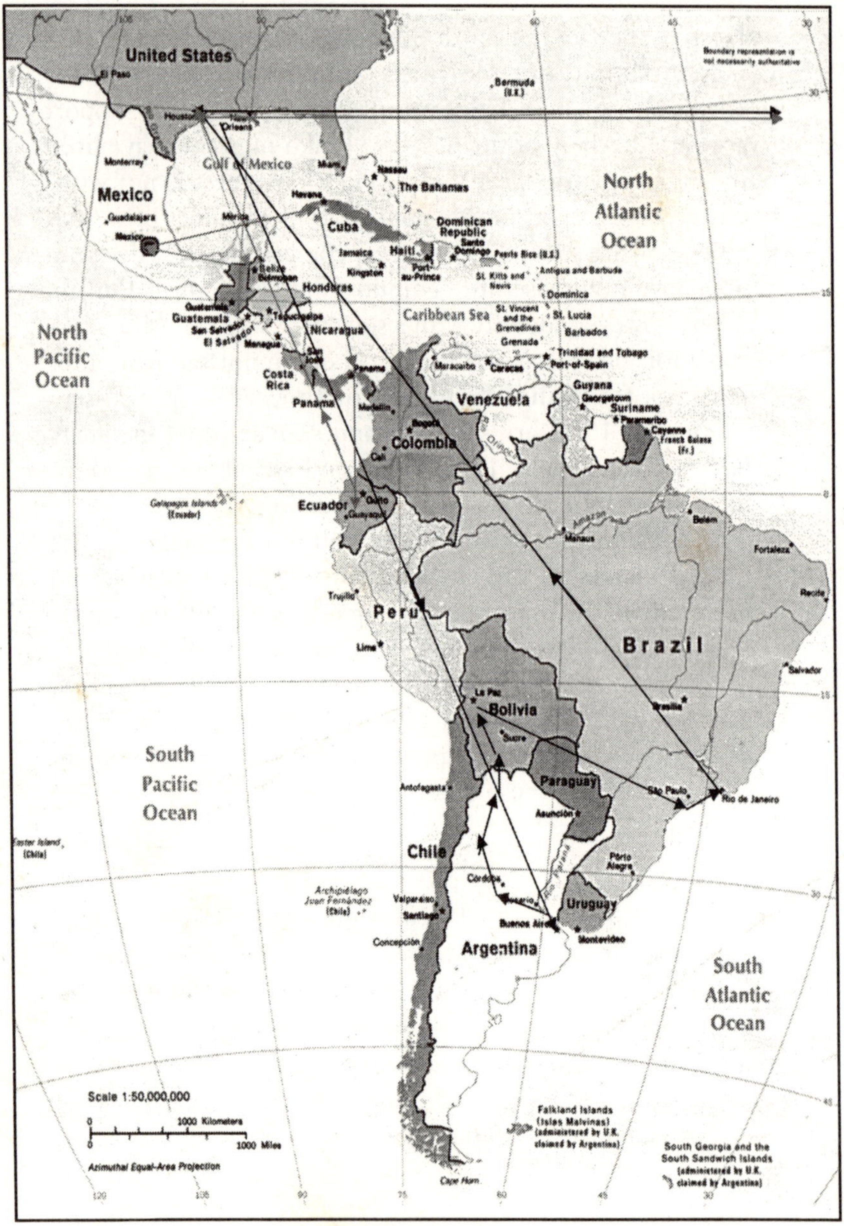

Figure. 4: Latin America—Author's Travels in two campaigns (2005 & 2006)

Aires via Sao Paulo (details under Travel Nuggets). Took overnight flight from Houston to Sao Paulo.

17 August: On arrival at Buenos Aires, Lia de Rodrigues, an Argentinian research scholar, met me. She had offered to put me up in her studio apartment which was vacant. It was a great help. Later in the evening I went to the Catholic University of Argentina where Lia de was speaking on 'Caste System in India'. Naturally, post lecture, I (or let's say my turban) got involved in the discussions. After that, I went for dinner with Tarsem Singh, First Secretary, Indian Embassy who had been very helpful in making my appointments with Indian immigrants.

18 August: Nora Singh, Head of Indian Society, took me to the Embassy of Bolivia as I needed a visa. Bolivia has no embassy in India. Nora does not speak much English or Punjabi. The visa lady at the Bolivian Embassy was very helpful. But there were serious problems (for details see Travel Nuggets). I had to rush to the Indian Embassy. Later in the early evening went to meet Har Rattan Singh who runs a healing centre. In the evening, I had dinner in the Indian restaurant, 'Kathmandu' with Nora, Esther Singh, Lia and others. Nora and Esther have Sikh fathers.

19 August: In the morning, I went to meet the travel agent with Euge for ticketing for the remaining part of my visits to Argentina, Bolivia and Brazil. Because of the local transport strike, I had some difficulty in meeting up with Euge on time. She lives way out in the suburbs. Later on I collected my new passport from the Indian Embassy and got a Bolivian visa endorsed.

20 August: I had lunch with Manoj Meghlani, the owner of 'Kathmandu' restaurant. In the evening Lia, Esther and her daughter saw me off at the bus stop. I almost missed the bus as the travel agent had booked me for Carlos Plaz, a resort town 40 km from Cordoba but had not told me so. We were all the time looking for a bus to Cordoba. (Even with local guides such things happen.)

21 August: The overnight bus travel was very comfortable with airlines type meal served. At the hotel in Calos Plaz, a small town, I had some language difficulty. A lady sitting at the next table came over to offer help. At my request, she telephoned about 20 'Singhs' of Cordoba in the telephone directory. We both felt disappointed as none of these Singhs spoke either English or Punjabi. Finally she got connected to one Singh family who could speak English. I talked with them and they readily agreed to come over in the evening. During the day, I walked around this resort town and did some shopping.

22 August: Carmen and Leandra came to see me off at the Cordoba Airport, from where I was taking a flight to Tucuman. Louis Singh and Dante Singh along with a university student (to act as interpreter—just in case I needed one) came to receive me. I had an Indian lunch with families of Louis and Dante. In the evening, I visited historic buildings from where the Argentinean revolution against Spanish rule had originated. Later at night I went to 'Yoga Centre' run by a second generation Sikh where we sang 'Japji' in a most melodious tune. Martha Singh, a lady with an Indian grandfather, was very kind in rushing home to get me a photocopy of her father Kartar Singh's passport.

23 August: Louis, a lawyer in Tucuman, saw me off at bus stop, for my travel to Rosario de la Frontera. I was met by Jiwa Singh and had lunch with Tara and Jiwa, who live in the same house. During the rest of the day, they introduced me to several Sikhs who were running retail shops or supermarkets. Jiwa and Tara, themselves own large tracts of agriculture land and some real estate. At night stayed at the gurdwara guest room.

24 August: Jiwa dropped me at the bus stop for travel to San

Pedro where I was met by Gurdial Singh. Besides introducing me to several Indian families, they took me to the sugar mill called 'Es Perenza' earlier owned by the British. In a memorial stone for the First World War, per chance I noticed mention of Arjan Singh who had died during the war. Architecture of the buildings, etc., was of the British colonial period similar to the one seen in India in old days. In the evening visited home of a Singh family. They gave me their father Naman's passport copies.

25 August: Hari Gurdial Singh drove me to Jujey, the capital of Salta Province, where I met some Singhs. All of them had Argentinean mothers, and they in turn (both ladies and men) had local spouses. They met me very affectionately and wanted to continue talking. I then went to the local cemetery where there are several Singh Burial Tombs. Earlier immigrants when they died had to be buried as cremation was not allowed. Hari, then took me to Guemes, a village where there are several old Sikh settlers. Some of them were new immigrants and others were children of earlier immigrants. Balbir Singh was particularly knowledgeable about the history of immigration. The family of Atma and Jujhar Singh had an *SGGS* at home. They gave me newspaper clipping of an article published a long time ago about the Sikh immigrants. Balbir dropped me in the evening at my hotel in Salta.

26 August: Met two Sikh immigrants, one Gurcharan Singh, who is a mechanic with the local Government Transport Company and another Suba Singh, a taxi driver. Later in the evening, I interviewed Zulma Singh, a girl who works in the Airport Traffic Control. I had contacted her earlier but she did not turn up at the hotel. It was by sheer coincidence that I met her in a public park.

27 August: Went to airport for flight to Santa Cruise, Bolivia. The flight was delayed by 20 hours. Had to stay back overnight, at the hotel. There I met a lady who spoke English.

On hearing about my project, she located a Singh who was a dentist. I met him and his recently divorced wife. She took me to another Singh lady lawyer's office but it was closed.

28 August: An interesting flight to Santa Cruise de la Sierra over the Andes Mountains—beautiful snow-covered peaks. Interviewed Amarjit Singh Virdi on arrival and later in the evening went to an Indian dance function organized by the Indian Society. A local lady of 50 years performed Bharat Natyam quite well.

29 August: Went to the gurdwara, 30 km away from the town located on the highway to Brazil. I met a few Sikh families there. Interviewed Prithipal Singh Dhillon, Kuldeep Kaur Bhalla, a widow, and the family of Satwant Singh Sandhu.

30 August: Flew to La Paz located at a height of 3,640 m (12,000 ft). The city is located in a bowl with the rich living at lower levels and the less affluent at higher levels. After some sightseeing, I came back to the hotel feeling a bit uneasy. Sham Kaur, earlier name Gisela came over in the evening. She was looking stunning in a white outfit and turban. Had an interesting chat. Later at night when I tried to sleep breathing became difficult. (More details under Travel Nuggets.)

31 August: Took a tourist trip to Lake Titicaca, elevation 3,812 m (12,580 ft)—a beautiful drive on an almost flat road on a plateau.

1 September: Took an early morning flight to Brazil. On arrival at Sao Palo, was met by Mit Mohan Singh Kahlon, a long time resident of Brazil. I had dinner with my ex-ICI colleague, Rolando and Helmund, who had stayed with us in India.

2 September: Flew to Riberao Preto, 300 km away, to interview a Singh descendant. Mit had located this important contact through Mr. Mehta, an Indian businessman. A most rewarding interview with Wagner Singh, grandson of Sansar Singh, an early immigrant to Brazil followed. Mr. Mehta acted as the interpreter.

3 September: Rolando showed me around the city and took me in the evening to Mit's house, in a distant suburb, next to a picturesque golf club. I had dinner with some of Kahlon's golf buddies.

4 September: Met a number of Sikhs and Indians at a lunch hosted by Mit at his house. In the evening took a flight to Rio de Janeiro. Went for a stroll to the famous Copacabana Beach.

5 September: Took a tour of the city and later in the evening went to a bar which was famous for its local music. Trust my luck; it was raining the two days I was in Rio. No famous Brazilian bikinis on display at Copacabana and Ipanema for me.

6 September: Flew back to Houston.

Note: I prefer to stay in hotels. The only exception was Rosario, where I stayed at the gurdwara in order not to hurt the sentiments of the Sikh sangat.

Second Trip: 25 August–20 September 2006

25 August: My friend, Lal Patel dropped me at Houston airport. I was met by Sabbi (Sarabjit, CEO of Tut Great Falls Farm) at Belize airport. The airport is small and old. After checking in at the hotel, Sabbi dropped me at the main market—Albert Street, which has a few Sindhi shops. I called up a few people for interviewing. Belize is a ramshackle town. Most people are black Africans. At dinner in the hotel, I noticed a mention of Har Simran Kaur, the Public Relations Manager. On checking, I was told that she had since left the job. I tried to trace her but without any luck. Someone told me about a Sikh boy from Chandigarh, who was earlier working at the Hotel Casino but had since left the job, and was untraceable.

26 August: Checked out of Palace Hotel (somewhat disappointing). Finally I could trace Simran's residence phone which was answered by her Muslim husband Mairuf. Both are from Mumbai but I could not meet Mairuf. I think, he avoided me—understandable. Har Simran was away to India including a short visit to Chandigarh. I took a photo of the closed Simran Salon. I then went to the market looking for two old Sindhi immigrants—Mahitani and Bhojwani. Got some leads on Sikh migrants' early history. Met in the evening Douglas Singh, Chairman of the Opposition Party. In the evening I went for a two-hour drive with Sabbi to the capital, Belmopan, 55 miles to the south-west (affluent houses). Sabbi's wife Gurpreet, had prepared a great dinner. The Sabbis have two young sons.

27 August: Left early to check in the Belize Hotel again but first stopped at the Tut Farm Office, which is almost a mid-way point. Met Balwinder Singh (the Chandigarh Casino guy), at Tut Farm. Phillip Singh, son of late Chanan Singh, came over to meet me at the hotel. He brought a copy of his father's passport: The first entry was dated 1930. Phillip's other brothers and sisters have migrated to USA. Heard of another old immigrant Singh in the North but couldn't visit him.

28 August: Early check out to rush to San Pedro Island, about 60 km away by boat via Cay Caulker Island. Belize has the second largest reef after Australia. Enroute saw an island with only a golf course. As no glass bottom boat tour was possible, chartered a boat for 1.5 hr just to see the reef. Nothing spectacular, a lot of people enjoying scuba diving, etc. The weather was very hot. Returned to Belize to meet Shira Singh, who preferred to meet outside her office but never turned up. Sabbi with his family picked me up and took me out for a meal at Radisson Hotel. Stayed the night a Sabbi's house.

29 August: Left early for the 2.5-hour drive to the Mexican border. Had problems with Immigration (details under Travel Nuggets). Sabbi was of great help—dropped me at the airport in Chetumal from where I took a flight to Mexico City. Mexico City has a large population (largest city in the world), plenty of traffic slowdowns despite several flyovers which have come up since I last visited 20 years ago. The infrastructure is vastly improved not only in the capital but all over, specially the highway network. Satinder Pal Singh of Shell had sent a car to the airport. The hotel was in the historic centre. Within minutes after my check in, I was looking at the Cathedral—every Western city has these. Walked to the National Arts Centre and watched the National Opera competition—a delightful evening at the beautiful theatre. I returned almost at midnight. There was a long ongoing strike by the Opposition party, who had lost the national elections narrowly. The entire main street, a wide avenue stretching several kms, was occupied by sloganeering supporters with sleeping bags, portable toilets, tv, make-shift kitchen and music, etc. The protest was generally peaceful.

30 August: Visited the Indian Embassy and met Ambassador Bhatia briefly along with Sukhvinder, the Visa Consular. Took a long walk through Palenco, a rich shopping district, a park and visited the Contemporary Arts Museum, followed by lunch of 'keema' and rice. Thereafter I took in the Anthropological Museum with Jagdish Singh, father of Satinder Pal. I later went to their house and met his wife who is a Kathak dancer, and two young kids. Local restaurant owner of 'Koh e Noor' Jassi had invited a few of the local Sikhs for dinner at his establishment to meet me. It was nice meeting several Sikhs and talk about my project. A very late night again. In Mexico City distances are too much and driving time is equally long.

31 August: Interviewed Arjan Singh (wife is Mexican, also named Arjan Singh), a very interesting person. He is now running the Sikh Centre of Yogi Bhajan. Tried to locate Chadda, with whom I had dinner in 'Koh e Noor', but he was not available. I was really tired. For the first time slept in the afternoon for a couple of hours and later on caught up with my correspondence on the internet.

1 September: Woke up very early and went by metro to the bus station. Mexico City is 2,000 m above sea level. Took a luxury bus to Acapulco, a five-hour journey amidst a hilly tract having forests of low height trees but few water bodies. Crossed the last small hill through a tunnel and wow! there was the Pacific Ocean. Acapulco, although famous, is like any other beach town with high rise condos and hotels on the sea front. It was a hot day—I am told all days are hot and hence its attraction to the tourist from the West. After moving around the beach, I had a breaded chicken and rice lunch—tasty. After spending three hours, I took a bus to Mexico City arriving there at 10:00 p.m. Not a worthwhile trip but wanted to feel—'Have been to Acapulco'—objective achieved.

2 September: Woke early and took a five-hour bus journey to Xalapa, a town one hour away from Vera Cruz. Met a handsome 3HO Mexican Sikh with two Patka-wearing sons (15 and 5 years). A fascinating story as to how he became a Sikh. He took me to a nearby town to meet another Mexican Sikh convert family. Took the midnight bus and arrived at Mexico City early morning. Hung around the bus station for a couple of hours—rather uncomfortable but bearable—before checking in at the hotel.

3 September: Rushed to see Mexican dances at 9:30 a.m., which was a real treat. Quickly took a round of three museums. The Gaudi show in one private Palace museum was interesting. Besides being a revolutionary architect (Barcelona in Spain is full of him), Gaudi was a musician too.

4 September: Met Dyal Kaur, a young Mexican Sikh undergraduate, who is working on a thesis on 'Sikh Identity in Mexico City'. I offered to help her on global Sikh migration study and overview of Mexican-Sikh connection. She accompanied me to the offices of the two northern states of Sinaloa and Sonora to seek their help in locating old Sikh immigrants. The officials sounded helpful and promised to revert back but nothing really came out of the visit. I have yet to tackle the province of Baja California, which I am told, has a few Sikh immigrants. Invited Dyal Kaur for lunch at a vegetarian restaurant—all 3HO Sikhs are vegetarians. Later on I met another Mexican Sikh along with Arjan Singh. I had to rush to buy some presents before meeting the Indian Ambassador along with his senior staff. I suggested to him that India should encourage the local university to have students undertake a PhD in India-Mexico migration and cultural relations, etc. I met SP for a brief final goodbye. In the evening when I was walking back through Polenco, a car with a Sikh family beckoned me. I had met them earlier. They invited me to their house. Surjit Singh, had just returned from India. According to him, recent immigrant Sikhs came from 1990 onwards through a garment exporter called Pali in New Delhi. Several of his employees and partners are now running independent businesses mostly in Mexico City but also in Guadalajara, Monterery and Cancun. A gurdwara has also been set up in Mexico City recently. I had to cut short our meeting to rush back to the hotel before midnight.

5 September: Came early to airport to catch the afternoon flight. Everyone had advised me to come at least three hour before check in but all formalities were over in less than half an hour. The long wait enabled me to write this diary entry and sort out my papers which are always in a disarray. I was ready for Cuba where I had no prior contacts at all.

A rather unwelcome reception awaited me both at the Immigration and Customs. My luggage was strip searched and it took me two hours to complete the formalities (details under Travel Nuggets). Havana is a run-down city but has beautiful buildings and wide avenues with a great sea front. A Washington DC type Capitol Hill building dominates the city and a sea front like Mumbai's Marine Drive. Except for going around the city, I did not do much. The hotel, like any other building, has had its hey-day—very colonial facade and interior.

6 September: I headed for the Indian Embassy to meet the lady Ambassador, Vashista Mitra. Everyone in the Embassy was running around making arrangements for Prime Minister, Manmohan Singh's NAM visit. Although they had e-mailed that there are no Sikhs in Cuba, I did get useful leads which I followed up partly. The Embassy wanted me to check in a couple of weeks after the PM's visit was over. I located one Ajit Singh who preferred to talk only over the phone.

It was useful meeting a yoga teacher, Prof. Pimental, a professional yoga instructor. He handed me a newspaper article on old Indian immigrants which was published three decades ago containing interesting information.

Later in the evening I met up with a Canadian Sikh, the son of the ex-Indian High Commissioner to Canada, S.J.S. Chatwal (now settled in Delhi). He has interests in various businesses, along with other partners, mainly Canadians.

7 September: Tried contacting one Castilla Singh of Guantanamo, a TV commentator. I tried to fly to the east but had to abandon the plan owing to unreliability of flights. Since I was getting bored in Havana, I arranged a visit to Trinidad, a six-hour bus journey—fairly comfortable. It gave an opportunity to see the countryside.

8 September: Returned late at 9 p.m. and then went to the Parisian Cabaret, courtesy Chatwal.

9 September: Cuba is an interesting country. The people seem happy and help one other. I hung around Havana, waiting for my flight to Panama City. Panama surprised me as a big city and its busy airport—Central and South American hub of Copa Air. The country is Spanish-speaking and is a less affluent version of the USA. Many restaurants have free wi fi internet. Arrived in the late afternoon and later had dinner with my laptop as company.

10 September: Narinderjit Dhaliwal in his late twenties, picked me up at noon to take me to the large and well constructed gurdwara. A 'sangat' of about 80 or so attended. Good 'langar' as usual. A Sindhi is the President of the gurdwara. I was barraged with a lot of quick shooting information of various earlier immigrants. Parkash Singh later on recapped some of the profiles of earlier immigrants in his house. The hotel helped photo copy the telephone entries under 'Singhs' in the directory—quite a few.

11 September: Visited the Embassy where I got the names of some of the important persons belonging to the Indian community there. In the afternoon I met Koreena Bajwa, Kolkata born and educated, whose mother and grandmother were living in Panama. She is married to a Colombian and running the Masala Restaurant. Her grandfather Gursharan Singh had migrated around 1915. Later I visited a local shopping mall.

12 September: Early visit to Dr. Gupta from Hissar, Haryana, Head of Pharmacy Deptt., University of Panama. I borrowed a book from the University Library on Indians in Panama. Although the earliest immigrants were Sikhs, the dominant community now is Gujaratis, including a large Muslim section and of course Sindhis. Parkash Singh took me to the Canal—last lock called Mira Flores on the Pacific coast. What an enterprise! In the exhibition centre, there was a large mural of the workers. I could spot three turbans (details under Panama country profile). I then visited the old American colony township and offices, including the Canal library. Despite help by the supervisor, I could not get information on the earlier Singhs. However, the supervisor informed me that there were several Singhs working presently in the Canal administration. Parkash gave me a long tour of the city including the old parts where the President lives. The dinner was at Surjit Dhaliwal's house where there were several invitees both Punjabis and the local people.

13 September: Narinderjit took me to their 'Sher e Panjab' farm, 50 km away. It is basically a cattle ranch spread over

2,000 hectares and two hill with a ranch house. On return to the city, I met Julia (pronounced Hulia) Singh, daughter of an early immigrant—Balwant Singh (*c.* 1911). She said she misses 'bakra' meat cooked by her father. Later in the evening I met Balbir, an executive with a car agency. His sister works for the Canal Company.

14 September: Narinder dropped me to the airport for my flight to Quito. The approach to Quito is beautiful—lush meadows, mountains, valleys, etc. Before leaving Panama, I had been warned that there were no Sikhs in Ecuador. On arrival in Quito, as I approached my hotel, a sign 'Indu Restaurant—Indian Cuisine' raised my hopes. Search in the telephone directory threw up only one Singh. Indu Restaurant is owned by Azim Ahmed from Karachi. There are a few immigrants from Pakistan, all of whom came here in the late 1990s or early 2000s. Aziz took me to another Indian restaurant owned by one Mahinder Bhai from Gujarat, who in turn introduced me to Joginder Singh working across from his place. I was advised about a retail shop run by a Sikh called the 'Labhu Shah Boutique y Darshan International, Boutique the de la India'—a long name indeed for a miscellaneous goods retail shop. Regarding setting up of 'Khalistan' headquarters in Ecuador in 1985, I looked up the telephone directory but could get no leads. Had minor breathing stress—below 3,000 m (9,350 ft) height.

15 September: The purpose of visiting Ecuador was to get information on the formation of Khalistan in the 1980s and recognition of the same by the Government of Panama. Earlier on I switched to a better hotel. Visited the Ministry of External Affairs, Government of Ecuador where I met a helpful young officer, Christion. They had never even heard of Khalistan. On my insistence a quick internet search surprised them. The Archives Section Head was unavailable, so I returned later in the day after visiting the historic city centre, the church, museum, plaza, etc. At the Relaciones Exterior

Ecuadorian, there was no old correspondence with their Embassy in New Delhi—neither any mention of Khalistan in the files. However, my persistence paid by searching the correspondence on Khalistan HQ with Ecuador's UK Ambassador. No direct mention of Khalistan but London had passed on news items on the subject to Quito which covered news items in London papers of Ecuador connection. Also an intriguing report was sent on Rajiv Gandhi's meeting with Margaret Thatcher on Sikh extremists. Basically no useful information could be obtained but I did get some leads for me to follow up in the UK. It was nice of them to have shown me their old files. I attended a Jazz concert in Teatro Nacional Plaza—good performance by the Trio.

16 September: While standing at a plaza before going to Otavalo, a Sikh came running across to me to say hello. We exchanged greetings and decided to meet later. I took a bus ride to Otavalo along with Jinda, who was on his sales (*pheri*) mission—a pleasant two-hour drive. The town has a big weekly market selling native Indian handicrafts, etc. I got busy with souvenir hunting. Took the return bus to a point short of Quito and then took a taxi to what is called the 'Centre of World'. Mindo town is on the Equator. The name Ecuador is derived from Equator. On returning to Quito, I went to meet the 37-year old Sikh Bhullar, staying at 'Hare Krishna Temple'. Heard the sad story of his several efforts to migrate to the USA or Canada via Thailand, Cambodia, Vietnam, Malaysia, Dubai, Argentina, Brazil, Peru and now Ecuador. He had been wearing his turban so far. Two months back he cut his hair (and as he says, got into more trouble than ever before). A nice guy who is in a pathetic situation but who won't give up.

17 September: Took the rail motor coach to see the snow-clad Cotopaxi mountain. As usual, I ran into bad luck with clouds and rain but saw some beautiful landscape with a very fleeting glimpse of the mountain. Interesting logistics of the bus-cum-train journey with more tourists on roof of the rail car than inside. On return overcrowding inside because of the rain. Sunday—Quito is dead in the evening. An opportunity to complete my Panama and Quito diary.

18 September: At the Catholic University Library, I looked up all the newspapers of July 1985 to see if there was anything pertaining to the setting up of Khalistan in Ecuador. I did not find any news coverage. It seems it was an innocuous effort to sensationalize an issue by some overseas Sikhs. Met up with an Ecuadorian mother and son who showed me around the city. Met up briefly with Kalam Singh, owner of a small discotheque.

19 September: The best was the last day in terms of sightseeing. Went 175 km (4-hour bus ride) to Banos, south of Quito, a small town situated in a valley, a typical Alpine scene. The famous volcano Tungurahua, still active, had devastated several parts of the town. Saw lava ash and browned trees. Could not have a good look at the volcano as it was a cloudy day—tried to see the volcano from two vantage points. One can hike up to the volcano top or almost. Lava flows like a river and affects areas on its way, leaving the adjoining countryside unaffected. The website of the volcano is interesting.

20 September: Early morning flight to Houston.

Final Comments from Quito/Houston Flight—5 hours

End of an interesting sojourn. It is difficult to interview people in a structured way due to lack of interest and at times diffidence and in some cases outright fear of being probed. At times I felt lonely—that's why I have to keep moving otherwise I get bored in a jiffy. Language was a barrier. Panama was most interesting from the Sikh diaspora angle, scenically Ecuador was tops. Cuba was a disappointment. Ecuador and Panama use US currency (paper notes). Coins interestingly are their own, with one side having the US motto, 'In God

We Trust', and the other side some local insignia. Lal's packet of chocolates, etc., came in handy. Laptop adds to the weight but was useful. Latin America is very wi-fi friendly—free in most hotels or reasonably priced in internet cafes. People all over seemed happy and helpful. Very few people know about India and hardly anyone knows about Sikhs. Turban to them denotes 'Arabia' possibly because of Osama bin Laden being in the news. So I had to clarify on the street greetings of 'Salaam' or 'Allah' to 'Le India' and 'Namaste'. Hotel and other travel costs are reasonable and some countries can be travelled really economically especially if one spends longer period in each country. Visas, airport taxes add to costs for quick fire visits. Public transport and taxis are reasonably priced.

The most memorable experience was of meeting Guru Sewak Singh in Xalapa, Mexico. All hotels were good except in Havana. In Cuba, the sight of people queuing up for ice cream and people with placards offering home bed & breakfast accommodation as a bus approaches a city was innovative. Sikh hospitality in various countries visited is gratefully acknowledged. The vendors selling their wares were mostly enjoyable in Mexico's metro and in bus travel in Ecuador.

The theme that came out loud and clear is that every Punjabi migrant's ultimate destination is USA or Canada. UK is not any more top of the chart. So, as the Leftists say in India—

Yankee Go Home
But Take My Son Along

TRAVEL NUGGETS

As mentioned before, travel for this study had both interesting and at times annoying moments. Since travel to the countries visited is generally not common with tourists from India, some sharing of my experience might be of interest and useful to future travellers.

- Question asked by Brazil Embassy when I went to get my visa—Why are you visiting Brazil as a tourist and why is your wife not accompanying you? Reply: I thought the only way to visit Brazil is to go alone, beautiful women there are the reason for travel. The Embassy processed my visa immediately. At least they seem to have a sense of humour.
- Bolivia: Visa had to be obtained in Buenos Aires as they have no Embassy in India. On visiting the Bolivian Embassy in BA, the visa processing lady was most helpful—I believe it was because of my turban. She even filled up the form for me. When I came to collect the visa three hours later, she is sad faced and tells me that there is a big problem. I get worried too. She tells me there is no blank page on my passport for stamping the visa. I had to rush to the Indian Embassy to get an additional booklet for my passport. Knowing some officials helped me in getting a new passport by the next day.
- I had bought a ticket from India to Sao Paulo and back. I needed a Sao Paulo/Buenos Aires connecting flight ticket. Since Indian travel agents could issue only expensive tickets, I asked through a friend for help from a travel agent in Buenos Aires. I got a confirmed ticket but when I tried to pay in San Francisco through credit card, the agent told me that credit card payment could be accepted only in Argentina. Since cash could not be paid, the agent suggested remitting money via Wells Fargo. WF levied a minimum charge of $50 to remit $150—tantamount to a highway robbery. Ultimately after spending considerable time and effort, I could manage to book alternate tickets on internet through credit card.
- On checking in at the Continental Airlines in San Francisco, they would not agree to tag my checked bags to Buenos Aires as they had no inter line agreement with Air Lingus (SP-BA sector carrier). Later on they took the position that even luggage cannot be booked to Sao Paulo unless I had a valid visa for Brazil. The connecting time

between the two flights was only 90 minutes or so. This meant I had probably to clear through immigration, collect my bags after customs clearance and check in the bags to Buenos Aires. I was getting worried about missing the flight. Luckily I had a Brazil visa but single entry. Continental in-flight staff could not or would not help except to say that on arrival their agent would help. Luckily for me, there was an Air Lingus representative at the arrival gate for another passenger. This agent helped me out by issuing the necessary Boarding Card and getting the luggage re-tagged to Buenos Aires.

- I took a luxury bus from Buenos Aires to Carlos Plaz, a resort 30 km beyond Cordoba, the second biggest city in Argentina. Since I was the only passenger left at Cordoba, the bus driver wanted me to get off and take another bus. When I refused, he had to take the bus with me as the sole passenger.
- At the Hotel in Carlos Plaz, at breakfast I wanted jam, instead the waiter kept bringing ham—confusion in sounds of J and H in Spanish language.
- La Paz in Bolivia is at a height of 3,000 m. I did not take rest on arrival but instead took a city tour. At night I was okay when sitting on the sofa watching TV but as soon as I tried to lie down and sleep, I had breathing problems. I had to go to the hotel receptionist who kindly provided oxygen cylinder. Cocoa tea was of no help. Now I understand how an 'Oxygen Bar' can be a delight.
- While travelling in a taxi to catch the early morning flight from La Paz, a couple was frantically trying to thumb a ride, just on the outskirts of the city. When I stopped my taxi to take them to the airport, they were very grateful. Apparently nobody stopped since the last half an hour to help them as their taxi had broken down.
- While in London for a stopover, friends took me out for a post-dinner drink to the Dorchester Hotel. The lady pianist was playing beautiful jazz. On applauding her good

music, she came over to thank me and said she was 'Dhillon', same surname as my wife's. What a coincidence.

- Mexico is probably the only country, which asks visitors applying for a visa whether they would be visiting border areas in the north and south. I do not know whether this condition is applicable only for Indians or is more widespread. I had said 'no' for both cases while applying for the visa. However, nearer the visit, I found that there are no flights from Belize to Mexico City or any other city in Mexico. The only alternative was to cross over by land at Chetumal in the south, only a couple of hours drive from Belize City. Chetumal had regular flights to Mexico City. The person at the Consulate in Delhi assured me that I can cross over but I was a bit sceptical. As a cautionary measure, I sent an e-mail which the Consulate acknowledged (a pleasant surprise), confirming that I can cross over by surface. As feared, at the Chetumal border checkpost, the Immigration Officer refused to allow me entry. He said he would have to check with New Delhi as the landing card attached to the visa was for arrival by air and hence the objection. Luckily for me, I was carrying a print-out of Mexican Consulate's clarification. I was allowed entry.
- While booking a hotel in Havana through the internet, I received confirmation from three different sources, causing me concern of being debited thrice for the same room. After several reminders, I finally got the clarification that all these agencies were working for the same hotel.
- On landing in Cuba, my luggage was thoroughly checked after keeping me waiting for what seemed to be an eternity. Later when I changed money at the airport bank, I was short changed by the cashier. Fortunately for me, for once I checked the change. The girl tried to be defensive but she knew what she had done. So Cuba arrival was not a good experience.
- When arriving at a resort town in Cuba by bus, there were a dozen or more people with placards. I thought they were

striking or protesting about something. But I soon discovered that they were advertising their Bed & Breakfast accommodation for the arriving tourists.

- Visa application for Ecuador was particularly fastidious, asking for health certificate and police clearance. More details are given under country write up of discrimination against Sikhs.
- In Belize when I was trying to locate Har Simran's salon, I asked someone for directions. He said he can help me provided I paid him some money.
- In Cuba travelling long distance, the bus driver would stop the bus to hug a friend on the roadside at a non-descript village or town and even gave free rides to known faces. A friendly gesture to his countrymen but somewhat annoying to fare paying passengers. I am told earlier on all state transports were obliged to give ride to hitch-hikers which was quite common. A socialist gesture, no doubt!
- In many cities especially Rio de Janeiro, the tourists are strongly advised not to venture out alone or with valuables. I decided to take a local bus in Rio but the Hotel receptionist was horrified. When even the hotel manager could not dissuade me, he tried his final gambit, 'Sir, are you not afraid of dying?' Even that did not work for him—I am still alive.
- Petty cheating is quite common, i.e. if you were to give a $5 bill by mistake instead of $1, they would merrily accept the same. Taxi negotiations are almost a universal pattern but many are quite honest charging fare similar to what they would charge the locals. Not returning change by the bus conductor till you remind are some other common practices. But by and large tourists are treated reasonably. Turban was a help in most cases in Latin America except for immigration or customs departments in some countries.
- The Sikh immigrants were generally welcoming particularly those who were well off. The second generation of Argentinian Singhs were especially nice mainly because they

wanted their children to know the Sikh and Punjabi culture.

- Most early Sikh immigrants who married locally had a large number of children—birth control was either not known or practised.
- Touristy highlights:

  a. Most striking are the Andes Mountains. Many cities in South America including their capitals are located at high altitudes, e.g. La Paz and Quito, the former at plus 12,000 ft. Cocoa tea is considered an antidote. Previously its exports were banned (Cocaine connection) but now tourist packs are allowed to be taken out. Bolivia, being a poor country with harsh living conditions, needs cocoa, a natural antidote for such harsh conditions.

  b. Most countries have beautiful sea fronts, beaches and hills next to the sea, providing beautiful vistas.

  c. People are generally fun loving with a passion for drink, dance and music. Population-wise there are a lot of mixed races called Mestisas. The bureaucracy, police and army are still powerful. People seem contended, happy, and fun loving. Many are getting married at young age in some cases due to unwanted pregnancies. The church seems to be somewhat lax on allowing divorces, which have become common. Slums are a major issue especially in big cities. Catholicism is the major religion and each city has churches located in prominent places, main squares or hill sides and many with magnificent architecture.

  d. Latin America has some really large cities, e.g. Mexico City (20 million people) and Sao Paulo (15 million) and some famous cities like Rio de Janeiro and Havana (Le Habana) which were and still are fun cities. Carnivals though the most famed one is at Rio, are prevalent in all the Latin American countries

  e. Language is a big barrier particularly to be able to get to know the local people.

CHAPTER 3

Sikhs in Argentina

INTRODUCTION

Trust the Sikhs to locate the farthest country from Punjab to emigrate to! As has been pointed out in an earlier chapter, end of the nineteenth and early twentieth century was a period of active 'outward look' by the Sikhs to South-East Asia, China, including Hong Kong, Australasia and North America. It is, however, not well known that Sikhs started to migrate to Argentina in small numbers in the late nineteenth and early twentieth century along with the Sikh incursions to North America. The reason for selecting Argentina could have been that besides the USA and Canada, the only other prosperous country in the Americas at that time was Argentina. Although not English-speaking but it had British influence especially in industry, commerce, business and railways. The Sikhs in Argentina have been substantially assimilated into the local society and the third and even second generations may not call themselves Sikhs. But emotional bonds exist and a gurdwara was commissioned in the early 1990s. Fresh immigrants keep coming albeit in small numbers but turbaned Sikhs are a rarity. Some of the first generation immigrants got married locally; many in the second generation and almost all of them have done so in the third generation. New immigrants though are more ambivalent in this respect.

It is interesting to note that Argentina is one of the few countries in the world (excluding California in USA, Canada and now Italy) where out of the total Indian immigrants, Sikhs formed a majority. They continue to form a very significant segment of the Indian community in Argentina.

THE COUNTRY

Despite being the second largest country in South America and the eighth largest in the world, Argentina has always fallen short of being able to establish itself as a major power which its size and range of industries suggest. Corrupt military governments and bad economic management has been the problem. Another factor is probably the pattern of immigration in earlier years as the land was owned by only a small section of the population in the form of huge estates which encouraged vested interests. The economic crisis earlier in this century forced major devaluation of the Argentinian currency in 2002. Argentina has almost an exclusively European population (in contrast to Bolivia and Brazil). The country has good farmlands, and grazing areas. Climate is moderate except on the mountains and in the South. Argentina was discovered by the Spaniards in early sixteenth century and declared its independence from Spain in 1816. The country had some charismatic leaders as San Martin, liberator of Spanish America and romantic rulers such as Juan Peron and Eva Duarte later Eva Peron of *Evita* (the Broadway musical) fame.

The High Level Committee Report has the following to say:

> Argentina was never a part of the British Empire and there was thus no post-slavery indenture system to take Indian labour to that country. But it seems some intrepid Indians went there around the beginning of the 20th century as employees of British owned railways, or as plantation workers for British or Anglo Argentina firms. Most of those who had gone to Salta or Jujuy in the northern part of the country married local women and settled down as farmers. They even adopted local names and became Argentine citizens. In time, some of these people and their descendants took up other professions such as law, medicine, finance, banking and trade. They are generally well off and are held in high regard.
>
> Many of the PIOs in Argentina have remained attached to their Indian culture and traditions. They have constructed a gurdwara at Rosarion de la Frontera in Salta province. Some of them are actively

involved in propagating ayurveda, yoga, Indian classical music and the Hindi language. They have established an Indian Association in the Northern provinces and organize social and cultural events to celebrate Indian festivals. Unfortunately, there is little interaction between them and those who have settled down in other parts of this extensive country.

A large number of the Indian Diaspora living in Buenos Aires are businessmen, doctors, financial or business executives, and employees of multinational corporations. Most of them have retained their Indian citizenship. Considering the small size of the Indian community in Argentina, its impact on the general population of its country of settlement is insignificant. Nor does it have any special demands or expectations from India. However, some of the prominent businessmen in the Diaspora have expressed the hope that the bureaucratic hassles often encountered by them in the course of their business dealings with India should be reduced, if not totally eliminated.

EARLY SIKH IMMIGRANTS

There is evidence that Sikhs started migrating to Argentina in the late nineteenth century. This premise is based on the following:

1. Hew McLeod writes in an e-mail to me,

> The second feature was the presence among the migrants of Ram Singh. Most of the Sikhs maintained contact with this man, revering him for his muscular piety and his devotion to the Sikh religion. Baba Ram Singh was born in the village of Bhulla Rai near Phagwara and first came to Australia in 1890 in the company of some other Sikhs at the age of 14. He returned to the Punjab after a brief stay and then journeyed to Argentina with his younger brother. Returning again to the Punjab he travelled once more to Australia in 1898. There he worked as a farm labourer in the Lismore area, living in various huts and shanties.

This would mean migration to Argentina of a Sikh teenager, an interesting feature of migration. It is my surmise that these youngsters must have followed or accompanied some older migrants.

2. Other than McLeod's reference, no definitive information is available but the national census of Argentina in 1895 shows the presence of six Indo–English persons as per Lia Rodriguez De La Vega, a Buenos Aires Researcher.
3. A house built in village Lagheri dating back to 1911 by Gunwant Singh on his visit back home would also indicate possible late nineteenth-century migration.
4. According to Baldev (Daniel) Singh of village Bopa Rai Khurd (see detailed interview below) who lived in Argentina for over two decades, the British who were setting up sugar mills were facing difficulties because of 'Veerappan' type brigands and sought the help of Sikhs to provide security for their operations. According to him the first Sikhs went to Argentina to work in the British sugar mills in 1879 in Jujey area. He states that there is a cemetery of 1900 where Sikhs are buried. This needs checking.

EARLY TWENTIETH-CENTURY SIKH MIGRANTS

Major arrivals were in first two decades of twentieth century. Several channels of travel have been noticed: (1) Some Sikhs came directly by ship to Buenos Aires. The ship sailings were from Singapore via Durban. Sikhs would first travel by train to Kolkata and then go by ship to Singapore. (2) The *Clansman* affair of Fiji has been detailed under 'The Passage to Tina' later on. This version is of Sikhs being taken to Fiji instead of Argentina and how they finally managed to reach Buenos Aires via Wellington, New Zealand. (3) In another version, it is told that the Sikhs were brought in by the British to help build the railroad system. (4) Still another version is of the Sikhs wanting to emigrate to the USA were dumped by the shipping lines on the Northern shores of South American continent from where they wended their way through Brazil or through Peru/Bolivia to Argentina. (5) Another channel of migration was to begin in Cuba and in time onwards via Panama Canal onto the Pacific coast of South America. When

Plates 1–2: La Esprenza Mill (top) First World War Memorial with Arjan Singh's name; (bottom) The Sugar Mill

Plates 3–4: Jujey—Sikh Burial tombs—cremation was not allowed

Plates 5–6: Nostalgic Sign Boards: (top) Ex-granthi's shop, (bottom) Sikh Supermarket

Plates 7–8: Nostalgic Sign Boards: (top) Retail shop;
(bottom) Sikh Auto workshop

the Canal construction got completed in 1914, the Sikh workers were apprehensive of being sent back to India. Looking for new pastures to inhabit, they literally walked their way to Argentina. What an effort. (6) There are accounts of Sikhs who migrated to Brazil but moved onto Argentina—some by getting appropriate visa and others just crossed over. The persons going to Cuba, Panama or Brazil sailed via European ports.

But why did the Sikhs go to Argentina in the first place which was the farthest away country in South America? Restrictions on entry to North America, detailed earlier on, led the Sikhs to look for opportunities to settle anywhere south of USA. Argentina in the early twentieth century was a prosperous country, called Europe of South America. Furthermore its farm land and climate was similar to Punjab. The patronage of the British who were constructing and running the railways and some sugar mills was an added feature.

THE PASSAGE TO TINA

The earlier Sikhs heard of a country by the name of 'Tina', possibly easy to pronounce than by its full name Argentina. This created unintended problem at least in one case. In his biography as an immigrant to Fiji, Tota Ram Sanadhya, Fiji Museum, 1991 (book supplied courtesy Narendra Anuj of Australia) mentions in some detail the legal suit filed by some Sikhs in Fiji. The case of ship *Clansman* evidently got well publicized as a confrontation between a group of Punjabis (Sikhs) and a European lawyer named Berkeley. In 1911 some Sikhs set-off for Argentina but they wrongly came or were brought to Fiji thinking it was Argentina. Having realized their folly, they were determined to go on to Argentina. Berkeley was approached who agreed to get *Clansman* fitted to take them on their cross-Pacific journey. There are many turns and twists of the case including death of Berkeley in June 1912. The Sikhs lost their case but left later by another vessel for Wellington, New Zealand on their way to Argentina. One

J.J. Davies escorted the Sikhs till Wellington. An interesting mention by Davies is that the Sikhs had 2,700 pounds in gold before sailing for Buenos Aires. So this group of about 46 persons should have arrived in Argentina early 1913. Full details are given in the Appendix 6.

EARLY PROBLEMS OF SETTLEMENT

Just like the early immigrants to other countries specially the white dominated countries, the initial problems were colossal. Language and a totally alien culture were the main barriers. Lack of funds added to the misery and the immigrants had to seek any odd job that could be obtained. I have heard of some of them living under bridges before they could get jobs and earn some money. Those who came by boat headed north-west from Buenos Aires towards Salta, about 1,500 km away. Those stragglers who reached Bolivia either from Chile or Brazil moved down to nearby Tucuman near the border. It may be conjectured that it was comparatively easy to get jobs in the far out north-west, as these areas were not as attractive as big cities like Buenos Aires for the white immigrants. Living conditions up-country were easier and similar to Punjab. Sugar mills and railroad construction provided an initial secure income source before the Sikhs started working on farms and slowly graduating to being owner farmers and ranchers. Subsequently, trucking and transport, as is the familiar pattern for Sikhs moving out from Punjab, became the immigrants' new diversification. This was followed by owning shops and supermarkets in due course of time. As the early immigrants settled down, communications were established seeking more compatriots to join from the family or village to which they belonged. For many, the local booze and the pub was a welcome relief from solitude. Initially all immigrants were single. Only very few of them could get their wives to join in due course but at a much later date. As a result of this, most of them entered into local marriage alliances.

RECENT ARRIVALS

Immigration continues till today but in smaller numbers. There is a case of several Sikh youths who were dumped by their travel agent in Buenos Aires in the 1990s telling them that Argentina was, in fact, America, technically true but so very misleading. Most of them are still waiting to migrate to the real America, viz., US or Canada. They are now running small retail outlets to be able to survive. A second generation Sikh lady is helping them out. There is a case of a young man from Ludhiana who went on a tourist visa, took off his turban on arrival in Argentina, and married in 1992 the granddaughter of a well-established Sikh. Local gurdwara marriage could be registered only in 1993 when they already had a baby girl, Luciana Kaur. For a marriage to be registered in Argentina, the man has to be 21 years and woman 18 years. The couple returned to India in end 1999 for family reasons but has now migrated to North America. A typical immigrant story! The newer arrivals maintain their Punjabi identity much more and this helps keep alive their connections with Punjab.

There are some persons like Balbir Singh of village Guemes, Salta Province, who are passionately Sikh and Punjabi, helping out other Sikhs to immigrate to Argentina. Although he is clean shaven, Balbir's son of 8 years or so keeps 'joora'. He has couple of other turbaned Sikh immigrants working with him.

I met a so-called 'granthi' Sikh in Buenos Aires who immigrated a few years ago after having worked for a couple of years in a garment factory in Korea. His is a fascinating story. He is now a specialist in healing through yoga and nature therapy. His clinic in the centre of Buenos Aires has photos of Sikh Gurus and 'Khanda', etc., prominently displayed. Sikh chants from Japji, etc., are a part of the healing process.

Some Sikhs have recently moved southwards from Bolivia through marriage or otherwise because Argentina offers better economic prospects. The Sikh 'granthi' of Bolivia Gurdwara moved to Rosario as a 'granthi' of their gurdwara. Now he runs a retail shop.

SECOND AND THIRD GENERATION

The second generation of Sikhs who married Argentineans are totally assimilated locally and except for Singh as their surname, they have very little association with Sikhs or Punjab.

I had the opportunity to meet with a wide spectrum of Singhs. Except for the first generation immigrants or children of the first generation father and mother from the Punjab, the first names are usually local, e.g. Leandra, Dante, Louis, Carmen, Nora, Esther, etc. Hardly any of them have visited Punjab but when I met them, they were exuberantly friendly and wished to know about their Sikh heritage and Punjab culture. There were several gestures to show their emotional and sentimental pleasure at meeting a turbaned Sikh. A barrage of questions would follow and without exception they had a strong desire to visit Punjab—finances permitting. Some of the ladies even expressed a desire to marry Sikhs from Punjab. Most of the immigrants seem to be definitely better off compared to the weak economic background of the early immigrants. But there are not many 'rags to riches' stories similar to North America or UK. On the other hand, there are no stories of trouble-making or jailed Sikhs either. One would place the Sikh immigrants and their newer generations as professionals, middle income group, retailers, farmers and transport operators.

Establishing contacts for a visitor is difficult because of the small numbers and problems of language, as very few of them speak English or Punjabi. There are very few Sikhs with turbans. Amongst the first immigrants, keeping the turban was possible when working for sugar mills, etc., where a few of them were employed. A photo of Esperenza Mill workers (appearing in a newspaper article) shows all of them in turbans. However, Sikhs working in smaller numbers or in isolated places found it difficult to retain the turban to gain local acceptance. Despite the difficulties some of them kept the turban till their death. Marriage to local women was also an important factor. Getting a job with a turban except in the British enterprises who respected Sikh identity, could have been problematic. New immigrants are closer to Sikh and Punjabi culture and their arrivals though in small doses helps maintain the cultural linkage. Two Sikh brothers even though clean shaven and despite their modest homes in terms of living space, keep the *Sri Guru Granth Sahib* at home. The immigrant families have access to recorded 'shabad keertans' and of course Punjabi pop and bhangra music. A third generation girl who otherwise is Argentinian in all respects, wore 'salwar kameez', along with her mother, though probably as a fashion statement, on her law degree graduation ceremony. Cooking of Punjabi dishes is quite common. At a lunch at the house of a Sikh in Salta, parents were having 'daal roti' and the son beef steak, wearing an Argentina soccer tee shirt. I got the feeling that many of them are ripe to be inducted into Sikhism and Punjabi culture.

One heard stories of help and support by the Sikhs even from long distances whenever there are serious illnesses or accidents, etc., even if it is outside the family. It is really a sight to see shop hoardings such as 'Dasamespita Norte Supermercado' (supermarket), 'Almacen Singh Khalsa' (retail store) or 'Despensa Singh' (grocery shop). 'Singh' surname is well respected and even the third generation is equally proud to be a Singh.

Earlier immigrants when they died had to be buried as cremation was not allowed. It was quite a sight to visit 'Singh Family Burial' tombs. Cremation is possible now.

A gurdwara was constructed in the early 1990s and is proving a great anchor for the community. Regular functions are held on Sundays and 'Sangrads'. Important Gurpurbs are celebrated. On special occasions Sikhs come from long distances. Gurdwara also provides for get-togethers on marriages, deaths and anniversaries, etc., and is helping bring closer the various Sikhs and their families. Langar is served on all occasions.

MARIA EUGENIA CERVANTES: NOVEMBER 2002

Euge was an exchange programme trainee of AIESEC in Chandigarh when we first met her. She had not heard of Sikhs before coming to India. As we got to know each other, we invited her to stay with us towards the end of her tenure in Chandigarh. I encouraged her to go to Rosario on return to give me her observation on Sikhs settled in the town where a gurdwara is located. This was to come in handy as a preparation for my visit later on. Her notes on the visit are quoted below as it is interesting to see ourselves through others' eyes, especially a foreigner who had some exposure to Chandigarh.

EUGE'S REPORT

Saturday

We arrived on the Saturday 23rd of November, after twelve hours in bus, at Rosario, the city in the province of Santa Fe where my friend Eva lives. Rosario de la Frontera is a city of 5402 citizens in the province of Salta; situated 1500 kilometers away from Buenos Aires. In many aspects the town is similar to one of these villages (small towns) like the ones I saw in India, very different from the capital city.

The house of Jiwa, where we were going to stay, was no more than six blocks away from the bus station. I decided this mean of transport because I spent money in a tape recorder to make some interviews and thinking in one further trip to another Sikh community in the country [I had given some money to Euge for this trip of hers]. That day Jiwa was waiting for us at his front door. He is a man of medium height, robust but who walks with the help of a stick.

There we met some of the other inhabitants of the house: his daughter-in-law, Jasbinder and two of his grandsons, Sergio and Carlos who were seventeen and fifteen years respectively, and are studying in high school. They also introduced us to the woman who helps them daily with the housekeeping, Norma. The house is spacious, simple and has an interior patio full of plants, flowers and a small parcel where they still grow local and Indian vegetables in order to use them for the traditional dishes.

That day, after a good breakfast with Jiwa we were visited by Tara and

José Singh, both born in India (uncle and nephew), partners in business in the city, among is found (run) a supermarket. Jiwa has lands and properties that hires (rents out) and are his way of life, now that he is retired. They were asking me about my experiences in the Punjab while I was asking them about their lives in this country so far from the one that gave them life (born). Later we were conducted to our room in the first floor of the house that nowadays is empty. It was used by the other daughter-in-law of Jiwa, that (who) has come (gone) back to India again. The lunch was with Jiwa and Tara; women and youngsters ate in other place. This behaviour we could appreciate it the rest of our stay there.

I was asked about you (Swarn) and they're waiting (for) you and Livleen (my wife) with open arms.

When we were finishing lunch Mariana arrived, the eldest grand-daughter of Jiwa. She is twenty years old, and is living and studying in Tucumán, two hours in bus from Rosario de la Frontera. She's in second year of the university, in the way of becoming herself an accountant licentiate.

Some time later Yita arrived, of twenty-nine years; she's the daughter of Tara Singh. She is teaching contemporary Indian dances in a cultural centre of the town with a large group of students that includes girls from six years old up to teenagers, also including a student with Down's syndrome. She's looking for support in the Indian embassy, but until now she hasn't received any answer. In more than one case I was told the same. Its pitiful that Indians in Argentina don't feel heard by their representatives in the country. The story of this young lady I think shows very well the clash between two different cultures like Sikh and Argentenian society. She was married when she was nineteen years old in an arranged marriage with a Sikh boy born in India who she didn't know. She accepted the situation for love and respect towards her family. She lived in India for several months with her political (!) family and then moved to Canada with her husband. Couple (marriage) lasted for four years and since then she has moved to Argentina, living with her parents again.

Regarding new generations, they are respectful for the traditions although they don't fully agree with them. They go to the gurdwara on the special dates, besides that they declare that they don't have any particular religious believing (belief). The smallest children, of six, ten years, are delighted being inside a group of people in which women wear in a colourful and different way and they speak correctly in Punjabi as well as in Spanish. There is a big quantity (number) of kids in the community; some of them were born in Salta being both of their parents Sikh, and others directly born in India.

That first Saturday of our stay, José came for taking us to a short trip to 'Las Termas', a place where the water flowed normally at 99°C and it is said that has medicinal virtues. Returning home, we went to the gurdwara in which were taking place all the settings for the celebration of the Sunday 24th (Gurpurb). The place was fully occupied by women and children, all of them were helping in one way or another for putting colour flags and paper flowers inside and outside the temple. Some women were preparing the food (langar) that they all were going to share the next day. We stayed there hanging balloons and other until midnight, moment in which we were invited by José for dinner (late night get togethers are a common feature even at homes) and then we went back to Jiwa's home that is just across the street, for a well deserved Sunday rest.

On Sunday we woke up and went to the gurdwara, I took pictures and could watch a Sikh religious ceremony for the first time. [Pity, no one took her to a gurdwara in India—considering that the company she was working for in Chandigarh was owned by a devout Sikh.] Men were located against the right wall and women against the left side. Children were running in the middle of the two stripes, coming in and going out the place. The temple is really a small complex that includes the house of the priest and his family, a big lunch room and kitchen used by the community in special dates like this. The land where the gurdwara was built was donated twenty years ago by José Singh and the building was [constructed] with the support of all the Sikh families in the region. They also helped to build a Catholic church in Rosario de la Frontera, a really nice gesture and a descriptive example of the good relation with the rest of the population.

Nowadays, following the economic problems of the country, the donations are smaller but they still collaborate for keeping the gurdwara and for the requirements of the priest, his wife and children. This person (granthi) came from Bolivia, approximately four years ago and although he is not the ideal person for the job according to some members of the community, he will remain in charge of the temple because the present conditions would make very difficult the bringing of a new priest as the money is really little. José Singh has also donated lands for the first Sikh cemetery (cremation) in the region to be established in the future.

After the celebration, we moved to the lunch room where we were lucky in meeting the first Punjabi lady that came to the country, Gurna Kaur, wife of Gurdial and sister-in-law of Dan Singh. She agreed in answering some questions that I could record and I'll transcript in a next e-mail. She's an old woman, warm, soft spoken and very humble in the way she express herself. It was a pleasure and honour having a little chat with her.

After lunch (langar), that included dahl, spicy vegetables, dahi and several types of sweets, Eva and I went to a rehearsal that Yita had invited us the previous day. Her dance group was going to show up in a festival the following Saturday and these were the last adjustments. They were eight girls of different ages, with months of practice and the aim of making the best participation in the choreography. Only one of them, besides Yita, was Sikh. The remaining dancers were girls of the city that also attend classical and Arab dance classes. After the several hours that the practice took, Yita invited us to her home where we had the opportunity of meeting her mother, a shy and elegant old woman, also born in India. Although she spent with us all the time we were there, she barely spoke. It was the evening when we went back to Jiwa's home, Tara came with us. After dinner we went to an Argentinian typical arts street market in the central park of the town.

Monday

Monday was very quiet; I had a long conversation with Jiwa that I could also tape in cassette. He spoke about his life, of how, when and with whom he came to Salta, his activities during all these years up to now and his family.

Mariana had finished the 2002 period in the university and she was preparing herself for the finals, so she decided to stay with her family in Rosario de la Frontera instead of going back to Tucumán. This was very useful for us because we could ask her what were the opinions of other young Sikh women growing up in Argentina. In various aspects she shared Yita's vision, with whom she's joined not only by the common cultural origins but also they have a long-term friendship. She told us how difficult it was bringing her male friends to her house and other details that in any teenager result almost trivialities but are not so in a centenary culture like the one in which she was born, subjects regarding the freedom of will and arranged marriages.

Jasbinder, her mother, showed me albums of family pictures and remembered her husband with love. Kuldeep, as well as the other Jiwa's son, Charan, had expired several years ago; both of them in two different fatal accidents. Jiwa's wife also has died some time ago after being cared for her last fifteen years by Jasbinder that took the job with devotion and sweetness. Although she never worked outside the house, she doesn't feel that staying at home was a problem at all. She is very happy with her political family and still has a fluent communication with her sister that lives in India, although they haven't seen each other for many years. She's very proud of her children, the three of them with very good marks at school and excellent potential for their professions in the future.

Tuesday

On Tuesday, the last day, Jiwa was absent during the morning and first hours of the afternoon because he went with Tara to Tucumán for some medical studies regarding the diabetes that affects him. Yita invited us to have lunch with her and surprisingly her mother participated more in the talking. It was nice taking pictures and to watch her smiling. We saw snaps of a National Dance contest in which Yita won the first prize with her solo choreography last August in her category. Before leaving we went to visit José and his wife, to whom we showed the pictures in the CD we prepared in Chandigarh. We saved them in José's computer and in Jiwa's computer too. Mariana came with us to the station and we said good bye promising to see each other soon.

CASE STUDIES

The Real Dhan Singh*
And all His Namesakes are Standing Tall in Argentine

Argentina has many Dhan Singhs. One is a successful fleet owner who came some six decades ago along with hundreds of fellow Sikhs and hardly any savings from India. They have created a tiny, vibrant community here of just about 1,000 people of Sikh origin and many of them are products of marriage between Sikhs and Argentineans.

* For the newspaper clipping see Appendix 5, 'The Real Dan Singh', *Economic Times of India*, 12 July 1998.

There is also Dhan Singh, who at 81, is sprightly and mentally alert, the dean of the Indian community in Argentina.

And there is Dhan Singh, father of Virginia—a successful lawyer who has made an impressive but unsuccessful bid for more than six years to win an election to the national Parliament.

From time to time, the Argentine mainstream media seeks Dhan Singh's counsel. When Mother Teresa was ailing he was asked tc comment. And when she died, his views were sought.

About two dozen Indians had arrived in Argentine in the first quarter of the century. Though they were bound for America, they were dumped on the way on various Caribbean islands. It was largely by accident that they were able to make it to Argentina. They hoped to reach America through the land route after working in Argentina for several years. But most, like Dhan Singh, married local women and stayed put.

Dhan Singh's story is little different, born in Bhatinda district of Punjab and raised in Calcutta, he had no explicit desire to go to America. 'One day I read in a Calcutta newspaper of the possibility of migrating to Argentina', he says. 'The news story mentioned Argentina was looking for hundreds of workers for its farms. I also heard from some people in government who had visited Argentina that it was very much like India, very green and beautiful.'

He did not hesitate to use up his meagre savings and sail for the New World, along with four of his friends. After a journey that took nearly a year, they reached Argentina in 1937. Dhan Singh was barely 20.

'I did not want to work for the British in India', he says, as one of the strongest reasons for leaving. Naturally, he did not want to work for the British-run Argentinean Railway unlike two dozen Indians who had come to Argentina about a decade before his arrival.

In some ways, his entry could never have been as traumatic as the few dozen Sikh soldiers of the British Army who at the end of the Boer War sought to go to America and Canada in search of better job opportunities. Many of them were dumped by the greedy and conscienceless agents at various ports in the Carribbean or the coasts of South America. These men knew very little English.

So when Dhan Singh arrived in Argentina, the few Punjabis in Buenos Aires helped him find a simple and inexpensive place to live and cook Indian food. Singh believes that given his cosmopolitan and pragmatic outlook, he did not expect problems in Argentina. Besides, he explains, he was much younger than the men who had preceded him. And being young meant that he could learn to read and write fluent English.

'I blended with Argentina easily', he says. 'It was the human warmth that influenced my decision to settle.'

After doing odd jobs for nearly a year he became a truck driver. When he reminisces of his truck driver days, Dhan Singh laughs, saying it was a given thing in many towns and villages that if you can't make a decent living through education you should at least drive a truck and earn some money.

It took him over two decades to find real success. He bought a number of grocery stores and began purchasing land. Marrying an Argentinean woman certainly helped. Together, they raised seven children.

Despite his preoccupation with business, Dhan Singh still found time to establish the Hindustanica Association of Salta. Soon he would raise money to construct a small gurdwara in Rosario de la Front area in Salta province, which was converted into a gurdwara about a decade ago.

Attached to it is a community centre. Dhan Singh has also reserved a part of his estate for the cremation rites of Hindus and Sikhs.

The gentleman now leads a semi-retired life but says he cannot really retire, for he has been working even before he became a teenager and since he has seen his hard work yield fruit, he says he is superstitions about surrendering himself to full-time retirement.

FIELD VISITS

During a ten-day visit, I met a wide cross-section of Sikhs of the first, second and third generation. Each meeting was as interesting as the previous one. These were somewhat sentimental stories. In the second part, I have included interviews of some of the returnees from Argentina whom we met in the

Punjab villages. It is an interesting way of getting a sense of lives of first generation immigrants.

Interviews in Argentina

Carmen and Leandra Singh

I was staying at Carlos Plaz about 40 km from Cordoba, the second largest city of Argentina. According to the telephone directory 20 Singhs were listed. With the help of a lady (subject of another story as to how she was literally moved to tears when she read the books on Sikhs carried by me). No one except Leandra Singh could speak English (or Punjabi). Leandra along with her mother Carmen Elena Singh and Cousin Gabriela Singh met up with me in the evening. Carmen's father was Muncha (possibly Munsha) Singh who married Juana when she was only 15 years of age in 1917 in Cordoba. Muncha then 26-years old was working with the British Railways. Muncha had seven daughters and five sons. He presumably came to Argentina a couple of year's earlier and started working in Buenos Aires before moving to Cordoba. At his marriage, so far as Carmen learnt, no Sikhs were present.

It was a marriage of convenience as Juana was probably a house maid. Carmen kindly presented Muncha's photo in India on a horseback before he left for Argentina. Carmen and Leandra were full of excitement and as they said post meeting with me—'we are richer now as we belong to two cultures, one of Argentina and the other of Sikhs and the Punjab'. They insisted on seeing me off the next day at the airport. Carmen had not seen an Indian till she met me post Muncha's death in 1943 at the age of 52 years (Carmen was 6 years old). Juana died in 2001 at the age of 99 years. I provided them with telephone numbers of other Singhs in Cordoba—Leandra wants to establish a sort of 'Singh Club'.

Plates 9–13: Argentina, Singh Ladies. (top) (L) San Pedro, Naman's daughters, (R) Jujey-ladies who have Sikh fathers; (middle) Buenos Aires (right) Dr. Lia de Rodrigues, (left) Nora Singh and (centre) Esther Singh. (bottom) (L) A local lady helping to telephone Singhs in Cordoba, (R) A Sikh girl in Punjabi dress for her Law degree

Plates 14–15: Buenos Aires (top) Har Rattan Singh, Healer, (bottom) Euge with her mother and author

Plates 16–18: Tucuman (top) Dante Singh and Louis Singh families; (bottom) (L) Yoga Centre run by Angel Singh—*kirtan* is played; (R) Martha Singh (right front) who provided her father Kartar Singh's passport copy

Plates 19–20: (top) Munc(s)ha Singh in India prior to his migration
(bottom) Muncha's daughter Carmen Singh with son Leandra Singh
and niece Gabriela

Plates 21–25: Guemes. (top) (L) SGGS at devout Sikh's home, (R) Balbir Singh's family; (middle) Bikram Singh who brought SGGS from Punjab; (bottom) (L) Bikram's siblings; (R) A new Sikh immigrant

Plates 26–28: Salta (top) (L) Suba Singh, Taxi driver, (R) Suba in his village prior to migration. All brothers have migrated; (bottom) Gurcharan Singh with wife & son wearing Argentine soccer shirt. Parents eating daal roti, son beef steak

Plates 29–31: (top) (L) A Singh lady lawyer's office; (R) Zulma Singh, Air Traffic control, Salta; (bottom) Bridegroom sans bride—Rosario Gurdwara. Bride did not pay obeisance at the gurdwara but joined the festivities in the evening preceded by church wedding

Plates 32–35: Argentina Returnees. (top) (L) Daniel Singh, V: Boparai; (R) Surinder & brother in Chandigarh; (middle) Gurmeet Singh, V: Jandiala; (bottom) Navjot Singh Sandhu with wife, children and father, Ludhiana

Plates 36–37: Gurdwara—Rosario de la Frontera. (top) Tara Singh and Granthi; (bottom) Inside view

Jiwa and Tara Singh

Jiwa Singh (uncle) and Tara Singh (nephew) of village Bopa Rai Khurd are the leading farm owners of Rosario de la Frontera, a small town where the gurdwara is located. Besides owning vast acreages of farm lands, they have transport business and supermarket and other real estate. They were responsible for initiating and setting up of the Gurdwara. Before coming to Argentina, Jiwa wanted to migrate to North America but Dan (Dhan) Singh, an earlier immigrant from his village, requested him to accompany his mother to Argentina. On arrival in 1958, he started working with Dan Singh and then soon thereafter bought his own truck, etc. A partnership was formed between Tara Singh, Jiwa Singh and Dan Singh. Tara Singh stays with Jiwa Singh. For more details see the diary entries of Eugenia Cervantes earlier in this chapter.

In an interview on 23 August 2005 at his house, Jiwa talked about his interaction with an old immigrant, Bhai Bhag Singh, who was a 'puran Gursikh'. Jiwa met Bhag Singh in 1965. Bhag Singh told him that they had entered Argentina from Cuba via Bolivia. They faced difficulties, as they were unfamiliar with the language spoken in this region. They did not know the manner to ask for food. They used to talk in sign language. They got job in sugar mill, San Pedro. Before that they had worked in the railways. Gradually they settled in Gumes and LaDermo. Following is a transcript of the question-answer session with them:

Q. How did Bhag Singh group reach Cuba?
A. They reached Cuba from India directly. They were unaware about the destination; they were planning to go to USA. They reached Cuba in the name of America. They worked in sugar cane fields in Cuba. Thereafter, they entered Argentina via Bolivia.
Q. When did it happen?
A. I don't remember but at that time he was saying 25 years ago (may be around 1940).

Q. How did they come to Argentina?
A. How they came from Cuba to Bolivia is not known. From Bolivia they entered Argentina walking. They came along the railway track and reached Salta. Bhag Singh reached Guemes from San Pedro.
Q. What was their livelihood in Argentina?
A. He started working in Argentina along with Niranjan Singh, his nephew. They started selling vegetable as vendors. Niranjan was interested in land and hence they bought some land. Niranjan started agriculture and Bhag Singh worked as vegetable vendor. They prospered in business and built their own house.
Q. Can you tell about others who came along with them?
A. Chanan Singh and Kehar Singh came to San Pedro. They came before Charan Singh. They were from a village Jandi near Jagroan. Their children are living here. Chanan Singh's children are in San Pedro while Kehar Singh's children are in Jujey.
Q. Tell me names of some other villages in Punjab from where immigrants came.
A. Bhag Singh was from Lagheri village, Gurmit Singh (interviewed by me in India) from Jandiala. Rakha Singh and Basant Singh were the earlier immigrants. Now they are no more but their progeny is here. There was another one in Jujey, Dalip Singh's father. I have forgotten his name.
Q. Why did the people go back to India?
A. Sugar mill workers were entitled for pension. There was a provision that enabled the person to receive pension even if they are residing in other countries. There is a saying '*kamai pardes khao desh*' popular among immigrants. When they were old enough to retire, they returned and received pension there. People use to retire at the age of 60 to 65.

Jiwa's Travel to Argentina: An Adventure: When I came to Argentina, a dollar was equivalent to 3.5 Indian rupees. I reached here in sixty days from Bombay. My ship came via Naples and Genoa. Dhan Singh's mother was sick. The journey from Bombay to Genoa took 21 days and we were confined in ship for another seven days after which we were asked to disembark. A gentleman, Mr. Gulati from Bombay, helped us to get her hospitalized. We met a local Shipping Agent who had fought in the Second World War as soldier along with Punjabi soldiers. He helped us a lot. He arranged for us to board the ship from Genoa. We reached here via Spain, Brazil and Montevideo. Dhan Singh's mother was suffering from trachoma. They did not allow us to disembark the ship at Buenos Aires port. We were confined in ship for seven days. Dhan Singh took the help of some advocates. An agent familiar with certain official in the Embassy got us offloaded from the ship when it was about to leave. This Agent was sympathetic towards us as his mother had gone through similar experience. We were sea sick. Tara Singh's brother had earlier tried to get us offloaded from the ship illegally but could not succeed as there was police all around.

Chatu Ram was a big landlord in Argentina. He had 38,000 acres of land. He took care of us as we were deprived of Punjabi food for last 50 days. More than 50 Sikhs were here at that time. People who had retired from the railways were doing agriculture or dairy near Buenos Aires. Their progeny still lives in the suburbs of Buenos Aires. There were around 100 families in Salta. Most of the people stayed in Salta and San Pedro. Lesser number of them were settled in Guemes and Ladermo. Punjabis have a quality—they worked in sugar mills and railways even though they were unfamiliar with the local language. After that they went on to start their own businesses. They became vegetable vendors and retailers. Punjabis are respected here. None of them were jailed or involved in any anti-social activity. Singhs have a lot of credibility here. Shopkeepers trust them. The young generation follows on the footsteps of their elders in this regard. Singhs are welcome anywhere in Argentina. Earlier it was easy to get visa for Argentina but now the situation is different. Agents are responsible for this.

Q. How many people arrive every year?
A. First came Dhan Singh's brother and then came Tara Singh's brother. I don't know when Dhan Singh arrived here. Ten to fifteen people arrive every year. In 1990s, around 200–300 people arrived. Agents consider it a via media to reach America. Earlier immigrants have got their families re-migrated. Here

people are treated at par, irrespective of their colour and socio-economic status. Everybody feels at home here. I have been to England and Canada. People don't talk much to each other there. Here people are amiable to each other. This love binds you with this land. Here you don't find any hatred. You can choose your locality for residence according to your purchasing capacity. Your locality is immaterial as far as social behaviour is concerned. Rich and poor eat together here. The social bonds of this society make you forget the ancestral land. Here if you are going in a jungle, the people living in huts will insist you to have food with them. In Europe people leave you dying on the road. Here people help you if you are injured on the road. We people from erstwhile British Imperial countries go ecstatic when we see the social bonding here. Now the situation has changed. People have become money minded. People are migrating to Canada and America. Agents are minting money.

Suba Singh

A clean shaven, taxi driver in Salta city who migrated to Argentina as a teenager in the 1960s. An interesting feature of the visit to Suba was a photograph of five teenaged brothers in turbans and striped (night suit type) pyjamas in their village Saleempur Masrooda in Jallandhar/Phagwara area. They were evidently from a lower middle class background. But the significant aspect is that all five emigrated, two each to UK and Argentina and one to Australia. It just symbolizes the Sikh enterprise.

Zulma Singh (Pali)

A transcript of her interview in Salta Public Park at night is given below:

My name is Zulma Singh. I am 26 years old. My father's name is Parshotam Singh, who lives in Guemes. My mother's name is Sulanda who is an Argentinian. My father was born in village Lagheri and spent ten years there. He moved to Delhi where he spent eleven years living with his parents and sisters. The patriarch Kuldeep Singh migrated after his marriage and wore turban throughout. He had two sons Sarwan and Bikram. Bikram migrated after marriage to an Argentinian and Sarwan stayed back in India. Sarwan's son Parshotam migrated to Argentina. Bikram has four children, Atma Singh is in Argentina, Satnam migrated to Canada, Manjit Kaur married in India (migrated thereafter), and Jasbir Kaur married an Argentinian Sikh and migrated.

My father is 57 years old. He came here when he was 21 years old. It means he came to Argentina in 1958. He came here to look after his grandfather, Kuldeep Singh, who was a vegetable vendor (*rehri*). He used to live in the same house as Atma. I visited India for six months in 1992, when I was 13 years old along with my elder sister (17) and mother. We met my grandparents, Mr. and Mrs. Sarwan Singh. I knew about Sikhs as there is a gurdwara (in the house) in Guemes and I used to go there for festivities. Now *SGGS* is in Atma's house but earlier it was in someone else's house. I go sometimes to the gurdwara in Rosario dlF, but not always. I got to know about Sikhism in Spanish from my father as I don't understand Punjabi. This was before I went to India. I have been working for nine years and am in the Air Force, presently attached to Air Traffic Control at Salta Airport. My mother likes India and Sikh religion. My sister is 30 years old and has three daughters.

I am disappointed with people who talk ill of India never having visited India. They say there are too many people in India, there is no food and there are a lot of problems. Every country has problems and I don't like people who talk ill of India. Since coming back, we are in touch with only my uncle. I used to spend some time with our neighbours in Delhi. There was no e-mail or telephone at home. I am a student and am working as well since 9 yrs—I was 18 when I started to work. I live alone now but earlier on I used to live with some girls. Not because I don't like to share, but because sometimes I have another companion during the weekend.

I go to my father's house and go to gurdwara in Atma's house. All of Atma's family speaks Punjabi. I used to ask them to teach me. So I have learnt a few words of Punjabi from them. Talking of differences amongst Sikhs in Canada and Argentina, she thinks the Sikhs in Canada are more 'developed'. In Canada, they have been able to evolve and change from what they were in India. Despite the father and mother being Sikhs in

Canada they have adapted better to the changing environ of Canada. In Argentina even if one parent, mostly the mother was Argentinean, the adaptation to Argentinean society and environ, is less evident. She has been to Canada and hence these observations. Sikh community in Canada is so much like Indians. They go to the gurdwara, they say prayers together, have langar together. Here, in Salta I do not share my Sundays with the other Sikhs—maybe once or twice a month.

Last month a young Sikh got married in Rosario. Bride did not come to the gurdwara and that's a problem because the bride does not want to share the religion with the groom's family. Argentinean society is Catholic and they do not accept other religions.

When asked—Are you Catholic? She replied—Yes. My mother sent me to the church but I do not go to the Church now. Zulma thinks, economics are changing attitudes in the society. Canadians have more opportunity to go back to India and stay in touch with Punjab. In Argentina, after the devaluation of local currency, we find it very difficult to travel to India. For us it is cheaper to go to Canada than to India. There aren't many turbaned Sikhs in Argentina. The few, who are here, are mostly in the north of the country. In India the standard of education is very high. What my neighbour's daughter in Delhi was studying in school was what my mother studied in college. The schoolbooks in India are very detailed and comprehensive. My mother has a college degree but my father is not highly educated. My mother is a teacher. She teaches Biology and Chemistry in high school. Her parents were farmers. My father's parents were not happy with him marrying a non-Sikh.

There is a problem in Argentina about the young people. They don't want to work and want the government to look after them. This is why we have so many social problems. They don't want to study, get a degree or do a job. I am lucky to have a few friends who listen to the teacher and want to study. What kinds of jobs are preferred in Argentina? Boys and girls want to go to the Army because of the good job insurance and retirement benefits. Some other professions such as Medicine are also considered desireable. Doctors have to work in hospitals. But most don't want to work. That is why there are some sit-ins and protests.

Har Rattan Singh

Interviewed on 18 August 2005 in Buenos Aires at 6:45 p.m. in his chambers.

He stated, 'I was born in Jagraon. We had land in Haryana that is why we were living there. I was educated in Haryana, Jind city. Then I came to Punjab in 1986.'

Q. Where did you live and study?
A. I am under-matric. I took training in *SGGS*. I took part in twelve akhand paths. I was very attached and fond of Gurbani. I was always dreaming for Guru Nanak's darshan. Once I was taking a walk in my fields when suddenly an idea struck my mind—Where is the Guru? People say that Guru is always with you. But I could not find him within me nor is he visible.
Q. When were you born?
A. In 1957.
Q. Did you start agriculture after school?
A. I joined an ITI (Industrial Training Institute) in Jind but could not find any job on completion of the course. I got an offer from Haryana Roadways which I refused. Guru Nanak came into my dream. I joined kar-sewa in Patiala. We (brothers) bought two taxis and started business. After some time, we got in touch with an agent for migration. On landing in Hong Kong we got help from the local gurdwara. We were advised to purchase a ticket via Korea and Japan to Hong Kong as visitor. I had asked for a two-day stay in Korea and got the entry for two weeks but I returned after two years. I had a five-day visa for Hong Kong so I left within the stipulated period. I went alone. I went to Korea where I had a friend from Jagraon. I rang him and he sent a Punjabi speaking local (interesting information!) to pick me from the airport. I asked one of my friends in UK to help. He responded with a thousand dollars (note the generosity and helpfulness). Before leaving for Korea, I had suggested to my brother to visit China for a week and thereby get his visa extended for another week. On my brother's return from China, he flew to Korea. In those days visa was not required for travel between Hong Kong and Korea. We earned 80,000 to 100,000 (INR) per month and sent money home. We were working in a fac-

tory manufacturing swim suits. They did not inquire about the visa. Even when we planned to return after two years, they were requesting us to stay. I was working as inspector and had sixteen people working under me. My brother was working as operator. We were in Seoul and there were many Sikhs. My friend Jiwan Singh was staying there for last five years. We were 16 Sikhs in a house—three of us used to wear turban. We reached Korea on 22 October and returned on the same date after two years. It was Diwali day.
Q. Does it mean I have to go to Korea too to study the Sikh immigrants?
A. You can get the exact information about Sikhs from Jagraon.
Q. Tell me the village?
A. There is a Raikot stop in Jagroan. There is a gurdwara called Ajitsar. Jiwan Singh's father was president of this gurdwara. You will get to know the exact whereabout from there only. Radai Agwad is an area in Jagraon where they know about many boys in Korea.

I took my parents to Hazoor Sahib for pilgrimage. I got married in 1987 and had two daughters and a son. We were in India from 1995 to 1998 trying to go abroad. Talking of migration to Argentina, Har Rattan told that he got to know about the country in Korea. When we tried for visa to Argentina, the Malta Boat Tragedy happened because of which the visa procedure became stricter. American Embassy refused us visa thrice. Our agent got us the visa to Argentina on payment of Rupees three lakhs. My brother went in advance. I followed him three months later. It is difficult to survive in Argentina. I am the only Indian having work permit. At that time my brother was working in Salta for 300 Pesos. I came to Buenos Aires and could not find work for six months. I exhausted most of my funds. An Indian, Surinder Singh, put me in touch with some people working on Yoga therapy. I had experience of Yoga and they were looking for an Indian looking person. They asked me to join after two days on commitment of paying thirty dollars per patient. On first day I attended four patients and got 120 dollars. Next day I got

210 dollars after attending seven patients. I worked for seven months and earned handsome amount. I cleared the debt of 2000 dollar and sent 2500 dollars home. I thought that bad days are over now. I had 7000–8000 dollars as bank balance.

Everybody showed me respect. I got work permit while working there. They closed the centre after seven months. I happened to meet one of my old patients in the street. Doctors had warned her that she would not be able to walk properly throughout her life. However, I was able to make her walk through massages. She remained grateful to me. This case made me popular all around. She offered me a place to open my own centre and promised to mobilize patients. I consider that day of 1998 to be lucky for me. Starting with 400 dollars per month earning, I reached 1200 dollars per month. Today I worked from 9 a.m. to 6 p.m. and earned 400 pesos. I got myself registered in 1999. I got work permit in October 1998. My patient's husband got my permit renewed through a pharmacy. I got permanent work permit after three years. I visited India afterwards. Now I am a permanent resident here. I can get Argentinean passport but there is a condition of being without a turban (Ministry of External Affairs to note), which is not acceptable to me. I am confident that I will get Argentinean passport as turbaned Sikh. People from President's House to Income Tax Department and Human Right activists visit me regularly. They have faith in me and are getting relief. I have now heard from him that he is the first Sikh to get Argentinian passport with photo wearing turban.

I went to India after two years to see my father. I cured him of kidney problem through massage. I returned to Argentina —my Guru Ji invited me back home. After selling the oils and other articles used for Yoga therapy I returned to India within two months. I stayed there for 19 days.

An industrialist from Delhi visited here. I cured him through meditation. He insisted me to visit his home in Delhi. I went with him and took his family to my Guru.

I faced many difficulties in getting the visa for my family members. On my request the Ambassador helped me to procure Family visa. My family came here in 2003. They found it difficult to adjust—my daughters are 16 and 14 whereas my son is 12. I got them admitted in the university and took care of their needs. They are Puran Gursikh. They bring my meals here. I am thankful to God who is providing us good livelihood in a poor country. My children are happy and computer is their best friend. My father-in-law is in USA. He has applied for our immigration and we are expecting immigration visa very soon. (He has now moved to Seattle.)

I have helped many people to settle here. A Partap Singh came to this place and started asking for money like a beggar. He was an old man and married to a Peruvian lady. I asked him to deliver lectures in Spanish. He earned handsome money and went to Spain. We are not in touch as I scolded him when he asked for money. (Partap Singh of Peru now lives in Delhi —see under Peru).

Q. Did you know about General Satinder Singh?

A. He used to meet me on the way but did not talk to anybody. I used to ask him, 'You are a Punjabi brother—do talk to me'. He used to smile in response. I have not seen him for last one year. At times he used to have flute in his hands. He used to sit in a park and play the flute. He used to respond with eyes without speaking even a single word. He was afraid of disclosing his identity and making associations with others. He was very strong internally. He never shook hands with anybody, just smiled.

Q. Do you know anything about other Sikhs in Argentina?

A. I don't know much as I am busy in my own business. I don't socialize much. There is one 'Sardar Lamba' who has a shop here. I don't know his address but his telephone number is there with me at my home.

Balbir Singh of Guemes

Interviewed on 25 August 2005, Guemes.

Balbir Singh studied in his village Lagheri. After passing matriculation from Mahilpur, he received residency permit from

Argentina in 1974. He worked four years on the farm, after which he ran a grocery shop. Thereafter he moved to Buenos Aires in 1979 where he worked for four months in the Indian Embassy there. While in the capital city, he worked with the Hemnani Group who had started business of export-import from Nigeria. Balbir travelled around the world in 1981 covering Spain, UK, Iran and India as a bachelor. He spent two years in UK from 2002–4 but did not like the lifestyle. His wife is British born Punjabi. According to Balbir, one of the first ladies to arrive in the area was Gurnam Kaur w/o Gurdial Singh (1952). Another lady who came along with Gurnam was Nasib Kaur w/o Pyar Singh with a child. The daughter Marina is a journalist and exponent of local dancing. Another lady Husbeen, a doctor, had been to India three or four times.

According to Balbir, the maximum immigration to Argentina took place during the period 1924 to 1930. He further estimates the following population of the first generation Sikhs at present; Guemes—12; San Pedro—8 to 10; Pariko—3; Yuta—1, Caimensita—4; Laderma (largest sugar mill)—3; Salta—3; Rosario dlF—10 to 12; Metan—3; Gulpa—2 to 3. The first *SGGS* was brought with the help of the British of Rio Grande. The first generation population is at a standstill, some leaving the country and similar number coming. Immigration regulations have become strict.

Alberto Singh

Interviewed 23 August 2005, Rosario dlF.

Seventy-eighty per cent of the Sikhs are born in Argentina only. I have been to India thrice. I am from Boparai Khurd. We are very few people here. There were more families earlier but many have left due to devaluation of currency. Those who are living here are accepting the situation but the Sikhs coming from outside feel that their earning capacity is low when compared internationally. They also find UK, USA or Canada more attractive. I will not like to leave Argentina even if there was an opportunity to migrate to these countries. We like it here. I don't like those countries because of their lifestyle. We work very hard, 12–14 hours a day. I did not study very much and took over the business from my father who was not keeping good health. We are five brothers and sisters.

Gen. Satinder Singh

He was a Major General with a good family background who migrated to Argentina post his retirement. Not much is known about the reasons for migration except for an alleged unhappy marriage and a very dominant wife—as per the people who served with him in the Army (and Chandigarh has plenty of them). On arrival in Argentina he probably bought some farm land. He also taught English at the university. According to the Indian Embassy he came to collect mail or to meet some formalities regarding his pension. He has since passed away. He became a very private person—please see Har Rattan Singh's interview. An e-mail from his son after my visit says it all. I have done no further probings—respecting the departed soul's privacy.

As to my father's odyssey in Argentina, your information is correct, he migrated to Argentina in 1976, at which time he bought a farm in Viedma. In about 1978, he sold the farm and moved to Buenos Aires, where he wrote for the *Buenos Aires Herald* and taught English to professionals planning to travel abroad.

As to the details, Dad, as all in the family know, was a very private person and as such guarded his personal life from public discourse. Hence, I am honor bound to refrain from delving into his personal and business dealings in Argentina.

I do hope you understand, and if there is any other information that I can provide please do not hesitate to contact me.

Best regards,
Muttoo.

Interviews in Punjab

Village Boparai Khurd a large village with three hundred houses, has a High School, a Sikh gurdwara and a Hindu temple. The streets are well paved. A large number of people from the village have migrated. It is known for its well entrenched anti-British revolutionaries. One of the residents was involved in the *Komagata Maru* incident while several others were involved in the Ghadar movement. Baldev was interviewed in this village.

Baldev (Daniel) Singh

Interviewed on 29 September 2002.

Baldev Singh migrated from village Boparai Khurd in 1972 at the age of 22 years but returned in 1995 due to personal reasons. His migration was because of his uncle Dhan Singh. According to Baldev, the first Sikhs went to Argentina to work in the British sugar mills started in 1879 in Jujey area. Argentina has sugar cane, mangoes and jamuns. The sugar mill was under Veerappan type attacks and the Sikhs agreed to defend the mill. There is a cemetery from 1900 where several Sikhs are buried. There were about forty single Sikh men in Argentina around 1930. Dhan Singh left for Argentina in 1930s. Around 1910 or before that date about fifty people landed in Port Allegre, Brazil, and from there went by train and walking or by other available modes of transport of the times to Bolivia, and from there to Argentina.

Dhan Singh, whose brother was a taxi driver in Calcutta, went to Argentina around 1936, along with five others. They went to work in a farm. The wages were 50 cents per *bori* (sack) for harvesting corn cobs. Many were living under railroad bridges. Dhan Singh married a local woman by the name of Maria. Baldev Singh migrated to Argentina in 1972. According to him Argentina was a rich country. In 1953 some other people including Gurdial Singh went to Argentina. Hardit Singh Sidhu left for Argentina around 1954. In 1963,

Hardit's brother Tara Singh left by KLM Airways accompanied by four others (Surjeet Singh, brother of Daniel, Piara Singh, nephew of Dhan Singh, Bikram Singh and Nihal Singh). In 1958 Jiwa Singh left for Argentina with Dhan Singh's mother. They went by ship, which took two months. Dhan Singh's mother came back in 1969. Dhan Singh had visited Boparai village in 1955, and again in 1972. Others who emigrated from the village were Sukhdev Singh, nephew of Tara Singh around 1967–8. Daniel arrived in Argentina on 14 June 1972 at the age of 22 years and returned to India in 1995. Daniel had studied at Siddharth College in Halwara.

Village Lagheri, Mahlpur

A village of about 500 houses, electrification took place in 1964–5 and landline telephone connections became operational in 1993. Now every house has a telephone. Every house has two to three members overseas and in some cases entire families have migrated, mainly to UK and Canada. The village has a middle school. A high school and college is located at nearby Mahlpur. The latter is famous for its crop of professionals in politics, diplomacy and teaching. The village has six gurdwaras, four constructed by the Jats and two by the Ramgarhias. It has two temples also.

The following persons were interviewed on 6 October 2002 (along with Eugenia Cervantes of Buenos Aires).

Harbinder Kaur, wife of Jaswant Singh. Harbinder's brother had migrated to Argentina as their grandparents were already there.

Niranjan Singh: Sardar Niranjan Singh, now dead, migrated in 1921, at the age of 18–19 years. He had eight children, four sons and four daughters, through his marriage with an Argentinean lady. Niranjan Singh never visited India. He wanted to come back in 1975 but unfortunately died in an accident before that. Niranjan Singh was accompanied by two other

Sikhs from his village, Kuldeep Singh and Malha Singh. Ajit Singh went in 1971 by air and shifted to the UK in 1980. Balbir Singh (interviewed in Argentina) went in 1975 when he was sixteen years of age. He later sponsored two young men for immigration to Argentina and sent them air tickets.

Kuldeep Singh: Kuldeep Singh, father of Bikram Singh, went after marriage and visited India three times. He kept his turban. He had two children, Bikram Singh and Sarwan Singh. The latter did not migrate and lives in Delhi. However, Sarwan Singh's son, Purshotam, is married to a local lady, a professor, in Argentina. Purshotam runs a dairy (see interview of Zulma Singh).

Bikram Singh: He migrated leaving behind his children (two sons and two daughters), whom he later sponsored for immigration to Argentina. One son Atma Singh is in Argentina and the other son Satnam Singh migrated to Canada. Among the daughters, Manjit Kaur got married in Lagheri and then migrated. The other, Jasveer, was married to a Punjabi in Argentina.

Gunwant Singh: Uncle of Niranjan Singh went to Argentina, possibly in 1891, returning in 1911 after twenty years and built a house (a three-storey house with concrete benches and photos of gurus all around. The house had coloured glasses, but is now dilapidated). He married an Argentinean.

Ajit (*Gurmit*) *Singh*: Interviewed on 6 October 2002 in Village Jandiala, Tehsil Garhshankar (along with Eugenia Cervantes of Buenos Aires).

Ajit Singh left for Argentina at age 16 in 1951. Ajit's passage from Singapore to Buenos Aires cost a meagre Rs. 45 and the ship touched Java and Durban enroute to Argentina. There were five other Sikhs travelling with him. His journey took him almost seven months including the waiting period in Calcutta and Singapore where he stayed free in gurdwaras.

He had to spend more than two months each in Calcutta and Singapore before he could get a passage along with five other Sikhs. Ajit was married to Norma, an Argentinean whom he has left behind. Ajit Singh, whose original name was Gurmeet Singh, returned to India in 1994, after about forty years. He was married in Guemes in 1986. Norma was evidently not well off and was working in a hotel when they first got to know each other. However, he made it clear to Norma at the time of marriage that he will ultimately be returning to India. He was sponsored by his uncle Rakha Singh living in Jujey. Rakha Singh was born in 1910 and migrated at the age of 20/22 years (in early 1930s) after he had beaten up a police officer in the village (another of the many reasons to migrate). Ajit started working together with his uncle selling and trading in vegetables. They bought some trucks to start a transportation business. On arrival in Beunos Aires, he lived in a Hindu mandir. From Beunos Aires he went to live with Dharam Singh in San Pedro in Jujey. His journey by train from Buenos Aires to Jujey took three days. According to him some Sikhs travelled from Panama to Argentina overland during the early Ghadar period.

Navjot Singh Sandhu

Interviewed at 1723 New Prem Nagar (Near Hathi Complex & PAU), Ludhiana 141008.

Wife: Harpreet—d/o Charan Singh s/o Jiwa Singh of Argentina.

Children: Ms. Luciana Kaur (10 yrs). Master Nicolas Navkaran Singh (8 yrs.).
Father: Sardul Singh Sandhu, Retd. Registrar, Bhatinda Engineering College. (Sardul, a refugee from Lahore had settled in Samrala).
Mother: Died in 1999. She was a teacher.

Navjot has two sisters, the elder one is a teacher in Ludhiana and the younger is engaged to a computer teacher in Canada. Navjot studied in Ludhiana, Guru Nanak Engineering College for a diploma course. He was engaged when he was studying in his first year (17 yrs) to Harpreet (15 yrs) of Boparai Khurd. He went to Argentina on 17 December 1991, on a tourist visa for one month. He was wearing a turban but removed the same on arrival in Argentina. He flew British Airways, and had to stay at Heathrow. He did not know English well but the flight crew was helpful. He was sponsored by Jiwa Singh who had also sent him the ticket. Navjot had his first Punjabi meal on arrival after a long journey and felt safe.

According to him, Jiwa Singh (at present 72 yrs old) and his wife had two sons, Charan Singh and Kuldeep Singh. Kuldeep Singh migrated with two sons, Gurpreet and Amandeep. Charan Singh stayed back and died in 1989 just before his planned trip to Argentina. His wife migrated with daughter Harpreet (17 yrs) and two young sons on a one-year visa. One son stayed back but the younger son returned after schooling. Navjot, having gone on a one-month visa in December 1991 married Harpreet in the gurdwara as per Sikh ceremony. This was not official according to Argentinean rules as both were underage. They were married in January 1992 at Rosario de La Frontera. Their marriage was officially registered in 1993 (under Argentine law the minimum age for marriage for men is 21 yrs and for woman 18 yrs). Their first baby was born in November 1992, but was registered only at the time of their official marriage. Harpreet's grandfather, Jiwa Singh, had bought a house for Navjot and wife-to-be (Harpreet). They stayed in this house though not officially married with Harpreet's brother Amandeep.

SOME REFERENCES

Two references are of great interest, the first written by Bilka and the second a newspaper article which appeared in a

Argentinean newspaper. The original version is given in Appendix 3B.

An account of Sikhs in Argentina by Bhagat Singh Bilka

In his book *Unfole Warke* in Punjabi, Baba Bhagat Singh a Ghadarite writes about the Ghadarites' Argentinean branch. According to him, Sikhs came to Argentina in 1910–11 and started working in the sugar mills and railway workshops of Buenos Aires and Rosario up in the north. The economic conditions though poorer than North America were better than many other Latin American countries and employment was easily available. In 1914–15, they were getting the Ghadar literature but did not participate actively. By 1925, Argentina became the last destination for many Punjabis. Sikhs left India in the hope of settling in the USA via Calcutta, Burma, Malaya, Indo–China, Japan, Panama but none of the countries allowed them to disembark and hence some had to land in Chile and move on to Argentina via Bolivia. Another group travelled via Bombay, France, Cuba, Mexico, Panama and Brazil to reach Argentina. One has to see a world atlas to admire the distances they covered by ship, foot, train or bus under totally alien conditions. It was no less an effort than that of Columbus! In and around 1930, several senior members of the global Ghadar movement visited Argentina in places such as Rosario, Jujey, Tucuman, Cordoba and Salta indicating a widespread presence of Sikhs in central and north Argentina. Some of these afficionados came to Argentina from Brazil. During the world gathering of Ghadarites in Moscow, out of a total of 71 delegates, about 20 per cent were from Argentina. (To place in context, it has to be noted that delegates from several countries particularly from the British Commonwealth countries were denied passage to Moscow.)

The Hindoo Cowboys

(By Gustavo Javier Wrobel; Photos by Alfredo Calascione) (A newspaper article in Argentina–Spanish version with photos in Appendix 3A).

On a morning in 1924, Bikar Singh had a sleepless night. Each second seemed an eternity. With the break of the first rays of the sun, he washed his face, recited a few lines from the *SGGS*, had his breakfast in silence looking at his family as if he was seeing them for the last time (describing the scene at the time of his departure from Punjab). In reality also, this was not far from the truth. It was after several years before he got to see a familiar face (it was when his son joined him). After a little while he left by train to a port city in India to catch a boat for Cuba.

After staying in Cuba for three years, he left for South America. He could not pronounce the name of the country he was migrating to but he liked the land of this new country. He was a farmer and wanted to remain to be a farmer. He was dark complexioned, was wearing a long flowing robe, a turban and a long beard. On seeing the new country, he exclaimed that this was what he was looking for. In the year 1927, he arrived in Salta province. He lived in Argentina till he died 57 years later. Bikar, though not the first Indian to migrate to Argentina, was certainly one of the earliest immigrants. He had a farm on the Jujey/Salta border in Ojodeagua village. It is now looked after by his children. He had developed an expertise in cultivating a special type of tobacco called Virginia which had a ready market for exports. The local Governor had also complimented him for his expertise. According to Bikram Singh (his son), this land was as dear to him as his own sons. According to Bikar, Argentina was the best place in the world. After 50 years in Argentina, he thought of paying a visit to India. Till his death at age 85, he was physically fit. All the jobs including purchases were done by him personally. He used to go to the church with the Evangelists and liked it as he felt that their teachings were similar to those of Sikhism, such as ban on smoking and drinking. He adhered to his principles till his last breath. He believed in practising the teachings and principles of his religion.

Bikram Singh is also considered a trendsetting individual in Guemes. According to Bikram, he came to Argentina at the age of 44 to a place where he had no relatives. He stayed for three years after which he returned to India in 1969 (for a visit). In 1973, he called for his wife Gurdev and children (two sons and two daughters) here. The first few years were very hard. In the beginning he felt homesick as he did not know anyone and nor did he know the local language. On top of it, the local traditions seemed strange to him. 'I was bored and missed my family quite a lot. The compensating factor, however, was that I had a job and was busy acquiring property', he says. In India the situation in regard to these two aspects was difficult for him. 'Soon I started liking being in the new country', he said. Till 1978, they were cultivating their own land but thereafter moved to Guemes to set up shops. These developments of owning farms as well as shops gave a lot of confidence to the younger generation. As a result, their children could go to schools to study. The remaining 10–12 families are now occupied in running bakeries and other shops. With time they felt settled as they got familiarized with the local customs, etc. Now Bikram has retired and lives a relaxed life spending time praying in the mornings, shopping for his wife, and cycling to socialize with his neighbours, etc. According to Bikram, 'Argentineans are very good people and we get along well. They invite us over for meals and we return the compliments.' Jasbir Kaur, his daughter is now running a retail business.The Sikhs collectively meet at their house for religious functions since they keep the *SGGS* in their house. Bikram Singh leads the prayers followed by others, and later *prasad* prepared by his wife is served. *Prasad* is made from atta, sugar and butter. His wife Gurdev Kaur runs the kitchen and spends most of her time in household chores. For cooking meals, she does not get the right ingredients at times. She, however, prefers the Argentinean sweets once in a while. She sometimes makes *samosas* with chicken stuffing as beef is prohibited by the Sikhs.

Atma Singh, Bikram's elder son, migrated to UK to live with other relatives who had migrated there prior to India's Independence. His other children continued to live in Salta. The eldest daughter's marriage was arranged through post with another Indian. This is a common practice in India. They ask their relatives to look for a suitable match for their daughters or sons and exchange photos for this purpose. This is how Jasbir Kaur and Rajinder Singh got married, by seeing each others' photos only. They now have two children who were born in Argentina—daughter Sonia Monica and son Franco Alberto. Rajinder looks after the bakery named 'Nueva Delhi', where he gets an opportunity to meet local Argentineans. According to Rajinder, the local people are very good and they are on good terms with them. Customers get curious about happenings in India or when they hear the Indian music being played at his bakery.

Satnam Singh, the younger son (of Bikram Singh) came to Argentina when he was five. According to Satnam, though a Sikh, he has imbibed a lot of the local traditions. 'To keep a beard and wear turban in India is common but I feel uncomfortable to follow these traditions here. My father has no objection to my not keeping a beard or wearing a turban but he insists that I do not eat beef or smoke. I do eat meat once in a while, he confesses. Satnam had his entire education in Argentina and broke away from the traditional professions of his family to take up medicine. He has now migrated to Canada. Amongst all the family members, Satnam has the best command of the local language 'Castellano'. His best friends are Argentineans and he enjoys their company including playing billiards with them. He plays football (soccer) too and has been part of the local team. 'My mother does not object to my being friendly with the local girls but would want the relationship to develop no further', he rues. According to Satnam's mother, she would not like him to marry a local girl because she does not understand the Argentinean language very well and won't be able to converse with her daughter-in-law freely. She appreciates that Indian women do not cut their hair and are not overly fashion conscious. The Hindus living in Guemes do not overly mix with Argentineans in social or sports functions. But they do gather together on Sundays amongst themselves to share their issues and problems. If a new Indian movie has arrived, they watch the same together. The fourth generation children (Monica and Franco) are comfortable with the local language. For Bikram Singh, it was okay to insist on following Indian traditions but it is not the same for his sons Atma and Satnam as far as their children are concerned. Seeing all these inevitable changes, Bikram does get an urge sometimes to return to India. However, the politically unstable situation in Punjab (1980s), has put a question mark for permanent return, and he makes do with only visits. Bikram says that he is comfortably placed here and does not prefer to go back.

SUMMING UP

Out of all the South American countries, Argentina has the strongest Sikh connection both historically and in terms of numbers. There is total assimilation of the Sikhs into the local culture and a vast majority have married locally. Knowledge of Punjabi is disappearing but the setting up of a gurdwara is providing a rallying point and helping in spreading Sikh ethos and Punjabi culture.

CHAPTER 4

Sikhs in Belize

INTRODUCTION

What was once British Honduras is now known as Belize. The country has an old connection with Sikh migration. Early twentieth century when Sikhs started arriving on the West Coast of Canada in large numbers, the Canadian government got a bit worried. Sikhs being British subjects, the Canadian authorities did not want to appear to deny immigration. So they thought of offering to the Sikhs to settle in British Honduras, now called Belize. The Sikhs, however, refused. Thereafter, Sikhs came as direct migrants from India to the Honduras and prospered. Late George Singh, son of a Sikh immigrant, rose to achieve the high office of the Chief Justice of Belize. His son Douglas Singh is the Chairman of the Opposition party of Belize. The Tuts of California (originally from Jalandhar) own a large farm purchased recently. Visa for Belize is issued by the British High Commission in India. Belize is very poorly connected by air to its neighbouring countries and the convenient connections are mainly via North America. In the 1990s Belize became popular with Indian migrants specially Punjabis and Sikhs to further migrate to North America legally or illegally. Since Belize is not very well connected by air, some of these migrants have had to charter small aircrafts (from Cuba) to reach Belize. What enterprise!

Singhs, some of whom seem to have black African features, are proud to trace their lineage to Punjab, e.g. Phillip Singh, who is an IT technocrat with a local telephone company. Except for the recent immigrants, most Sikhs and the siblings of old Sikh immigrants are now totally assimilated with the local population.

THE COUNTRY

Belize consists mostly of flat, swampy coastal plains, in places heavily forested. The Caribbean coast has about 320 km long Belize Barrier Reef, the second longest in the world after the Great Barrier Reef. The climate is tropical and generally hot and humid. The rainy season lasts from May to November and hurricanes and floods are frequent.

It is a small country bordering only two countries—Mexico and Guatemala. The Spanish arrived in the sixteenth century and considered it as a backwater. The English and Scottish pirates started invading Belize during the seventeenth century. A British force routed the Spanish Armada off St George's Caye, in 1798, delivering Belize from the Spanish rule. In due course, Great Britain declared Belize to be a colony of the British Honduras. The capital was moved inland to Belmopan in 1970 after Hurricane Hattie all but destroyed Belize City in 1961. After its independence in September 1981, British Honduras officially became Belize, a member of the British Commonwealth. Belize gained some notoriety due to its becoming a trans-shipment point for cocaine heading into the US from South America. There are stories of aeroplanes landing on roads, dropping the consignment and then taking off. Earlier, the economy was dependent upon farming, logging and fishing but now tourism is the predominant industry. Closer ties to other Central American countries mean Belize is being gradually Hispanicized. The country is prone to hurricane damages. The population is mainly black African.

The Singhvi High Level Committee Report has the following to say:

> The Indian Diaspora in Belize consists only of PIOs as there are no restrictions here to the acquisition of local citizenship. Most of them had gone there in the 1950s, when Belize was still a British colony. They subsequently invited some of their relatives, as well as some of their employees, to join them from India. The community is comprised al-

most entirely of Sindhis and so there are few differences among them. They are mostly retail traders and are well accepted. They have little interest in local politics, but their economic strength assures them an influential position in Belize.

The PIOs maintain close and regular contact with India through frequent trips to visit friends and relatives back home. Some of these visits are connected with their quest for Indian brides for their children. As in all other countries of Indian settlement, Indian music and Hindi films are popular here and have been useful in nurturing friendly relations with the local people.

In addition to the community described above, there is a fairly large group here of persons who trace their origin to India. These persons live in villages scattered all over Belize. Like the indentured Indian who founded the Indian community in the Caribbean, the ancestors of those persons had reached Belize in the nineteenth century as cane cutters. As they were a small group, they intermarried with local people and lost their language and original religion. However, they are still identifiable through their physiognomy and are known as 'Hindus'. They live in reasonably compact rural communities. Re-establishing their linkages with India is a useful and necessary endeavour as they number between 10-15 thousand, which is more than 5 per cent of the population of Belize. It is also necessary because this effort will create another strong bond between India and this region.

GEORGE SINGH: NEW CHIEF JUSTICE
SWORN IN ON 2 FEBRUARY 1998

A news item: 'The new Chief Justice, George Singh was sworn in this morning by the Governor-General, Sir Colville Young in Belmopan. Justice Singh replaces Sir George Brown who retired at the end of January. According to the office of the Attorney General, the new Chief Justice qualified as Attorney-at-Law in 1978 from the Norman Manley Law School in Jamaica. He has held posts of Chief Magistrate, Solicitor General, Director of Public Prosecutions, and Judge in Family Court.'

Plate 38: Belize, Ex-Chief Justice, George Singh's widow with son Douglas Singh's family. Douglas is leader of opposition

George Singh (Late)

George's (born 1937) father Mann Bawa Singh came here in early 1930s along with three others—Raphael Singh, Chanan Singh and Lal Singh. George's father had married a local lady. His father moved to Honduras when George was two but he stayed back with his godparents. As recollected by George in an interview, he heard that his father gambled too much and had too many women around. He lost his shop and went to work as an agriculturist with Hofius. He then got a job with United Fruit Company in Tela, Honduras. They were a big operation and it was a big deal then to have a job with United. Since his godparents were devout Methodists, he went through Methodist Schools and ultimately became one himself.

That's why I never knew what my father looked like until I was 15 years old. It was then that he came to Belize on a two-week trip and I 'met' him for the first time. I never saw him again—he was killed in Honduras about five years later. I was working for Customs at that time and could not go for the funeral. Two months later I went to Honduras and saw my mother for the first time in twenty years. She hugged me but I didn't feel anything like you see in the movies. She was a stranger to me. It was then that I also saw my sisters for the first time.

While at school I was an oddity—one of the few East Indians going to a Methodist school. I was called 'Black Spanish' by the other boys (that was one of the nicer names). I didn't have many friends. I guess I have always been shy because I didn't want to be made fun of just because I looked different. I took comfort in books. There was nothing else to do. I went to the public library when I was too young to be a member. I gained a good command of English. I started work after graduating from Wesley College. The big thing then was to qualify for the Civil Services where I got selected. I worked in Customs, Lands & Survey, as a Magistrate, Solicitor General, Public Prosecutor, Judge and finally Chief Justice.

George married in June 1964.

Douglas Singh

George's son, Douglas is the Chairman of the Opposition, United Democratic Party of Belize. Born on 9 November 1966, he went to a local school and then to California for undergraduate degree and finally an MBA. Douglas has been working with the Development Finance Company for a number of years. He also has his own offshore company called International Corporate Services. George devotes considerable time to political activities. The United Democratic Party, under its Chairman, Douglas Singh, was re-elected in 2008. Presently, Douglas is the Leader of Government Business.

EARLIEST IMMIGRANTS

Mann Bawa Singh

George Singh's father, Mann Bawa Singh, came to Belize in the early 1930s from Honduras as an employee of Chiquita Company which owned banana plantations. Three other Sikhs came along with him during the same era—Praphael Singh in Pentagora, Chanon Singh in Belize and Lal Singh in Corozol.

Plates 39–40: Belize, Some Singhs (top) New immigrants with second generation Singh; (bottom) Tut Farm, Sabbi with his Indian staff

Chanon Singh and Phillip Singh

Met Phillip, whose father Chanon Singh was one of the earliest immigrants. Chanon Singh had land and a house in India that he gave to his brother. He had come to Belize via Panama, El Salvador and Honduras. He continued wearing turban in Belize for quite some time. On examining his old passport it is mentioned that Chanon Singh travelled on British passport No. 1878 issued at Belize, British Honduras on 11 March 1940, which shows that he had left India much earlier. According to B. Mahitani, who came to Belize in 1966, he found him to be old and frail. He was then around 70 years old. He had nine children, many of whom now live in the USA. He had married a Spanish Belizean lady and had forgotten his language. In due course, he bought 100 acres of land. His farm was 55 miles from Belize City. He also acquired a few houses in Belize which were rented out. For some time he was living on the farmland and later moved to the city. Before his death, he was finally able to visit Punjab along with his son Paul, who is a taxi driver in New York City. Chanon is buried in Belize.

Phillip is an electronics technician with a local telecommunication company.

I also met his brother Alfanzo's widow (Alfanzo had died recently in an accident), Julia Singh, along with one of their daughters. Phillip recollected having met a Sikh from India (probably in the 1970s) who was touring Americas on a bicycle. (Later, I learnt that it was Inderjit Singh Jaijee, now settled in Chandigarh, who was our neighbour in Calcutta in 1968. His account of Argentina is given separately.)

YOUNG NEW IMMIGRANTS

During the 1992–5, there was an influx of immigrants from India who were using Belize as a transit point to migrate to North America. At one stage, there were about 150 of them, 70 per cent of whom were Sikhs, some with turban and others

Plates 41–42: (top) Late Chanon Singh (2nd from left) in his village in India prior to his death; (bottom) Chanon's son Phillip Singh, an electronics engineer

had become clean shaven. They were brought there as clients of various agents, both Punjabis and Sindhis. Some of these adventurers were able to reach their ultimate destination, some were put in jail and some others were deported back to India. The Belize authorities did finally crack down on in-transit immigrants. At present there are only a few young immigrants. I heard of two young men, Balraj and Goldy and two girls Ranjit Kaur Mangat of Ludhiana and Rama from Hoshiarpur. The entry strategy is planned by immigration agents and in their case, admission obtained in Belize University, which is almost non-existent.

However, this helps them get student visa which is later converted to residence permit. Change of status is possible but somewhat expensive because of the legal charges. Thereafter these boys and girls look for jobs or odd business. For example, the two girls are running a sort of 'dhaba' in a small town—all the time waiting to move to North America. There are instances of highhandedness by the police and immigration authorities but once you have left the country, there is no turning back in most of the cases whether they like it or not. The motivation is basically economic improvement, which is supplemented, in some cases, with independence.

There is an instance of a Sikh, sponsored by his brothers from the US, who came to Belize to get married to a white American. The woman came from USA to Belize for a few hours to get married. On return to USA, she applied for his immigration. Of course, it was not an easy process and there were long court cases but all these adventurers do not mind prolonged hassles so far as they see even a remote possibility of reaching North America. Local Indians do help here and there, but experiences are mixed for the hosts.

As an interesting aside, the normal route of travel to Belize involves changing flights through the USA which necessitates a transit visa which is not easy to get. Even the so-called 'students' in Belize had to make use of chartered flight from Cuba costing around US $4,000 to 6,000. The agents can be innovative if you are ready to pay. Sabbi's wife Gurpreet had to travel to Cuba from where she came to Belize by a chartered plane (detailed story given later).

Deepak Luthra

Deepak of Chandigarh, could not clear his engineering and medical entrance examinations in India. It was suggested to him by an agent of Delhi, to go to Belize in 2004. He paid US $6,000 for tuition and US $1,000 as expenses, in addition to the travel expenses including travel by chartered flight from Cuba. On arrival he found that the university had no students. Since it was a lucrative business for the university, they were initially reluctant to allow him to seek work permit. There are some other students from Punjab.

Harsimran Kaur

In the Palace Hotel there was a mention of Harsimran Kaur as the Public Relations Manager. On further enquiry it was learnt that she had quit the job and was running a beauty salon. With great difficulty I could locate her shop which was closed. It was found that she was away to Mumbai where her parents reside. She seems to have some relatives in Chandigarh also. After a number of tries at her residence telephone number, her husband Mairuf answered. I could not get much information from him. It could be surmised that one of the factors leading to her migration might have been the inter-religious marriage which could be problematic in India but is of little consequence outside. This is only my conjecture, to highlight the various possible motivations of migrating from India.

TUT FARM

Niranjan Singh Mann, a businessman from Punjab, was running a restaurant in Belize and was involved in immigration of young people from Punjab to North America via Belize. He advised the Tuts of California that Big Falls Farms was on sale due to the default in payments by the owner to the Belize government. The Tuts bought the farm in 1992 giving Mann some shareholding in the venture. The Tuts and Mann were on different wavelengths and soon decided to separate. Mann moved out of Belize. The size of the landholding was about 37,000 acres. The farm came along with machinery and water system, etc. The attraction for the Tuts was that 80 per cent of the rice was imported in Belize and they saw an opportunity in meeting the local demand. The exact figures are not available but the farm deal was worth a few million dollars. When the farm was purchased, about 14,000 acres had already been cleared. The remaining land was a Mahogany forest, which is a hard wood tree and is a specialty of Belize. The farm is being run as a corporate entity and has to pay corporate and other taxes, which are quite high. The purchase of the farm in Belize was the first geographical diversification for the Tuts beyond USA and India. The Tuts belong to village Paragpur of Jalandhar in Punjab. They are four brothers—Amarjeet, Surjeet, Pritam and Ranjit—all in their fifties or early sixties by now.

Amarjit first migrated to Canada in 1960 in his early twenties and soon thereafter moved to California. His other brothers joined him later. They are basically into farming and trucking business. They were sponsors of 'Kar Seva' at Golden Temple for the water filtration plant. On purchase of the farm, Ranjit stayed in Belize to manage the affairs for two years before the present Managing Director, Sabbi, was brought in for induction, training and finally taking over.

Sabbi

He was a fresher from college in Jalandhar, and only 19 years old when he came here. Sabbi was a bit shocked on reaching Belize, as it was not a highly developed country. He travelled from India via Amsterdam, Panama and El Salvador. He was naturally quite excited to migrate and had enough self-confidence that he would be able to make a success of his job.

In the beginning, the Tuts had a local guy as the CEO till Sabbi took over. Having migrated in 1992, Sabbi's first visit back home to India was in 1997 for three months. This initial period of five years in Belize was a bit tough for Sabbi as there was no Indian community to mingle with. Food-wise also hardly any Indian ingredients were available. Sabbi used to eat in the canteen which meant a basic diet of rice, beans and meat which was wholesome and tasty but very different from Indian food. Sabbi's visit in 1997 to India coincided with his sister's marriage. During the visit to India, he met Gurpreet and got engaged to her. Sabbi returned to India in 1998 to get married. His wife joined him next year. Tuts now visit Belize only for short periods as Sabbi is operationally quite independent. On major policy decisions such as diversification to new crops, Tuts provide the lead. Such a need has arisen because rice cultivation has become uneconomical. There are a number of Mennonites from USA settled in Belize, who have also got into rice cultivation in a big way. This has resulted in rice production exceeding demand. Unfortunately, export of rice is uneconomical because of high input costs. The Tuts have therefore decided to diversify to papaya cultivation.

The farm was initially profitable but of late the profitability is under pressure. About 2,000 acres is under rice cultivation employing about 40 persons. The yield per acre is about two tonne. The farm has a number of cattle and a few citrus trees. They also grow some corn and beans. They have dug their own canals for irrigation purposes. There are two other Immigrants at the Tut farm—Buta Singh, who came in 1992, and Resham Singh (Buta's wife's brother) who followed. Buta's parents now live with him.

CHAPTER 5

Sikhs in Bolivia

A MISADVENTURE OF THE JAT SIKHS

The lure of land combined with bravado can be a deadly combination which can get one to achieve great heights and occasionally can result in disaster. In Bolivia, the latter was the case of Sikh immigrants in Santa Cruz de la Sierra, a city in the south-east of Bolivia where more than a hundred of them migrated in the 1980s in search of their El Dorado.

Many of them have sad stories to tell and most have either returned to Punjab or migrated onwards to North America and other places. Although bad luck is always a factor and an important contributor, unfortunately the worst traits of the Jat Sikhs came into fore as adversity hit them. The remnant immigrants still have their faith in the 'Waheguru' and have a gurdwara (probably the earliest in South America) to turn to for the monthly 'sangat'. Turbaned Sikhs are almost nonexistent. From an all time high of 150–200 families in the 1980s and 1990s, presently there are only a few families left with a population of about 30 or so Sikhs.

An interesting meeting with a Bolivian Sikh lady in La Paz with white turban and white flowing dress was a heartwarming experience as to how people find solace through the Sikh dharma and how Sikhism is catching up albeit very slowly in South America as followers of Yogi Bhajan's 3HO.

EARLY SIKH IMMIGRANTS

Bolivia was a transit point for the Sikhs going to Argentina, from the early twentieth century, but they did not establish roots in the country. There are references of Sikhs landing in

Chile (earlier, the port was part of Bolivia) or Peru and moving on to Argentina via Bolivia. But nothing is mentioned about any of them settling down in the country. Harsh climate, relatively poor economic situation and unfertile land might explain Sikhs' not establishing early roots in Bolivia. It is the author's belief though that some Sikhs must have settled but there is no specific information available. Names of some Sikhs, as early settlers were mentioned but more investigative effort is needed to get details.

THE COUNTRY

Bolivia is one of the poorest countries of South America and topographically may be termed as the Tibet of the Americas. The Spanish conquered the country in the 1530s and silver was struck in 1544. Silver mining was an important pillar of the Spanish economy. Bolivia won independence from Spain in 1825. However, Chile annexed part of Bolivian territory including its only port of Antofagasta leaving the country landlocked. Since the 1950s, the country has been ruled by 'in and out' governments of civilians, army, leftists, etc. Cocaine production in the country in the early 1990s complicated relations with the US followed by acute recession and unemployment. A huge gulf still separates this divided society, with half the population immersed in the contemporary world and the other half who remain subsistent peasants. La Paz is the world's highest capital city at 3,600 m above sea level. The adjacent city of El Alto, at 4,200 m above sea level, is growing at a fast pace. Santa Cruz, the commercial and industrial hub of the eastern lowlands, is experiencing rapid population and economic growth.

THE EIGHTIES' IMMIGRANTS

According to the *Lonely Planet* travel guide:

> Santa Cruz's long-standing reputation as a drug-trafficking Mecca is now being eclipsed by an agriculture boom. The region boasts rice-

growing Japanese colonies as well as settlements of Italians, Indian Sikhs, and thousands of German-Canadian Mennonites. The region has attracted Brazilian opportunists, foreign oil workers, agribusiness tycoons, drug traffickers, scientific researchers, missionaries and environmental activists.

Into this conglomerate and diverse environ and a scenario of conflicting interests and politically unstable country, rushed in the Sikhs of Punjab. Jat Sikhs have a passion for owning farm land and what could be more attractive than owning hundreds and thousands of acres at dirt cheap prices—$30 per hectare. The prospects were all the more tempting for the Sikh immigrants from the Gulf countries with ready cash and the steep prices of land in India. Another major attraction for Gulf workers was that their families could join them. The Sikh problem in India in the 1980s was a powerful trigger for migrating and settling abroad. In this background a proposition of buying land to settle abroad, never mind how far away the location (or in some emotional way the farther from India the better) struck as an opportunity not to be missed. In this emotionally charged times, caution was thrown to the winds. There was already a talk by Sikh separatists of setting up Khalistan Headquarters in Ecuador, also in South America.

International magazines and newspapers had tempting advertisements for vast areas of farm land being sold in Bolivia at cheap prices. Many Sikhs started buying land. The entire project seems to have been masterminded by small groups of immigrants many of them working in the Gulf countries but some involving even government officials of Punjab since retired. It was a well spread-out network but with limited investigative scrutiny prior to venturing out. Even in my interview, words were used to the effect that 'Punjabis are expert farmers and that they were bound to succeed'. It was with this high moral stand that they rushed in. The initial years were good but instead of consolidating their gains, most opted for buying more land, machinery and chemical inputs in the hope of harvesting gold. The problems got compounded due to inadequate rains. With heavy loans for machinery and debts for fertilizers, pesticides, etc., the immigrants faced hostile creditors and government agencies. While the original defaulters had run away, the compatriot guarantors were in deep trouble. Some had to face jail terms. With the arrival of bad times, it is clear from the interviews, that it brought the worst amongst the immigrant community in terms of personal values, relationships, jealousy, backbiting and generally a poor community spirit. This is in contrast to the earlier initiative to set up a gurdwara there. The immigrants did not seem to have done their homework properly and failed to learn lessons from earlier immigrant experiences. The alternative of buying more costly land but with better irrigation prospects was not pursued by any of the immigrants. There was more of herd mentality and attitude of bravado rather than an investigative and properly planned strategy. Many invested large funds in co-operative ventures with no proper accounting. Some of the negative traits of the Jat Sikhs came to the fore. However, the faith in 'Waheguru' still exists amongst those who have stayed back.

The Singhvi High Level Committee Report has nothing to say about the country.

THE GURDWARA

In the 1980s, Sikhs built a gurdwara, 30 km from Santa Cruz in a picturesque location along the railroad track to Brazil. The community cannot afford a full-time 'granthi' any more after the earlier incumbent moved to Argentina. A part-time clean-shaven Sikh helps run the Gurdwara.

Although earlier on most Sikhs used to attend the gurdwara on Sundays, 'Sangrads' and Gurpurbs, it is now only the very devout who visit the gurdwara regularly. But 'langar' is available for a visitor and the gurdwara does still provide a gathering venue. During my visit, a few of them turned up.

Plates 43–44: Bolivia Gurdwara

A FAILED COOPERATIVE VENTURE

This is a story of one of the larger ventures. It would appear that two brothers had masterminded one cooperative group of about 35 persons. The project involved units of 200 hectares each but partners were free to subscribe to any number of units including part units. There were 38 units, each with an initial purchase price of $6,000 making a total investment of about a quarter million dollars. Additionally, all partners were asked to contribute about $30–50 a month totalling about $1,500. A bulldozer was used to uproot the trees and they themselves cleared up the debris to save labour cost. Some of the partners did not migrate themselves but sent their representatives to Bolivia. A tented village about 130 km from Santa Cruz was set up for living. Provision for water, which was problematic, had to be made. There were a lot of mosquitoes and living conditions were tough. It was a slow process of development but money was coming in from the partners. When the funds got exhausted, additional contribution was asked for against which some partners contributed but some did not. The first call was for $500 per partner which later became $1,000. This was repeated for two years. The project investment mounted to almost a million dollars. Since no profit was in sight, disenchantment soon set in. Some people went away feeling disgusted. Although initially everyone was enthusiastic, fissures started appearing within a couple of years. Infighting, bickering and quarrels became the order of the day. The complaints were in regard to absence of proper accounting by the sponsors. The project was bound to create inter-personal problems due to lack of transparency, cost overruns, and absence of a systematic accounting and reporting system. The professionalism needed for a project of this size and complexity was totally missing. It was run more like an HUF by a 'Karta' and not as a corporate entity with 38 shareholders. It was decided in 1992 to sell the land and distribute the money so received amongst the partners. It is alleged that only those who were present in Bolivia got paid, some fully and others in part, who left in disgust. Hardly five to six people remained back. The sponsors figured that nobody would come from India to collect their paltry share of sale money. They decided to buy a petrol pump. It is alleged that there were malpractices in managing this new enterprise also. One of the sponsors died and thereafter the petrol pump was sold off. When the news spread, several partners exerted pressure on the sponsors to refund their share of the sale proceeds. The story becomes murkier as everyone including the two sponsors or their inheritors claimed bankruptcy. Consequently, one of the sponsors has returned to India and the dead sponsors' children have migrated to Argentina. A sad ending!

CASE STUDIES

The case studies are divided into two parts. The first section deals with people interviewed in Bolivia and the second the returnees in their villages in Punjab. These interviews give a glimpse of what motivates outward migration. Details about the feelings, etc., have been incorporated to highlight that migration is not all smooth sailing. The early years are universally tough for the first migrants. In case of Bolivia, the problems continued and in fact became more acute over the years. A unique feature is that besides interviews of immigrants in Bolivia, we had an opportunity to talk to a few immigrants who have returned to their villages in Punjab. Most of them both in Bolivia and Punjab are sad about their experience.

Interviewes in Santa Cruz

Amarjit Singh Virdi

Interviewed on 29 August 2005 at 8 a.m. in Hotel Las America.

I am living in Santa Cruz for the last 26 years and came to Bolivia for agriculture from Germany, where I was working. I purchased land to farm but there was no water and the language was also different. Water is 120 to 140 m below the ground. The living conditions were not good, particularly in 1979, when I came here. There were no tarred roads. We had to face several difficulties but now by the grace of 'Waheguru' we are finally on our feet. We heard in Germany through newspapers that Bolivia was selling land. Bolivia wanted agricultural manpower and technology and suggested that all one needed was a tractor. We Indians are good at agriculture. Bolivia sent us the necessary forms, etc., based on which the land was registered in our name. With these documents, we were issued the visa in Germany.

I was the first one to arrive in Bolivia for agriculture. One Darshan Singh (I could not meet him) was the other Sikh, who had come earlier but he was into restaurant business. He later set up a cinema. In our group 5 or 6 people were initially interested but only three of them finally bought land—Baljinder Singh, Nirmal Singh and me. We paid $6,000 each for the land. I had $10,000 with me on arrival in La Paz. When I arrived, there was a strike in the country. I had to wait for four days in La Paz Airport after which I could travel to Santa Cruz. I stayed in a hotel for the first week and then moved to a cheaper rented accom-

Plate 45: Bolivia—Amarjit Singh Virdi

modation. Initially I was on a tourist visa with the proviso that it could be extended if I decided to settle down on the land. I came alone to Bolivia—the other two came after 2–3 months as they had gone to India to meet their families. On arrival in Bolivia, I advised them (while they were still in India), about the initial difficulties including the language issue. I also mentioned that such difficulties are faced by all new settlers—Sikh settlers in Kenya and Terai area of UP in India had faced similar problems. The land was purchased from Bolivian Land and Forest Company Ltd. and is located about 107 km away from Santa Cruz on the Brazil Road. Our contract stated that if we did not like the land, money would be refunded. Later on, when we were dissatisfied, we approached the Company for refund but by that time the promoters had fled to Costa Rica. The promoters comprised three partners—a Swiss, a German, and a Bolivian. They sold these lands to Americans, Canadians, and Swiss. They had promoted the lands all over the globe including the Philippines and Pakistan. I was the first to arrive. Others arrived within a month. Since the one-year time limit for refund of money if dissatisfied, was coming to an end, the promoters fled. The Swiss guy was jailed for a couple of days but he managed to leave the country. Because of language problems we could not file a legal suit. We decided to stick on because we had already put in a lot of money. The land is fertile and good for agriculture but there was no water and the country had no policy for developing agriculture. Inputs and seeds were difficult to get, and marketing of produce was also not easy. Additionally during the first five years, we had major problems because of run-away inflation. On arrival, we had to sleep on the railway station with no proper shelter in the cold and rain. Local people tell lies and one cannot trust them. So we had to think on our own as no advice was available. In the face of so many difficulties, we began to discuss options of going back. But the stigma of failure was difficult to face. We couldn't even go back to Germany because of the changed laws for immigrant workers. Option to go to the USA was also ruled out. We therefore decided to make the best of the existing situation. A start was made by clearing 600 hectares of land. We planted corn and had a good crop of 40 quintals per hectare. Due to inflation we could not sell the produce. We then decided to diversify into poultry and piggery using corn as feed. We faced the same difficulty in selling chickens and pigs. Now we had neither the corn nor the chicken or the pigs. After four or five years we gave up farming and related ventures. In the beginning, our visas were extended for 1–3 months at a time. After a year it was extended for two years and finally I got a visa for indefinite stay. We abandoned the land and decided to move to the city around 1985–6 to do business. In 1990, I got married to a Bolivian. She is a teacher in a school. I have a son and a daughter. With hard work I have made some success of the business and I was able to visit India with my family last year. I am presently a construction contractor having ten employees. Subsequent to abandoning the land, our ownership was cancelled.

The majority of Sikhs came in 1984–5 when the Punjabi population here grew to about 400. Subsequent migration was basically transitory, the final destination being North America. Several of such immigrants had to cool their heels in Bolivia for four to six years during which period they did odd jobs or businesses. Most of them were on tourist visas, which were easily extended but the authorities have become stricter now. Local Sikhs were always helpful to sponsor their visa extension. Most of these migrants were from the Gulf who did not want to return to India.

Satwant Singh Sandhu

I came to Bolivia in 1987 from village Rarha, district Hoshiarpur. After working in Dubai from 1975–85, I returned home. Although I did not own much land but I had six trucks. I had moved to Chandigarh for my children's education. My relative and village mate, Santokh Singh who was in Dubai contacted me to advise that land was available in Bolivia at a very low price. I was reluctant to move as I was well settled and children were in good educational institutions. Santokh, however, persisted in inviting me to join for the Bolivian venture. I consulted my father who advised me to go ahead but asked Santokh to visit Bolivia first. Accordingly, he went to Bolivia and continued to press me to join him informing that the land had already been purchased. Santokh along with his brother Buta and friends (about 35 of them) had already joined the venture. The group had purchased some land prior to their migration to which they added subsequent purchases on arrival. I went in 1987 and after one year our families joined us. More Sikhs of our group arrived and all of us worked very hard. The country was backward and soon a feeling developed that Bolivia was not a good place to stay and work.

Plate 46: Bolivia—Satwant Singh Sandhu

After two to three years, some people started returning to India and others moved to USA and Canada but we stayed on. And then we could not leave! Our initial love for each other in the group started to fade and we started falling out and began to go our separate ways. As a result the land was divided into individual shareholdings in 1992. I ventured out on my own. I cleared 700 to 800 hectares of land and started planting different crops from time to time. Rains were satisfactory and agriculture started generating some income. We got some money from India to buy machinery and increase the landholding. Weather then changed—rains were inadequate for almost five years in a row. This resulted in heavy losses. In a year chemical inputs including pesticides, etc., could cost as much as over one lakh dollars. Consumption of diesel alone was 40,000 litres a year, a heavy investment to pay back when the crops failed. The suppliers gave us credit for a couple of years but then pulled back. The first really bad year was 1998 but we continued to make heavy inputs which resulted in further losses from 1999 to 2002. The situation became desperate in 2003. We had to surrender our houses and land, etc., to pay back the loans. Various country compatriots were unfortunately happy to see us suffer and started spreading rumours that we might soon have to go to jail. I had to send my wife to India on short notice on a secret mission to bring Rs. 35 lakh, i.e. $75,000, by selling all investments there. These funds were invested in the crops with the hope that we could make good income. Now for the last couple of years we have not sowed anything, as each sowing requires $80–90 thousand. In a good year I had employed 150 workers for three months at a time. Last year I planted 1,500 acres of sesame and 400 acres of cotton. Because of lack of rains, cotton crop broke even but I incurred losses against the sesame crop. Now I have about 60 people and am planting only 150 hectares.

Q. What was the intentions of Santokh Singh?
A. Originally he was okay but when he made a lot of money, he changed. Price of one hectare was $30 (Rs. 1,000). We thought we would spend another Rs. 5,000 to 10,000 per hectare to make it cultivable. Santokh told us that he had purchased it for $20 and we did not mind his making $10. But the land was not worth more than $2–3. A suspicion arose that he had bought his own land at $2 only. We were all equal partners sharing profits and expenses. This differential pricing was unfair. We were 35 to 36 people in partnership. We used to earn $40,000 to 50,000 a month. Some of the partners did not come themselves but sent their representatives to Bolivia. All the partners were contributing about $30 to 50 a month amounting to about $1,500. Two hundred hectares was considered one unit, but each partner was free to have less or more units. There were 38 units, each contributing $14,000 as initial expenses per unit, a total collection of half a million dollars. A bulldozer used to uproot the trees and we ourselves would clear behind the dozer. We thus saved on labour expenses. We set up tents to live. There was no arrangement for water. We had to make some provision. When the project was started in September, there were a lot of mosquitoes, and life was real tough. It was a slow process but money was coming in from the partners. So we felt comfortable except that

there was no proper accounting by Santokh who was the project head. When we ran short of funds, additional contribution was asked for to which some partners contributed and others did not. The first call was for $500 per partner, which later became $1,000, which was repeated for two years. Since no profits were in sight, disenchantment set in with regard to expenses and future prospects. Some people went away feeling disgusted. It was decided to sell the land and distribute the money so received amongst the partners. In 1992 everything was subdivided amongst the partners. I got my money back as I was in Bolivia. Others present in the country also got some money back.

As per Santokh, the land was sold for $3,30,000, which meant $8,000–10,000 per partner. But the truth was being doubted. Money was not paid to everyone and instead it was used to set up a petrol pump. Most of the people left in disgust and hardly five to six people remained. Santokh realized that nobody would come from India to collect their paltry share of sale money. As it turned out, the earnings from the petrol pump were not enough for the maintenance of the two or three involved parties. The business lasted 2–3 years. When failure loomed ahead, they sold the petrol pump after three years for $4.5 lakh. When the news spread, other partners pressed them to give their share. Soon thereafter, Santokh died. The assets were subdivided between Mrs. Santokh and her brother and Buta Singh. Santokh died before the sale of the petrol pump. Buta insisted on keeping some funds for distributing to the partners. However, it is alleged that Buta never parted with these funds. Buta told Satwant that he had paid back to the partners but the partners had a different story to tell. The reality was somewhere in between as only part of the money had been paid ($4,000–5,000 per party). A small retail shop was started by Buta. Whenever anybody asked him to return their money, he would argue that his own position was precarious. They visited India and Buta returned to Bolivia as a baptized Sikh.

Regarding other immigrants Mukhtiar came earlier than Santokh and became an agent. Having the advantage of knowing Spanish, he invited more people to come and collected commission from everyone for each transaction. Jagdish S. Sandhu of Bharatpur came as a part of the Mukhtiar group but was exploited by him. Jagdish's brother Sarna was also in Bolivia but he died later on in India. Jagdish returned to India in 1998 and Satwant bought part of his land. Buta and Mukhtiar made a lot of money. Mukhtiar finally went to America. Sharma, the present counsel had his own group. Parminder Sandhu had another small group, but Parminder had honest dealings. Talking of agriculture, he told that in a good year, one can make $2 to 3 lakh in a five-month period. Losses could also be equally heavy if there are no rains. In the north, the rains are better, enabling two crops a year. Though price is higher at around $1,000 per hectare, it can be a good proposition for those who have enough money to invest. He would prefer to sell the present land and buy land in the north rather than migrate to Canada or the USA. Two hundred hectares is a good economic unit. Rains were good at the time they bought land. In fact, the north was not considered good because of heavier rains. Now the weather pattern has changed to make the north more viable. When asked whether he would encourage new immigrants for the lands in the north, he said that nobody accepts advice without assigning blames if things do not turn out as per expectations. By incurring expenses of $30,000 to 40,000, profit of $20,000 to 30,000 can be made if the rains are satisfactory. Regarding permanent families in Santa Cruz, he named a few, e.g. Chachi Dhillon, Buddha Singh, Sharma Kalyani, Satwant, Amarjit Virdi, Jarnail S. Dilawar and Nirmal Singh. He mentioned that there are six-seven families with ladies (Dilawar and Nirmal Singh), four-five south Indian families doing odd jobs and eighteen bachelors. At one stage there were about 150 family or single units.

INTERVIEWS IN PUNJAB

Buta Singh Sandhu, Village Rarha, Hoshiarpur

A matriculate, he went to Dubai at age 30 in 1978. He helped his younger brother Santokh migrate to Dubai. He saw an advertisement about cheap agricultural land available in Bolivia. He had the money and in addition had a desire to become big landlord like most Punjabi farmers. He along with others purchased a large acreage of forest land at $30 per hectare. They got their families to move to Bolivia on resident permits. With agricultural infrastructure not well developed and scarcity of irrigation resources, their hard labour could not bear fruit. The alien language and backwardness of the country were also hurdles. After years of hard work and large investment in earth moving equipment, they realized that the venture was a failure. They decided to start retail shops with the entire family participating. Despite supplementary remittances received from Punjab, life was still not comfortable. Buta lost his father and younger brother in Bolivia. Buta and his wife Ranjit Kaur got baptized in India in 1998. Buta Singh recollects that when they first arrived in Bolivia, there were around 10 turbaned Sikhs but when they left Bolivia only Jai Singh wore turban. Almost all the Punjabi immigrants are going through the same ordeal. He is uncertain about his future as to whether he will ever return to Bolivia. Buta Singh kept on underlining the economic losses and emotional crises he went through during his stay in Bolivia. He seems to be a defeated man.

Jaswinder Singh, Village Heon near Banga

My brother Dilawar went to Jordan in 1980 after matriculation. After two years in Jordan, he purchased land in Bolivia along with Buta and Bhupinder. They ordered heavy agricultural machinery from Dubai. This whole endeavour failed due to lack of irrigation and non-support from the Bolivian government. Subsequently, Dilawar took up a job as a driver and in time graduated to having his own transport business along with me when I joined him in 1991. Our transport business flourished as we had three buses and used to ply between Santa Cruz to Cairo in Brazil. We could save up to $2,000 per month in a good tourist season. We used to stay in village Pylla near Santa Cruz. Unfortunately, the business collapsed because of two road accidents and my ill health. We spent a lot of money and time on fighting legal battles pertaining to the road accidents and my treatment which culminated in our present poor financial position. During my first visit to Punjab in 1995, we were financially well-off. I have now finally returned to India and work as a driver for a private school bus. I have tried my luck and have worked hard but could not save money.

Dilawar Singh in Bolivia is also not keeping physically fit. He plans to come back, being single and wants to stay in Punjab permanently. Dilawar and I managed to call our nephew to Bolivia who has since migrated to Italy. Most of the Punjabis in Bolivia are living hand to mouth and trying to migrate to any rich white country. Earlier on there were about 300–400 Punjabis but now there are only 25–30 Punjabis left. Most of them are locally married and are permanently settled.

Gurnam Singh, Village Appowal, near Banga

Gurnam Singh went to Bolivia more than three decades ago. He had some problems with his wife. He stressed to his parents that either they should send him abroad or get him remarried. As told by his wife Ajit Kaur, he went abroad around 1970 when their younger son was two years old (now 37 yrs old). Gurnam had two sons and a daughter was born after he left for Bolivia but the baby girl died soon after. He visited Punjab twice during this period; firstly about 25 years ago and then again three years back. During his first visit, he got his sisters married and brought his other brother Gurmit Singh along with him. Gurmit is married to a Bolivian girl and has an adopted daughter. Gurmit has not visited India since he left.

When Gurnam Singh left India, his parents were alive. His father died 22 years back and mother five years ago. He used to send money back home till his mother was alive. He does not send money any more. The house was built with the money he had sent. According to his wife, it cost him around Rs. 30,000 when he went to Bolivia for the first time. Gurnam has not talked to his wife even once since he migrated—not even during his visits home. During his recent visit, he stayed with his sister who is married in village Sodian. Their two sons, Kulwant and Kulwinder, are married now. The elder son has three daughters and a son. During Gurnam's recent visit, his daughters-in-law and grandchildren got the impression that he does not have any association with the family here. He has some faint association with his sons. During his visit most of the time he was drunk and was chain smoking. His granddaughter, Rajwinder Kaur, is very hurt by his cold behaviour towards the family. She feels that he does not respect their grandmother and hence cannot expect respect from them. Socially they do not denounce him but do not feel any attachment. Rajwinder went to drop him in Delhi. She says it was more an outing to Delhi with her cousin. It was stated that Gurnam Singh does not have good relations with his brother in Bolivia.

Gurnam Singh has occasional telephonic contacts with his sons here. These contacts are very much formal and are devoid of any warmth. His wife is a withdrawn lady and does not have any interest in him. She feels repentant about having wasted her life. She is helpless as her parents are not economically well of.

Roop Lal of Khalwara Colony, near Khalwara Village, Phagwara

Roop Lal went to Bolivia eighteen years ago (1986) and has yet to make his maiden visit to his family. He has two sons, a daughter and a wife. Roop Lal used to make furniture before going abroad. He had good business when he left for Doha,

Qatar. He started as a carpenter in Doha and earned handsome money and visited his home every year. Roop Lal attended the marriage of his younger brother, Kashmiri Lal, from Qatar about 19 years ago. He visited again after four months and stayed for a month. During this visit, he said that he had got land in Bolivia and was going there to cultivate the same. His wife Pyari remembers those days, as he used to say that she would be called to Bolivia along with the children very soon. They went together to Ludhiana to purchase the seeds of spinach and lettuce, etc., to cultivate in Bolivia. That happened to be his last visit. Initially he sent some letters about the efforts to make the land fertile turning futile. He asked for money and Pyari sold her jewellery and borrowed from relatives to send him money (Rs. 70,000–80,000). After trying his luck in agriculture, Roop Lal turned to the profession of his training, i.e. making wooden furniture. He started his own shop but could not succeed. Subsequent to this failure, he made no contact with his family for many years. His eldest son, Buta Ram, established telephonic contact with him in 1995–6 with the help of his mother's brother. They came to know that he had to really struggle in Bolivia. He tried his hand in driving but met with an accident. A Bolivian girl got killed under his vehicle. All his earnings and time went into the legal battles because of this accident. He had sent small amounts of money home after re-establishment of contact—a total of Rs. 30,000. He claims that he is comfortable now and wants to return. He stays at Santa Cruz. His younger brother Kashmiri Lal has gone to Dubai as he found it difficult to feed the joint family here. He has sent only about Rs. 10,000 during his stay of 7–8 months. After his graduation, Roop Lal's eldest son runs a STD booth. He is 22 years old. His 18 years old younger brother is a school dropout, and is presently looking for a job. Buta Ram is in touch with his father in Bolivia and talks to him on phone on regular basis. He wants to go to Bolivia and onwards to America or any advanced country. His father is encouraging him to come over to Bolivia and is promising to do the needful. Buta Ram thinks that his father was now married to a Bolivian and is least bothered if he is facilitated to reach his destination, i.e. north America via Bolivia. He has sent the Xerox copies of his documents to his father to pursue his case. Buta Ram thinks that in Bolivia all the earnings are exhausted in fulfilling the daily needs. Some people have returned from Bolivia and do not want to go back. While in Bolivia they were in touch with his father and told about the difficult situation there and of the remarriage of his father. His only concern is going abroad by any means. His father's second marriage means nothing to him.

The interviewer met Pyari (born 1949) in her home. Her wrinkled face and blank look told the ordeal she has gone through. She had seen prosperity when her husband was working in Ludhiana when they were staying there. When her husband shifted his work to Kartarpur, the city known for furniture, they shifted their residence to Jalandhar where they have their own house. When Roop Lal shifted to Doha, Qatar, they moved to their present residence, which is built on a large plot. The house was planned to be big but the economic downturn has reduced it to a mere utility house.

She got her daughter married four years ago as she found the wait for Roop Lal futile. She borrowed money from relatives and other sources. Most of the money taken from close relatives is yet to be returned. Now she talks of the lost cause. She is convinced that her husband is remarried in Bolivia and she is not very hopeful of his return. She wants him to take care of their sons' future. She has survived by rearing buffalos for selling milk. Her two brothers have supported her, one of them is a bank employee and the other is settled in Greece. Her husband's brother Kashmiri Lal has been a great support to her family. She rues her husband's decision by saying, 'Why do people go to such poor countries?'

AN ANGEL WALKS IN

In contrast to the scene of Santa Cruz, there is a Sikh lady in La Paz who is teaching Kundalini Yoga and is a follower of Yogi Bhajan's 3HO. Sham Kaur (Gisela), a Bolivian by birth, wearing a white turban and 'khanda' emblem and white flowing robes, walks into the hotel in La Paz and the hotel staff (me included) go into a spin. It was truly an angelic entrance. She had agreed to meet me at the hotel. Sham Kaur, a highly educated lady, provided a contrast in practice of Sikh religion —symbols and all, without belonging to or having been to Punjab against the earlier encounter with the Santa Cruz Sikhs from the land of Sikh religion's origin and major following, Punjab. Despite the requirement on her to wear Western clothes during working hours, as a senior government official, she believes in and practices the Sikh dharma. She is single-handedly trying to propagate the Sikh faith in Bolivia. At 34 years, she finds great solace in following the teachings of the Sikh gurus and the words of *SGGS*. Her life story is detailed below.

SHAM KAUR (GISELA)

Interview on 31 August 2005 in La Paz, Hotel Apart Casa Real:

I was born on 26 April 1971. My family background is mainly Christian, both parents are Christians and I was born and raised in La Paz, Bolivia. I attended school here and later decided to go abroad to Chile where I studied for eight years. A degree in Industrial Engineering was followed by a Masters degree and an MBA in International Business, all from Chile. Thereafter I joined Brown University in USA for an Environmental Program. Presently I am working for the government on Green House Reduction Project. I have been working here for past five years and am now running the office since last year. I have also lived in Peru working in natural resources development specializing in climate change. I started doing Kundalini Yoga three years ago and at that time there was no regular teacher. Some people came to conduct workshops. At that time Nam Nidhan Kaur came from Chile and was training students to become teachers. I had this nice coincidence that I was

Plate 47: Bolivia, La Paz. Sham Kaur (Gisela), An Angel walks in

in Peru, where a course was getting started. I decided it was a wonderful thing for me to do. There was no teacher in La Paz and I thought I could propagate the technique to others. I studied in Peru for one year and when I came here I had this opportunity to open a centre with some friends to teach Kundalini Yoga which is new in this country. Since then I have been very involved in these issues. I wanted to know the origin and source of this wonderful and amazing technique and to find out more about Yogi Bhajan and the set up in Espanola, USA. I wanted to know about the Sikhs as this was more like a research for me. It was exciting for me to visit a place about which I did not know anything, i.e. Sikhs in Espanola. I stayed there with the community for a week and it was a wonderful experience. I took a 'Japji' course, and had the opportunity to meet so many wonderful teachers and people. It was amazing to see the radiance of Yogi Bhajan even though he was very ill at the time. In the second 'Japji' course, Yogi Ji appeared, and it was great to see him, be in his presence and to hear him. I also got to meet Bibi Ji and others. There were many people from Latin Countries (Chile, Mexico, Spain) living there. So I had a warm welcome in Esponala. It was my first time to attend a gurdwara and to learn about Sikh traditions. It was particularly fascinating as it is so far removed from our culture here. I learnt about 3HO from Nam Nidhan Kaur when she came 2–3 times to conduct courses. It so happened that I was in a very difficult situation at work as also in my personal life. When I was very young, I was always seeking answers to the question 'why am I here?'. When you are in a reflective frame of mind, you tend to look to the outside for answers. I tried Yoga and it gave me an inner consciousness, a different perspective of the world. So far I was into math and the real things, which do not help. I started to discover other aspects and it was really a blessing. That was the time that Nam Nidhan came for a weekend course in Yoga and I realized that this was the thing I was looking for. Not just the Yoga but also the way you feel when you are meditating and the connection with your inner self. I had the opportunity to attend a video course of Yogi Bhajan and wow it was really amazing how you felt with him. It was so strange. All of a sudden there was a certainty and I felt that there was no logical reason for uncertainties. Here it was, I became completely sure that this was what I want to do and practice.

During my Espanola visit, I got to meet and learn from many people. I wanted to provide access of these teachings to the Bolivians. You know our country has a lot of poor people who cannot go to Espanola but I felt that they should be able to get help through these teachings in their own country. I was alone in Espanola and I needed help to spread these wonderful things to people, to everybody. I did not understand the difference between Kundalini Yoga and the Sikhs. At that time there was a very thin line between Kundalini Yoga and Sikh tradition in my mind. There are many Sikhs who do not believe in Kundalini Yoga and vice versa. At the beginning it felt strange. When I returned, people here felt that I was strange, and continued to have that feeling because of the way I dressed (with turban). Yogi Bhajan has attracted over the years many Sikhs in the West. People are looking for something different and new. So they take to Yoga. More women are interested because they are disappointed with their existing faith and religion. They are looking for something new and different. It is mostly women who take to Yoga and its teaching. Almost 80 per cent teachers of Yoga in South America are women. For some reason I have got very much involved in this—the process of teaching Yoga. I met Gurubachan Singh Khalsa and started discussing with him and Nam Nidhan as to how to spread this movement. We should do subsidiary kind of things as teachers because we have access to mantras, music and the books. Since most of these are in English, it is difficult to spread the message as most people do not speak English. Many people in Mexico are working on the translations, but not as fast as needed by us. Many people are trying to serve and help out in this process. Gurubachan was very close to Yogi Harbhajan and they spent a lot of time together. Yogi Bhajan had nominated him to spearhead the movement in Latin America as Yogi himself could not do this. Gurubachan came here once last year and we did a lot of organizational work where two or three people would work together. It was decided that Paraguay would be the base. Someone will take care of the office in Paraguay. A website has been developed which is already online and the next step is to start a magazine where all teachers can send photos and articles. This challenge has united us and I have become the representative in Bolivia. Many teachers are willing to come to South America and La Paz. So in addition to my regular job, I do this work, organize workshops and everything else here. It has not been easy. We have to maintain the momentum. There has always got to be a leader. There are many other wonderful teachers but somehow I have taken the above responsibilities of the group in Bolivia. As an example, we recently had 11 women teachers and one young man for a course. Out of this group four or five are really committed. The movement is growing and it is necessary to grow. I was teaching at night as I have a job during the day time. Additionally, I have to travel for a lot for conferences, etc. So now I teach only on Saturdays. Rest of the time I devote to organizational aspects and keep pushing on the momentum. It has not been easy. It is hard and tiring and at times, I feel as if my energy is totally drained out. On top of that I have become a role model whereby people start looking up to me and want to know what I am doing. It is fascinating to see people and teachers grow. The teachers are gradually inducted into wearing turbans although for me it was very easy. I do not wear turban during the day. I have asked for permission at work to wear the turban at least one day in a week but I do not think it will be given. In a government job, it is difficult to allow that. That's understandable. I have to make a decision for the future that I propose to take the vows and 'amrit'. And when that happens, I will have to have a different way of earning my living. It will not be easy in this country because there is nobody in this country who wears a turban, not one. It is a process. There is another teacher who wanted to become a Sikh, she is older and is a psychologist. She is free to wear whatever she wants to. There is a wonderful teacher who came recently from Ireland named Harnam Singh and his wife, to give a lecture. He wanted to teach in South America and visited 4–5 countries with wonderful course content. He was teaching a little about what it means to be a Sikh and the values related to Sikhism while covering more generally the path people are taking via Kundalini. Harnam Singh said that this path develops courage and shows you how to become a better human being. He was basically describing how it was for him to become a Sikh and to follow the code of Sikhs and in the process become a noble person. It was wonderful as no one teaches you this. With all this happening, I am looking forward to a satisfying future despite the challenges.

CONCLUSION

It is sad that an enterprise by adventurous Sikhs failed causing misery to some well-meaning Sikhs of Punjab because of lack of professionalism and some bad luck. But what is inexcusable is the in-fighting, backbiting and downright meanness by many of them in times of adversity. While it was noble indeed to set-up a gurdwara on priority but the teachings and tenets of Sikhism were given a short shrift. South America though far away from Punjab continues to provide opportunities for settlements on farms but this has to be masterminded on a professional basis.

There is a new hope emerging from Yogi Harbhajan's followers who are setting up Yoga centres followed by gurdwaras in several of the South American countries. These Sikhs are following the Sikh dharma in an exemplary manner. They need to be supported.

CHAPTER 6

Sikhs in Brazil

INTRODUCTION

There are references wherein it is mentioned that some Sikhs who wanted to migrate to USA were made to disembark at the Brazilian ports from where they travelled over land to Argentina. Similarly, some of them who were already in Panama and Cuba, headed for Argentina via Peru, Bolivia and Brazil. There is evidence of direct migration of Sikhs to Brazil as early as 1912. In fact, Brazil even advertised in India for farmers to come to their country for promoting agriculture. Why the Sikhs did not establish roots in Brazil is not clear. Some accounts say that the land and climate of Brazil was not found attractive enough by them. May be the political climate was not very conducive for the Indians. Some references are available regarding Ghadar Party leaders' visit and their temporary stay in Rio de Janeiro on their way to Argentina or other countries. It would appear no branch of the Ghadar Party was set up in Brazil presumably because no supporters or cadres were available. Interestingly, Shaheed Bhagat Singh's uncle had lived in Rio for some time.

It is difficult to accept that all the Sikhs would have merely transited through the country without some of them not staying on. In this quest, I did meet an old Sikh immigrant's grandson which is covered as a case study later on. There are scattered Sikh professionals and businessmen in Sao Paulo and some other towns—a total of about 40 families. These are comparatively recent immigrants post-1970s or 1980s. Only a few of them as yet have struck permanent roots in Brazil. Sikh presence in Brazil is indeed insignificant.

One of the earlier establishments of Yogi Bhajan's 3HO in

South America was in Brazil. Subhag Kaur Khalsa, an American and her late husband, Gurusewak Singh Khalsa, a Brazilian, moved to Sao Paulo in 1987 bringing with them *SGGS*. They set up a Yoga centre in their apartment and finally a gurdwara in 2004. There are a few turbaned followers of Yogi Ji in Brazil. A friend from London, has a beautiful recording of a small group of these Sikhs with white turbans and flowing beards singing the Japji on a guitar on a Brazilian beach. Bravo!

THE COUNTRY

Brazil is the fifth largest country in area after Russia, Canada, China and USA and is the sixth largest in population. It is a country known for its Amazonian rain forests, exotic carnivals and the samba music. Beaches and bikinis are a national passion. The original Indian population has dwindled but some areas remain almost unapproachable even today. Portuguese is the language, being the only exception to Spanish in South America. The earlier prosperity came through sugar with the forced labour of African and native Indian slaves. Sexual relations between the masters and slaves were so common that a large mulatto population soon emerged. Coffee and rubber were other rich contributors to the economy in earlier times. Brazil is a part of BRIC countries, establishing its global importance. Economy has had its ups and downs and politically also it has had more than its share of military dictators, democracy of some sort, kings and their representatives. It is the only country which has had a European monarch ruling on its soil. In 1807 when Napoleon was at Lisbon's doorstep, the Portuguese Prince Regent decided to sail out with his entire court to Rio to rule from there. Cheap labour and underemployment abound in Brazil. No wonder most of the Sikhs migrants walked through the difficult country and did not settle in Brazil.

The Singhvi High Level Committee Report has the following to say:

Brazil is not only the largest and the most populous country in South America, but it is also the only one that is not Spanish speaking. That is because it was part of the former Portuguese Empire. It would be apparent from the statistical table that the size of the Indian community in this country is also the biggest in this entire region, marginally more numerous than its counterpart in Argentina.

There are 1500 PIOs and about 400 NRIs in Brazil. A small number of Sindhis had arrived here from Surinam and Central America in 1960 to set up shops as traders at a place called Manaus. A second wave consisted of university professors who arrived in the 1960s and also in the 1970s. Other PIOs migrated to this country from various African countries, mainly from former Portuguese colonies, soon after their independence in the 1970s. The number of PIOs in Brazil has been augmented in recent years by the arrival of nuclear scientists and computer professionals. A few Christian nuns and priests were also attracted to this predominantly Catholic country. It is not surprising that there are as many as 1500 PIOs among the Indian community in Brazil, as against only 400 NRIs. Foreign nationals can easily acquire local citizenship without any discrimination after 15 years of domicile in this country. Brazil has also no bar against dual citizenship. But in recent years, it has been granting immigration visas only in high tech areas. The fact that it is a monolingual country has also deterred aspiring Indian emigrants from attempting to go there.

In a country with a total population of 169 million people, the Indian diaspora must be regarded as miniscule. It is spread thinly over the vast expanses that constitute this gigantic land, so much bigger in area than India. The only exceptions are the Sindhis in Manaus (who have formed an Indian Association with about a hundred members) and the Goans in Sao Paulo. There is also an Indo–Brazilian association in the national capital at Brasilia. This is natural, considering that our Embassy is located in that city. Otherwise, it is not surprising that the Indian community has not been able, nor found the need, to organize itself into any single recognizable group. Besides its dispersal over this continental sized country, many of those that arrived in the earlier years have acquired Brazilian brides and are totally assimilated in the local society. The children born to such couples are Brazilians by birth.

On the whole, it would be right to conclude that the Indian diaspora in this country has good interaction with the local community and is held by it in high regard.

EARLY SIKH IMMIGRANTS

As mentioned earlier, there are several written and interviewee evidence confirming Sikhs transiting through Brazil on their way to Argentina. This, as the only scenario of Brazilian Sikh migration, is not convincing. Hardly any evidence was available till my visit regarding permanent settlement of the Sikhs in the country. In certain parts of Brazil, farm lands and climate are as good as in Punjab. Brazil also needed immigrants to help develop areas, particularly the Amazon country, attracting large migration of the Japanese. Perhaps in the early twentieth century, Brazil was not as prosperous and as immigrant-friendly on race considerations as the richer Argentina where the British tended to employ the Sikhs preferentially in their sugar and railway enterprises. It is to be noted that there were British railway companies even in Brazil and it is difficult to imagine that some of the Sikhs did not seek employment with them. A documentary on local TV on railways of Brazil, I am told, did show amongst the workers a turbaned Sikh.

Pursuing this line, I was fortunate to unearth information on early Sikh immigrants to Brazil at the British Library (India Office Collections), London. There is, indeed, evidence of Sikh migration even though it is true that some of them chose to return or move onwards to Argentina. Perhaps they did not find the working conditions suitable enough but several others did spread out to the countryside to settle down. There seems to be no concentrated settlement of the Sikhs in Brazil which resulted in isolation. It would appear that most of them lost touch with people back home and with each other within Brazil. Lack of new immigrants added to their isolation from homeland. These older Sikh immigrants and their descendants need to be located for further detailed study.

An indirect clue as to why Sikhs might have found the atmosphere in Brazil somewhat inhospitable for settling down could be gauged from the Japanese early immigrant experiences. Brazil was one of the largest, if not the largest settlement of Japanese outside Japan. Their experience in Brazil is described in a Ph.D. research paper, 'Zen Buddhism in Brazil: Japanese or Brazillian?' by Cristina Moreira Rocha, University of Sao Paulo. She writes:

> Japanese Immigrants first arrived in 1908 at the port of Santos. Emigrating to work at the plantations, they intended to return to Japan as soon as they had amassed the necessary means. In fact, at that time there was an ongoing debate in the Brazilian Congress about the ability of the Japanese to assimilate into Brazilian culture. Many senators wanted to stop Japanese immigration altogether. The discussion was public, and many newspapers carried articles picturing the Japanese immigrants as inassimilable.

Did the early Sikh immigrants sense this prejudice?

SOME REFERENCES FROM BRITISH LIBRARY PAPERS

The earliest correspondence available indicates a letter of 6 August 1920, from H. Abbott, the British Consul in Sao Paulo to the Foreign Office in London wherein he writes,

> While on the subject of emigration I may mention that some time ago I received a letter from a number of Indians in the Punjab who were desirous of coming to Brazil to work as labourers but that before answering I considered it desirable to get into touch with the Secretary of State for Agriculture and Commerce and to hear his views on the subject. He has informed under date of 6th instant, that there are no regulations against British Indian subjects coming to Brazil, and that the Local Authorities have already received in the Emigrants Hospice of the Department of Labor, 56 persons who arrived from Genoa on May 12th and 14th 1912 by *SS Sienna* and *SS Bologna*. As these Indians did not adapt themselves to agricultural labour in which they were engaged at different times between the years of 1912 and 1916, they finally disbanded; some coming to the capital and others going further

into the interior from whom, however, the Secretary of Agriculture has no further news.

In an interesting reference pertaining to repatriation of the destitute, the Sao Paulo Consul wrote to London on 17 September 1924, 'Indians came to Brazil but living conditions were not suitable so they got visas for Argentina but were refused entry to Argentina. So, eight of them wish to be repatriated to India.' It can be surmised that other immigrants settled down in Brazil either temporarily or permanently. The eight persons under reference were from Jalandhar and Kapurthala. In another reference, one Captain Francis McCullagh interviewed the President of State of Amazonas on 30 April 1924 at Manaos, when he was told by H.E. that the State wants East Indian colonists as white men had given up. He clarified that as per the Brazil Emigration Act of 6/1/1921, emigration was allowed on the basis of relatives and other persons.

It is clear that Sikh immigrants in general did not find Brazil suitable for settling down. Despite this, there is evidence to the contrary about Brazil continuing to pursue immigrants from India through immigration agents. As an example, an advertisement in the *Indian National Herald* of 20 May 1927 is interesting:

GOOD NEWS TO THOSE GOING ABROAD
BRAZIL WANTS INDIANS. FOLLOW JAPAN

Mr. F. De Santa Anne assures about 'no racial discrimination and good prospects in a fertile coffee plantation country'. Mr. F. De Santa Anne has come to India as an Agent for the Brazilian country. He is now in Bombay and has travelled [to] nearly all the countries and has studied the economic and mercantile conditions of all countries. 'Mr. F. De Santa Anne says that the special want of Brazil is men. Agriculturists and Indians from northern India are honourably welcome. Some years before the Japanese continued immigrating to Brazil and their number is increasing. If such is the case why should Brazil not welcome Indians who are more amicable with Brazilians than Japanese? If anybody wants any further information on the point he can write or seek the undersigned.

ISMAIL BHAI WAHID
Passport and Passenger Agent

HO
Dhobi Talao,
Opposite Xavier School,
Box No. 2022,
Bombay 2.

A news item of that period mentions, '130 emigrants left as a result of the advertisement. 15 more booked on 23 September. Actually 16 left per *SS Castalia*. The Emigration Officer was satisfied with the letters received from friends or relatives that there are openings for them.' From the above it would appear that a substantial number of Sikhs did migrate to Brazil. It is also established that some of them moved onto Argentina. There were no other attractive destinations to go to in the region. As it is, North America had erected barriers against Indian immigration. Of course, some Sikhs returned to India but others must have settled in Brazil. What do we know of them and their subsequent generations, needs detailed investigation? A case study of Wagner Singh is given below.

CASE STUDIES

The following interviews give a flavour of the background and present status of Sikh immigrants:

Wagner Sansara Singh

Interviewed on 2 September 2005 in Riberao Preto, Mr. Mehta's Office.

I had been pursuing various contacts to get information on old immigrants but without success. But persistence paid and it was possible to locate an old immigrant's grandson courtesy

Mr. Mehta and Mit Kahlon. Wagner's grandfather, Sansar(a) Singh, is registered as an immigrant arriving in January 1927 at Santos Port. Unfortunately Wagner knows hardly anything about Sikhs but was emotionally moved to meet a turbaned Sikh. I was presented several gifts including a pen and the watch he was wearing. Wagner mentioned that his grandfather came along with three others, Ram Singh, Ratan Singh and Watan Singh. Wagner feels that there are several more old Sikh immigrants in Brazil but he has no details. Wagner Singh's grandfather Sansara (probably Sansar) Singh was born on 20 March1902 in village Casado (pronounced: Delado) to Bogovani Singh (possibly Bhagwan Singh) and Aracor Singh (possibly Ar Kaur). Sansar Singh kept wearing turban (white) till his death when he was buried and not cremated. Initially Sansar worked with the British Railways in Sao Paulo. He moved upcountry to Olympia where he decided to start his own grocery retailing. Wagner remembers him as a somewhat quiet person. Sansar made no effort to teach Punjabi to his children but used to pray frequently. He was a vegetarian. His grandchildren remember him as a very loving and caring person. Sansar married twice, first to Judia and then to Waleska Venzel Caramento. He had two sons from Waleska—Walter Sansar Singh and Sansar Singh Jr. (Sansar Jr. looked like a Brazilian but Walter looked more like an Indian).

Walter (now dead) married Iracema Bafero, a Brazilian (presently 77 yrs old). They had seven children. Wagner, whom I met was the second born. Wagner's father Walter Sansara Singh joined a bank as clerk and rose to become the manager. He used to tell his children about the importance of honesty and exhorted them to do the right thing. He used to stress that all things are ours and not mine individually. Walter financed his brother's education, which helped the latter become a teacher, and finally the headmaster of a school. Walter was somewhat of an intellectual but his wife was not very literate.

Wagner was born on 18 August 1956 at Socotta, where he went to High School. He did not complete his college gradu-

Plate 48: Brazil: A Sikh immigrant's grandson Wagner Sansar(a) Singh and wife

ation as he had to take over family responsibilities because of his elder brother's death. Wagner joined a bank in Sao Paulo and worked for ten years. Living in a big city, he had the opportunity to see occasional Indian films as he felt great emotional attachment with India. Wagner met Nyela at a beach and got married soon thereafter. He left the bank and moved to De Guariba, the hometown of Nyela. After trying his hand at some business, he joined his father-in-law, who had a printing press. Wagner had to face problems because of competition with Neyla's two younger brothers. However, his father-in-law chose him as his successor in business. Wagner is presently also the Director of the local Commercial Association, while Nyela is the President. Nyela knows very little about India and did not have a good image of the country and the Sikhs. The only information they have is through television. India is considered as a backward and poor country. The Sikh image was negative because of Indira Gandhi's assassination and the secessionist movement. While seeing me off at the airport, they said they were richer now because of their two cultural heritages, one of Brazil and another of Sikhs and Punjab. They felt assured that the Sikhs are prosperous and well educated. Both husband and wife are now keen to visit India.

Mit Mohan Singh Kahlon

(*As narrated by Mit Mohan through the internet*)

My coming to Brazil, in early 1973, from Los Angeles, was bewildering and at the same time intriguing to my parents in Chandigarh. It was even more aggravating because they expected me to come back to Punjab after my graduate work in engineering at UCLA and start a professional life there. And instead, I was going to Brazil to work for an engineering and construction company. Where the hell is Sao Paulo, Brazil? Everyone has some idea about Rio but not Sao Paulo. Luckily in those days there was no Skype, internet; otherwise I would have been barraged by daily phone calls and messages. Let's understand their agony. In those days, thousands of students were leaving for higher studies to the USA and Canada, a euphemism to get out of India and settle abroad. A dream come true for Indians! In their opinion, I might have lost my faculty. But it took a while to get over this. This is how I landed in Brazil.

I have found the Indian community and especially the Sikhs very resolute. First of all Punjab is a land locked state. Most Punjabis had not seen a beach until they were above 25 years of age or even ever. This is in contrast to other Indian groups like Maharashtrians or south Indians who were more urban and outward looking. They had constant contact with foreigners; they would go to international restaurants and they would attend well-known educational institutions. On the other hand, Punjab was and still is a frontier agricultural state. Here we could either go to south Indian coffee house or a dhaba. Or once in a while we would go to see a movie. The only news source for us was *The Tribune* (no TV). But we Punjabis surprise every one with our diaspora numbers outside India. I also had a strong desire to go to the USA. I had neither relatives, nor friends in Los Angeles but was ready to face a completely new world. The reason I am saying this is not many students, beside Indians and Chinese did this. But to go to different place abroad is in our blood.

Plate 49: Brazil, Sao Paulo. Mit Mohan Singh Kahlon with other Sikhs in his house to meet author

Even today I think I can go to any country and adjust to their cultural environment, if opportunities arise, without much expostulation (even to Burkina Faso).

So my coming to Brazil was not at all strange or intimidating to me. In Brazil, I had a great and challenging job in engineering projects in areas of chemicals and petrochemicals and oil and gas. I was Project Manager at the age of 27, quite an impossible feat in India and, was very well paid. I went up the corporate ranks very quickly, faster than I could have achieved in US or in India. This was in spite of being a foreigner with the disadvantage of not knowing Portuguese. Brazilians are very friendly, generous, and hospitable people. I was accepted in professional and social life with open arms. I still remember an incident when I had to make a presentation to the Petrobras (state oil company) directors. They were surprised to find that an Indian was the Project Manager of Oil Shale project of the contracted engineering company. Petrobras owned confidential patents of the Oil Shale manufacturing process. Brazilians have always accepted foreigners with open arms.

One issue I am particularly flummoxed by is why many Sikh Jats from Punjab did not even consider coming to Brazil or Argentina, a developed country in those days? During the twentieth century, they tried US, Canada, UK, but not Brazil, a land of 8.5 million sq km (2.5 times bigger than India). What else were they looking for? It could have been the language. But Sikhs who went to Canada in mid-1900s, could not speak English either. Brazilian weather could not have been the problem. It is very similar to Punjab's—certainly a lot better than the North American freezing temperatures, where everyone wanted to go.

It could not have been the discrimination issue either. Brazil is a land of immigrants and has the largest Japanese community outside Japan. Racism is a subject that people often seek to avoid, it being deemed politically too embarrassing. Any suggestion of its existence often elicits a response of outraged indignation and immediate denial. Yet it is central to the discourse of most societies and Brazil also. Though there was slavery in Brazil, yet they have managed it well. The main reason is the population over the time got all mixed—Europeans, local Indians, Blacks and Orientals. Well, I will leave this issue to some perspicacious sociologists and others.

Brazil is well known for beautiful girls. On my visits to India, I always get curious questions on Carnival, girls and beaches. So what else I could have done here if not get married to a beautiful Brazilian Chinese engineer Mei Chi Teng. Again my parents raised eyebrows. Why can't I get married to a Jat Sikh girl in Punjab? My wife visits Chandigarh every year (I do so twice a year). I have a feeling that my family prefers her more than me.

Now coming back to my professional life again; I was getting tired of engineering and wanted to expand my intellectual horizons and look for more challenges. It may be another Punjabi trait. So I got admitted to an MBA course in Boston and joined a management consulting company, Booz Allen and Hamilton (now called Booz & Co). That was a very exciting job. In this job, one would be working on very different business segments every few months. Then I got the offer as a CEO of a ceramic tile company and later started my own company in hospital equipment distribution and service.

I often ponder what the world might be like in twenty years, or even fifty from now. India and Brazil would probably be the world's leading powers. They both make part of the BRIC nations. There has been an increasing interest between these two countries over the last decade. Umpteen number of Indian companies and businesses are arriving in Brazil. So I think I can help these companies to smoothly land in Brazil—not like the Sikhs who got stranded on Brazilian ports in the early twentieth century. I have helped a number of companies to establish in Brazil. Like many a people, at the age of 61, I have become a consultant also. This gives me opportunity to meet a number of people from India and especially Punjab.

One thing I miss is the gurdwara in Brazil. The first act of any Sikh who went abroad was to start a gurdwara. It is a place where all meet and socialize with each other. We all live in and through our history, however, distant it might be. I am born a Sikh and a Punjabi and I want to keep my religion; culture and language intact, though I don't wear a turban in Brazil more due to convenience in this modern world. But I always wear the turban in India. I am against any type of religious fanaticism.

There are about 40 Sikh families in Brazil. Many are in the business of import of garments and Indian artefacts. They have done well financially especially after a soap opera was shown on the local TV Glogo. We meet everyonce in a while at some family get-togethers. Once a year, we celebrate Guru Nanak's birthday at someone's house that has the *Guru Granth Sahib*. There are half a dozen professionals also who work with large corporations.

In summary, I am very happy and have had a very satisfying experience to come to Brazil. I have been professionally successful, met my wife, enjoy the company of my Brazilian friends, learnt new languages and cultures, travelled to fantastic and challenging new places (Amazon, Patagonia, and Atacama Desert). I will stay here and keep visiting Punjab regularly.

Subagh Kaur Khalsa

Interviewed on 1 September 2005 at 3.00 p.m. in Sao Paulo, Brazil.

(Of special interest is the emotional process she went through before becoming a Sikh and her passion in propagating the Sikh dharma and the difficulties she is facing.)

It all started for me through Yoga when I was 21. I was not looking for spiritual path consciously. I was looking for yoga. It makes you feel great and I felt good. During the next five years which I call my crisis years, I wanted to run away from the deep experience that Yoga at 3HO was taking me to but I realized that I could not get away from it. So I decided to go to India and try to find another teacher who would not quite shake me up like Yogi Bhajan. Before going to India, I went to Europe for a year mostly working with 3HO, French Group. During this period, I got to do 'Tantrik' in Amsterdam and that is where I met Yogi Bhajan. It was a very penetrating experience, the white 'Tantra' with Yogi himself directing. It was like another rebirth. It was hazy before the 'Tantrik' experience and from that point on I was clearer as to who I was or what my destiny was. On return to USA, I had the opportunity to attend Solicites in New Mexico. It was there in Solicites that I had a very deep experience in the gurdwara and that was another turning point. It was a very intense practice for about seven to ten days. I remember the gurdwara and I could not stop crying. It was another impact making experience. It was the first time I put on the turban. It was at that time just an act of putting on the turban and taking it off. There was no association of my turban with my role. But after a few times when I took off the turban I started to feel strange.

For another five years, I was in turmoil of having turban and kirpan, etc. It did not feel logical. Ultimately you have to throw logic out of the window. But that is kind of difficult to explain to the whole family. How do you explain to your mother who raised me as a Catholic and I had gone through the whole Catholic tradition? But now over the last twenty years they have started to respect my spiritual choice. On return from Solicites, I went to India. I was still trying to get away. I had some deep experiences but I was still on the run. In India I did meet some other spiritual teachers and I had the opportunity to switch. But there was no switching for me and it was in India that I finally made a commitment to Yogi Bhajan and Sikh dharma. I joined the Ashram in USA on return. Till that time (I was thirty), it was just a question mark for me in matters like why would anyone want to have children. However, on return it ignited in me to be a mother. Yogi Bhajan had given a formula as to how to find the right mate. He said there are two ways to go about this. One is you can go out and find which is what I was doing. This was not getting me anywhere. The second option is to sit where you are and do a

Plates 50–52: Brazil (top left) Subagh Kaur Khalsa; (top right) Gurdwara built by Subagh's late husband Gurusewak Singh; (bottom) Brazillian Sikh Khalsas with Arvinder Singh Garcha of UK

very intensive 'sadhna' and attract the person. This seemed such a far out thing. I was a sort of feminist and the idea of waiting, radiating and attracting and not doing anything was a whole new game plan. Nevertheless I decided to do this. I started to do daily a 2-hour 'sadhana'. Soon after joining the ashram I met an acquaintance who asked me to pick up a friend of her at the railway station. This was the Gurusewak whom I ended up marrying (big laughter). His English was really poor he was from Brazil. It was difficult to communicate with him. His packaging was different from what I usually went for. He was short and a bit plump. He was not quite yogic looking but he had a beard. He was a Healer. I had lost a lot of weight while I was in India and my metabolism was not good. I was not having my periods. I had never gone to a Healer. But for three months I had not had my periods, and made an appointment for a forenoon session. And that morning, I had my periods. I kept my appointment and told him that I had a reason for the appointment but I do not have that any more. So I do not know why I am here. Well, he laughed and had a huge smile. He said let us go for lunch and that's where he asked me to marry him. My husband was forty and I was thirty. At the first possible opportunity, we met with Yogi Bhajan when my husband asked for his approval. He had a huge smile on his face and said 'Blessings, Blessings'. He looked at me and said you get him back to Brazil—he does not belong here. So here it was. My destiny was signed, sealed and delivered. He said to us that we should do in South America what he did here. The enormity of the task created a lot of personal stress but the best part was that we made the commitment to put up the gurdwara. Before getting married in December 1984, Yogi asked me to take 'amrit' which I did. We had our first baby girl in the Ashram. To keep our commitment to Yogi Ji, we moved to Brazil when our daughter was 11 months old. My husband was uneasy in coming down at that time as Brazil was going through financial and political uncertainties. We were trying to have some money before moving. We had only about $ 3000—that was all the cover we had for the future. My husband had an apartment in Sao Paulo and we had made a commitment to build a gurdwara. So we brought the Guru and installed it in a very small closet in our first apartment.

That was our first gurdwara. Later on we moved to this beautiful place a little distant from the centre of the town. My husband worked very hard to get us established here. He continued to go back to the USA twice a year to carry out his healing work. Every time he returned he would bring back $5000–6000. One time he brought back $10,000. Basically that is how the gurdwara and the ashram got built. In the meanwhile kids kept coming, Hari Simran Kaur, Ajit Singh and then Gobind Singh. We were training teachers to reach more people quickly. A lot of 3HO followers in the USA were shy of introducing Sikh dharma. They questioned whether they were getting a religion or Yoga which was their interest. I can understand that very well. But we present this as

'Bhakti' Yoga with kirtan. It is an experience of meeting the beloved. So we founded Kundalini and Sikh dharma together. So until this day, gurdwara is a part of teacher training. We certify the people in front of the Guru and that's been our way. We had more women but still had a good share of men—say 3 is to 2 ratio. Yoga started to grow but slowly. On personal side we were five of us with three rooms only, including one for the gurdwara. This pushed us into the gurdwara project outside the residence area. In 1999 we broke ground for a new gurdwara building. Two weeks later, our neighbour approached us on his own to offer to sell his land which my husband had always wanted to acquire. With more space available the design and structure had to be changed. The first floor was 80 per cent complete by December 2000. My husband suggested me to visit my mom as she had not seen our two sons. Although we had literally no funds, we went to the USA in January 2001. My husband was going to spend two weeks with us and then go for his healing job. Next morning at my mom's house my husband said he wasn't feeling well.

Two weeks later we found out that he had prostate cancer. He was given 2–5 years. Me with three kids and the gurdwara only 80 per cent complete and him not having much time to live! We didn't know what to do unless the Guru decided to do something. We spent eight months in the States. The Guru opened all kinds of doors for the treatment. That was miraculous. We did not even have a health insurance. Somehow or the other my husband started feeling better. Later, on our return to Brazil, his health began to deteriorate. I started to get this message from above that this gurdwara needs to get going. I didn't want to deal with this on my own and hence I told him that we had to move on with the gurdwara project to which he agreed. So we started the construction of the second floor which was the gurdwara proper. Last year was a very bad year with gurdwara construction going on and his health deteriorating. He held himself in the body until inauguration in June of last year. You have seen the photos of inauguration. He held himself somehow or the other till 17 August 2004 when he left his physical form. In the meanwhile, the sangat has taken over my kids as we had no money. At the Council meeting someone offered to help send the two boys to go to Miri Piri School in Amritsar. Our daughter was over age and hence has gone to the ashram in USA. So the kids will get the benefit of sangat which they were missing here.

We have trained a total of about 150 teachers. There is an article which appeared in the Yoga magazine of Brazil which has covered our activities. The gurdwara is facing practical issues as there are hardly any followers. Another couple has the *SGGS* in their home in Sao Paulo. Other than that there is no activity. The task assigned to my husband of propagating Kundalini and Sikh dharma is now in my hands. In South America there is some progress in various countries. Presently not much is happening but I see myself as the guardian of the Sikh dharma in Brazil. I hold a position internationally as a guardian of Kundalini Yoga. I participate in the Group international meet twice a year. I am playing my role here to best of my ability and resources. Rest is up to the Guru.

RECENT IMMIGRANTS

Anup Singh Sabarwal: Sao Paulo, Brazil, 4 September 2005

I am from Delhi and was born in Pakistan. My son Kuldeep Singh known as Deepak (Deep Fashions) was here. Now the business under his name is called King Fashion. I came here in 2002. He came to this place eight years ago. One of our relatives, Pali, has an international business in ladies garment. My son was working for them. They sent him to Mexico and then to Brazil. Due to differences with his employer, he set up his own business. (See similar story under Mexico.) He started a wholesale business. There are eight to ten Sikh families in Sao Paulo. Nobody wears a turban here except me. Here people consider us bin Laden and greet us with a Salam aleikum. Language is big problem for newcomers as it is different from other languages. One Sikh came here as his son is in service in Sao Paulo. He met Atma Singh, a Brazillian converted to Sikhism, who brought him to us. It so happened that we knew him from Delhi. Last year Yogi Harbhajan's followers inaugurated a gurdwara and invited all the Sikhs. The founder, Gurusewak Singh, died soon after. We have given up important aspects of Sikhism but they are following it fully. There was a Sikh earlier on teaching in the university who has now migrated to Canada. There is another Sikh from Amritsar, who is working in a cashew company in Brazil.

TEJWANT SINGH (INTERNET SEARCH)

I have lived in Brazil for about nine years. During that time I found only one turbaned Sikh, who was the vice-president of McDonald's. This was in the year 1976. I used to teach English as a second language in a well-known school in Sao Paulo. An interesting thing happened one day. I saw a turbaned Sikh walk into the school with a suitcase in his hand. I was surprised to see him. It so happened that when he landed at the airport in Sao Paulo, one of the employees of the airline, who had been my student, told Joginder Singh (the man with the suitcase) that he knew another turbaned Sikh (me). Hence there he was. He had come from Canada to get his permanent status permit. This was my second encounter with a Sikh in Brazil. He was supposed to stay for a couple of days but ended up staying with me for six months before moving to his own flat.

CHAPTER 7

Sikhs in Cuba

INTRODUCTION

Sikhs have been migrating to Cuba from the early twentieth century on their way to the USA or Central and South American countries. There was also some movement to and fro from the Caribbean Islands. Some Sikhs did settle down as expected. But not much is known about them. Sikhs did not find Cuba an attractive destination because of the hot climate and poor working conditions on sugar cane plantations or as labourers on construction sites, be it railways, sugar mills or other industrial undertakings. There are some old immigrants or their next generations settled in the north-west in Santiago-de-Cuba and the Guantanamo Bay area. A special effort is needed to find them.

THE COUNTRY

Havana, the capital, is a mere 170 km from Florida's Key West in the USA. So is Mexico, only 210 km away. Cuba's other close neighbours are Jamaica, the Bahamas and Haiti, only 77 km away. Much of Cuba is made up of fertile flatlands known for its cattle grazing and sugar cane, coffee and tobacco plantations.

Christopher Columbus sighted Cuba in 1492. Soon thereafter Spain had conquered most of the country by 1514. Cattle ranching quickly became the mainstay of the Cuban economy. Large estates were established through enslavement of the native Indians. As the Indian population dwindled, African slaves were imported. Other European powers began to challenge Spain. Britain occupied Havana for 11 months. Besides tobacco, sugar had become a major industry and by the early nineteenth century, Cuba was the world's largest sugar producer. The Spanish-American war at the end of nineteenth century resulted in American victory and USA installed a governor. In 1903, the USA built a naval base at Guantánamo Bay. This is still in operation.

By the 1920s, US companies owned two-thirds of Cuba's farmland. Tourism based on drinking, gambling and prostitution flourished. In 1933, an Army sergeant, Batista seized power. On 1 January 1959, Batista's dictatorship was overthrown after a three-year guerrilla campaign led by a young lawyer Fidel Castro along with 'Che' Guevara and Camilo Cienfuegos.

Castro, as the prime minister began reforming the nation's economy. Relations with the USA deteriorated when he nationalized US-owned oil refineries that refused to process Russian oil (similar to the Indian story of nationalizing foreign oil companies). The Americans retaliated by cutting Cuban sugar imports, thus crippling the Cuban economy. Desperate for cash, Castro turned to the Soviet Union, which promptly accepted Cuba's sugar exports. Post-1961 Bay of Pigs fiasco, Castro turned full steam into socialism. The 1962 Cuban Missile Crisis, under John Kennedy, is said to be the closest the world has ever come to a nuclear conflict. The missiles were sent back to the USSR. USA declared a full-fledged embargo. Cuba began actively supporting guerrilla groups in South America and Africa. Despite the Soviet aid, the Cuban economy has been in trouble. The situation worsened in 1989 when Eastern Europe collapsed and Russia withdrew its aid. Cuba has built close relations with Venezuela and Hugo Chavez.

Architecturally, Havana is a beautiful city with the imposing Capitol Building similar to one in Washington, D.C. But most of the buildings are crumbling. However, interestingly poor people are living and owning prime buildings right in the centre of the city. Most can be seen sitting on their doorsteps or side streets. Rum is available in plenty. Dance and music abound here. They say if Castro goes things can be managed but if rum goes, there would be a revolution.

The Singhvi High Level Committee Report has no comments with regard to Cuba.

SIKH MIGRATION TO CUBA

There is evidence that Sikhs did go to Cuba in the early twentieth century but that they found the going tough in the country because of the heat, humidity and fever. So, most of them stayed for short periods, and then looked for better alternatives for settling down. As in other countries, some got left behind who settled down and have gradually got assimilated. I was told that there are some old settlers or at least their next generations in the eastern province of Santiago de Cuba and Guantanamo. A name of a TV announcer, Castillo Singh, was mentioned but in the short period I was there, contact could not be established. However, the Indian Embassy did mention that some years ago there were a few Sikhs, including one Jagtar Singh, who had contacted the Embassy to find out how they could claim their ancestral lands in Punjab. Details were not available. An old immigrant Ajit Singh gave some information about himself on the telephone. Another young Sikh entrepreneur, a Stephanian from Delhi, but now a Canadian citizen is doing well, business-wise in Havana.

In Argentina, I had seen some old passports with Cuban Immigration stamp. While visiting Panama later on, Prakash Singh told me that two Sikhs from Cuba had visited Panama eight years ago when they called on him as the President of the Indian Society. There is a newspaper clipping (provided courtesy Prof. Pimental) which gives details of Indian/Sikh immigration to Cuba. The interesting bits are that Amar Singh came in 1917 and worked at La Isabel Sugar Mill and married Felipe Esteria Ibanez. One lady Susana (Punjabi name could have been different) Singh came in 1917 with others and married B(V)attan Singh who presumably had immigrated earlier on. When interviewed in 1966, she said that when coming to Cuba she had brought along with her a 'Dopatta of the Sikhs'.

Battan was in Central Romelia and acted as the head of about 30–40 Indian workers. He later moved to Cruce de Benito. After her husband's death in 1959, Susana Singh has worn black dresses only.

SOME CASE STUDIES

The following interviews are of some interest, giving a flavour of the migrants.

Ajit Singh (Interviewed on telephone in Havana)

He was reluctant to meet me but agreed to talk over the phone. His first question to me was 'Are you keeping the turban?' On assuring him on that count, he started to relate his story. He came to Cuba in 1955 with the help of his uncle Udham Singh who had migrated in 1923–4 (died 1961). The uncle had sent him an air ticket.

He travelled New Delhi/Karachi/London/New York/Havana. Udham Singh came to Cuba along with 30–5 persons from Punjab and worked in the sugar cane farms in the province of Santiago de Cuba. Most of them had a tough life. Udham Singh later on got into the cloth business 'pheri' in Havana. Udham neither married nor visited India. However, he helped his family through money remittances including educating Ajit. One of the Sikhs, Asa Singh became quite prosperous and subsequently migrated to USA. A friend of Udham, late Dasondi Singh, gave him his house on his departure to India around 1952. Ajit continues to live in this house till today. In fact, looking for Singhs in the telephone directory, I came across Dasondi's name. Dasondi's sons Darshan Singh and Bhag Singh, though very old, live in village Mahlpur, Punjab. Ajit had met Dasondi prior to leaving for Cuba.

Ajit hails from village Manak Deri on Hoshiarpur–Jalandhar border. Amongst five brothers, he was the youngest. He studied up to middle school in Bhogpur, graduating with a B.Sc.

in 1953 from DAV College, Jalandhar. He has a brother in Delhi and several nephews in Canada, USA and UK. On arrival he started studying Medicine but was required to go through a Spanish language course. Those days the Indian Embassy in Washington, D.C. used to look after Cuba. During the 1956–9 revolution, the university got closed. He had a rough time making both ends meet. All he could do was odd jobs as no permanent positions were available. He then decided to do a Technical Diploma at the Radio & TV Institute and became thereafter, a technical apprentice. When the university re-opened, he was advised to continue with the job rather than go for a long duration study at the university even though education was free. When he was 32-years old, he got married to a Cuban and has a 35-year old son now who is a doctor. Ajit was basically unhappy living in Cuba but had nowhere else to go and envies others who moved on and succeeded.

Paramjit Singh

Paramjit Singh is an ex-Stephanian who is a Canadian citizen but is now settled in Havana as a business entrepreneur. His father was the Indian High Commissioner in Canada in the late 1980s. Having graduated from a university in Canada and with six years of work experience with Bristol Myer and Squibb, he moved to Cuba in 1994. He taught Accounting and Business in Havana University for five years before venturing out on his own. He has several partnerships with interests in mining, metals, shipping, printing and of course living well. His father and sister live in Delhi.

Prof. Pemental

He has been teaching Yoga for the last 35 years and has visited India. He gave a photocopy of a newspaper article from which I have quoted earlier and the excerpts are given below:

Excerpts from a Newspaper Article

Article published in *BohemiaCisco* 68, no. 24, 11 June 1976.

La Comunidad Indu en Cuba

'De La India Al Valle De Guantanamo' (From India to Guantanamo Valley).

The article mentions migration of Samuel Samkerr from UP to Cuba in 1903. He was amongst one of the first migrants from India, who were mainly employed in the sugar plantations. After First World War, the British offered free passage and help in employment in the Americas to the disbanded soldiers (many of who were Sikhs). (This started a wave of migration to the Americas, especially Latin American countries, as the doors were closed in the USA and Canada.) Some of these soldiers came to Cuba. Both the working and living conditions (including climate and diseases) were very harsh resulting in many of the migrants leaving Cuba after a year or so. In 1919, according to Samuel's son and as narrated to him by his father, there were more than 500—almost 1,000 Indian workers. The main wave of immigration was during the period 1906–16. Many migrants came first to Jamaica and then came over to Cuba hoping for better prospects and work environ. US companies were setting up and expanding their sugar plantations which generated employment opportunities. (The harshness of the environ can be gauged from the fact that Samuel had 14 children, out of which only four survived). The migrants had problems in their acceptance by the Cubans and had to accept their lifestyle at the cost of their own traditions. Their names even had to be changed in most cases. Many migrants left for Peru. I suspect most if not all of them went to Argentina which was more receptive to Indian/Sikh migrants.

Amar Singh: Reinaldo Singh's father Amar Singh was an earlier migrant to Cuba. Amar Singh's family owned a small landholding and that too of not good quality, in Punjab. The family situation was precarious and at a family conclave it was decided that Amar and his two cousins should migrate to the New World. The intention was that they would send money to alleviate the family's hardship. Accordingly Amar Singh, his two cousins and some other village friends, undertook the journey in 1923. At that time, waves of migrants from various parts of the world were coming to the Americas. Amar Singh, his companions and several other Indians tried to land in the USA, which was not possible. So they disembarked at Santiago. Initially Amar worked as a farm labourer and then graduated to peddling odd goods using a donkey for retail business mobility. Amar Singh got married to a local lady, Felipa Esteria Ibanez and had five children—two boys and three girls. There were several serious problems faced by Sikhs including Amar Singh. He was told that long hair is not acceptable and as a result he had to cut his hair. There were social issues including not being allowed to cremate their dead ones.

Susana Singh: According to the June 1976 article she has lived in Cuba for over 60 years in Cruces de Benito. She arrived in Cuba in 1917 in a boat along with several other Indians. Her husband B(W)attan Singh had arrived in Cuba much earlier. Her husband became leader of a group of 30–40 Indian workers and acted as interpreter also. Since the death of her husband, she has been wearing only black. When she arrived in Cuba in 1917, she wore a 'dupatta' but now wears a big scarf. Susana says that almost all Indians wished to go back as they were nostalgic about their homeland and wanted to be with their parents and other folks. But it was not possible.

CHAPTER 8

Sikhs in Ecuador

INTRODUCTION

The main interest in visiting Ecuador was to check on the so-called formation of Khalistan headquarters in Quito in 1985. The address given in various gurdwara websites is 'Khalistan Council, Khalistan House, PO Box 193-C, Quito, Ecuador Tel: 458 799'. KC is non-existent. Enquiries with the Ministry of External Affairs in Quito met with a complete surprise. When they carried out an internet search as requested by me, they were surprised to find references. Thereafter they agreed to look up old files in the archives. The search did not show up any correspondence on the subject between their Ambassador in India and the Ministry in Quito during this period. Because of the sensitivity of the issue with India, documents might have been destroyed—my conjecture. However, there were some indirect reference to the subject between Ecuador's Ambassador in London and their Ministry in Quito.

An internet version states that on 3 October 1985, an Embassy of Khalistan was established in Quito, the capital of Ecuador. About 70 officials of Ecuador participated in the inauguration ceremony. This Embassy was called *Casa de Khalistan* (Khalistan House). The news items which appeared in India and UK at that time on the subject could not be located. I vividly recollect having read the news in Indian newspapers at that time.

Bhai Balbir Singh Nijjar of Toronto was appointed the Ambassador. Passports of the Government of Khalistan in Exile were also issued. According to Indian government sources, Indo–Ecuadorian relations suffered a jolt in 1985 when, during the height of terrorism in the Punjab, news about

Ecuador granting recognition to so-called 'Khalistan' came to light. A high level delegation from Ecuador that included a former president of the country who was also the chairman of the ruling party, held discussions in London with various self-proclaimed 'Khalistani' leaders and allegedly offered to give agricultural land and settlement to 'Khalistani refugees' in exchange for substantial financial inducement. However, on account of diplomatic pressure from India, President León Febres Cordero formally announced within a few days that the team that had met with 'Khalistani' leaders was a private delegation and that there was no official support to the idea. Relations since then have been normal and cordial between India and Ecuador.

Another uncorroborated version is that the Indian government sent its commandos, with Ecuador government's concurrence, to get the Sikhs to move out from Quito. Inquiries with the few Sikhs whom I met could not throw any light on the subject. However, all the immigrants I spoke to had come to Ecuador much later. Various websites still mention that Sikhs even from countries whose nationals do not require visa but who belong to Sikh religion do have to apply for a visa. This needs to be set right. In my own case, Ecuador Embassy insisted on police clearance but I am told this procedure applies to all Indians visiting Ecuador. It was intriguing, to say the least, to hear from some Sikh immigrants that once a person arrives in Ecuador, getting a residence permit is not difficult (probably if one is not wearing a turban). Ecuadorians are quite friendly but opportunities for employment and business seem to be somewhat limited.

THE COUNTRY

From 1532 onwards, the Spaniard Pizarro spread terror among the indigenous people, the Inca leader, Atahualpa, was executed and the Inca Empire was effectively demolished. Spain ruled the colony from Lima, Peru, and later by the viceroyalty of Colombia. Independence was achieved by Simón Bolivar in 1822. Over the last 100 years, assassinations and political instability have increasingly invoked military intervention. The twentieth century has seen more periods of military rule than of civilians. In 1941, neighbouring Peru invaded Ecuador and seized much of the country's Amazonian area. The new border between the two countries was finally recognized through a treaty in 1998.

The Singhvi High Level Committee Report has the following to say:

> As in the case of Costa Rica, there is hardly any Indian presence in this remote Andean country that is situated to the south of Colombia and faces the Pacific Ocean. Nevertheless, five NRIs are currently located here. All of them are engaged in trading. Although this country has a fairly relaxed and non-discriminatory immigration policy, none of the NRIs has attempted to acquire local citizenship, which would probably imply the transitory nature of their sojourn in Ecuador. With their small size, they maintain a low profile and concern themselves only with their business.

SIKH IMMIGRANTS IN ECUADOR

Getting no information about Sikhs in Ecuador, I got to hear while I was in Panama about a Sikh restaurant owner in Seattle, USA. He was believed to have lived in Quito for some time. On contacting him, he warned me that there were no Sikhs in Ecuador and that I need not visit that country. So I landed in Quito with great apprehension. However, as I approached my hotel in Quito, I saw a sign of 'Indu Restaurant' which on visiting turned out to be owned by a Pakistani—Azim. He took me to a nearby Indian restaurant owned by Mahinder Bhai of Ahmedabad who in turn introduced me to a Joginder Singh working in an eatery across the road from his restaurant. I was also told about a shop owned by one Gurmeet Singh. The telephone directory search showed up a Jaswinder Singh also.

On a Saturday when I was standing in the city square, a gentleman came rushing to me and introduced himself as Dilbagh Singh Bhullar. While walking in the tourist area in the evening, another person greeted me with Sat Siri Akal and he turned out to be Kalam Singh from Delhi. I felt relieved that my visit was not a complete wash out.

CASE STUDIES

Joginder Singh

Joginder Singh, son of Atma Singh, hailing from village Bhagwanpur, Kapurthala came to Ecuador in 1995 at age 35 in a group of eight persons. All others have since managed to reach USA. He continues to rue his misfortune by saying that he got stranded in Quito. He has had a very tough time and is financially quite weak. He had no money and no job till an Iranian employed him for making 'samosas' at a wage of $100 per month.

At least he could survive, which was otherwise becoming difficult. A lady, Louise, helped him out and he is now living

Plate 53: Ecuador. Joginder Singh, a restaurant worker

with her and has four children, interestingly named Balwinder Singh, Tahinderjit Kaur, Paramjit Kaur, and Sukhjinder Singh. Back home in Punjab, Joginder was from a family of eight brothers, one of whom has migrated to UK. The eldest, Inderjit Singh, is a farmer in the native village. Joginder was married in India with two sons and a daughter. Not being educated, he decided to try to migrate to USA for better prospects but instead landed in Ecuador courtesy his travel agent.

Jaswinder Singh

Despite several efforts, I could not get to meet him. He promised to email his details but no communication was ever received. I was told he is a part-time teacher.

Gurmeet Singh (and Family)

They belong to village Hussainpur, Nakodar. He left India in 1990, arriving in Ecuador two years later after having been to Argentina and Peru. Obtaining a residence permit within a year in 1993 was not a major problem but legal and other charges had to be paid. Gurmeet initially stayed in a hotel and faced language problems. He soon started 'pheri' business in garments and other knick knacks which was soon expanded to servicing the retailers, which is their focus presently. He managed to get his family to join in 1995. Wife Manjeet and sons Sukhjit (27), Sukhjinder (25) and Harvinder (23) live and work together. Business takes him to India regularly.

The elder son Sukhjit got married in India but his wife has yet to join him in Quito. Back in Punjab, Gurmeet's younger brother runs a dairy from the village. They do not like the Ecuador culture and prefer Indian social mores. The sons are not well educated but are actively helping in business. They have a small retail outlet named 'Labhu Shah Boutique India' in the main square shopping complex but emphasis continues to be sourcing to retailers.

Plate 54: Ecuador. Gurmeet Singh's family at their retail shop

Plate 55: Ecuador. Jinda, Gurmeet's son on a *pheri* to the famous Otavala open air market

Plate 56: Ecuador. Kalam Singh, a Disco owner, with wife and daughter

KALAM SINGH

Kalam Singh is a chef from Delhi who claims to have worked with the Oberois in Mumbai before going to the USA in 1986 for five years. Thereafter he shifted to Colombia from where he moved to Ecuador to set up a restaurant in Quito. He got an opportunity to move to Canada which he did by selling his business in Quito. The move to Canada evidently was not successful and he returned to Ecuador where he is running a small discotheque. He is married locally to Imena and has two children, son Azad and daughter Preeti.

A WANDERING SIKH: DILBAGH SINGH BHULLAR

It is a tragic tale of a fine and enterprising young man, victim of the terrorist period in Punjab who is desperately trying to reach North America. He was born in 1969 in a village in

Plate 57: Ecuador. Dilbagh Singh Bhullar, a wandering Sikh with mission to reach North America despite travails

Amritsar district and studied up to matriculation. It would appear that the CRPF and Punjab Police shot 17 persons in their family village in a so-called encounter in 1992. This traumatized him to leave Punjab. He managed to migrate to Doha where he worked as a mason with a CDC company from 1993–9. During this period, he visited India several times. He was married in 1997 and has a son and a daughter. On return from Doha, he stayed in his village for two years. His aim was to go to North America. So he travelled as a tourist to Thailand and further on to Cambodia and Vietnam looking for opportunities to make a living but basically seeking a route to the USA. He had to return after 5–6 months with no success. The next time he sought the help of an agent, M. Singh who was paid Rs. 7 lakh with promise of another Rs. 3 lakh on arrival in North America. The travel agent set about planning his migratory route. The path chosen was a familiar one, i.e. to first go to a country where either visa is not needed or is easily available or issued on arrival. This is called getting an entry in 'kabootarbazi'.

The agent got him to travel on another passport, of one A. Singh, to Thailand (exiting from India with his own passport). He entered Thailand with A's passport which had a Canadian visa which was expiring the next day. Thai authorities would not let him travel onwards to Canada because of imminent visa expiry. So he used his own passport to enter Thailand. The travel agent, through his contacts got him a Malaysian passport. He was put on a flight to Dubai where Malaysians did not require visa for 72 hours. He stayed with a relative and managed permission to stay for a month. The agent in the meantime brought another four persons via Bangkok, arriving just three days before Dilbagh's one month visa expiry. In the meantime, Dilbagh had bought a ticket to Toronto for Rs. 55,000. Two of the new arrivals got through the immigration check but other two got caught. Since the Dubai Police got alerted, three of them were not allowed to board the flight. They were put in jail for three days after which they were deported to India.

Making another attempt, he went to Malaysia in 2004 as a tourist. A Chinese agent got him a two-year work permit on payment of 500 Ringits. He managed to earn about 800 Ringits by doing odd jobs and managed to stay at the gurdwara. While in Malaysia, he obtained a visa for Brazil arriving there in May 2005. He met Subagh Kaur Khalsa (see article on Brazil) who put him up and helped him. He worked in an Indian restaurant for three weeks. Thereafter he went to Bolivia, La Paz. Since he could not get visa for Peru, he crossed over the border and moved on to Ecuador illegally. He cut-off his hair in Ecuador and did away with his turban. Thereafter he lost his luggage. He tried to go to Guatemala by ship but Immigration Police raided the gathering point arresting 70 or so persons, mostly South Americans and put them in Manta jail. Two Sikh boys Jassal Singh and Lakha Singh Khore, were among the group. With the help of an attorney, he got out within a couple of days and managed to get an entry permit till 14 October. An Indian businessman, Gautam, is helping him. He is presently staying at the Hare Krishna Ashram. Wages in Ecuador are low and he is still hoping to go to the USA via Mexico or whatever it takes.

His view on his escapades is somewhat simplistic. He feels he was hounded out of his village because of police brutality and is afraid to permanently settle there. So he is seeking refugee status in a developed country, which is known for its asylum help to the politically oppressed.

The above is not the only sad story as one comes across many such adventurers including single girls in, say Belize, who want to better their prospects financially or otherwise. I am not sure what the way forward is for such desperados.

CHAPTER 9

Sikhs in Mexico

INTRODUCTION

Earlier, Sikh migration was connected with priority for settling in USA. When it was difficult to get legal entry into USA, Punjabis used Mexico as the route to cross into the USA. This is still continuing though with greater and greater difficulty. There were a lot of Sikhs who married Mexican women as it was not possible to marry whites. Karen Leonard (in her book *Making Ethnic Choices*) and others have covered this aspect of Sikh-Mexican connection in USA in great detail. Some Sikhs even settled down in the northern states of Mexico, but most migrated to USA. Some are settled permanently in northern provinces near the border from USA, which needs further study. Another major development has been the conversion of over two thousand Mexicans to Sikhism through the efforts of Late Yogi Harbhajan Singh's 3HO. These Khalsa surnamed Sikhs are indeed devout Sikhs and were the first to set-up a gurdwara in Mexico City. The older generation of Sikhs living in the Northern Provinces is largely assimilated with the local population. There are new immigrants in larger cities that are mainly into business since the 1990s. Additionally there are a few expatriate professionals and one old immigrant from Punjab who has grown up with the 3HO movement of Yogi Bhajan. Jassie, owner of the Indian restaurant, 'Koh E Noor', had generously invited the Sikh sangat to dinner to meet with me.

THE COUNTRY

Mexico has an unrivalled ancient history before even Christ. Around the third century, the Mayas built stepped temple pyramids, followed by the Aztecs in the early fourteenth century. With the conquest by Spanish Hernán Cortés in 1519, the 3,000 years old civilization got demolished in just two years. The indigenous population fell from an estimated 25 million to 1 million by early seventeenth century. From the sixteenth to the nineteenth centuries, a sort of stratified social hierarchy developed. The small numbers of Spanish-born colonists became the nobility in New Spain (as Mexico was then called). Next in rank were the crillos, followed by mestizos, and native Indians and black Africans at the bottom. By the eighteenth century, the Spanish settlers became very wealthy because of mining, commerce, ranching and agriculture. With Napoleon occupying most of Spain, the direct Spanish control over New Spain ceased. Miguel Costilla's rebellion resulted in Spain agreeing to Mexican independence in 1821.

Two decades of instability followed independence—the presidency changed hands 36 times. In 1845, the US Congress voted to annex Texas, leading to the Mexican-American War with US troops capturing Mexico City. Under the Treaty of Guadalupe Hidalgo, Mexico ceded Texas, California, Utah, Colorado and most of New Mexico and Arizona to the USA. By 1862, Mexico was heavily in debt to Britain, France and Spain, who sent a joint force to collect their debts. France decided to go one step further and colonize Mexico, sparking yet another war. But soon Mexicans regained control of the country.

Under P. Díaz, a dictator (ruled 1878–1911), Mexico made some progress. It was followed by ten years of violent civil war when roughly one in eight Mexicans lost their lives. After the revolution there was some progress. Civil unrest by the University students in 1966 was followed by massive and violent protests in the run-up to the Mexico City Olympic Games.

The oil boom of the late 1970s helped improve the economy, but the later oil glut led to a recession followed by an earthquake in 1985. Mexico signed the North American Free Trade Agreement (NAFTA) in 1994.

The Singhvi High Level Committee Report has the following to say:

> There are in Mexico, about 80 Indian families, constituting a total number of about 400 NRIs. Most of them are recent arrivals in the country. Almost all of them have settled down in the capital city. Mexico has a non-discriminatory policy with regard to the grant of its citizenship. The spouse of a Mexican national would generally not face any problem in acquiring local citizenship. Although a few of the NRIs have married Mexican girls, they have retained their Indian citizenship.
>
> The Indians in this country are mainly businessmen or professionals. Many of them work with one or other international organizations or a multinational corporation. There are also some understanding between India and their host country. At present, Dr. Raja Ram (a distinguished Indian scientist and Padma Shri recipient) is also in Mexico, working at CIMMYT. Some of the Indians work for ISPAT Mexicana. This company is part of the Laxmi Mittal group, well known in this region for having turned around a sinking steel company in Trinidad. The Indian presence in Mexico has been greatly appreciated as fifty other business ventures have invested around US $1.58 billion in this country during the period 1994–2000. There are also about 20 to 25 Indian Christian missionaries in Mexico.
>
> The Indian community in Mexico has no divisive factions in it, although its constituents come from different parts of India. It has jointly established an organization called 'Sangam', under whose auspices it celebrates important festivals and cultural programmes. A Sai Baba temple, a Vaishnav temple and a gurdwara have also been constructed by it in Mexico City. Most members of the diaspora speak Spanish and have adapted themselves admirably to their foreign environment.

CASE STUDIES

The following case studies mainly of Yogi Bhajan's followers are interesting. The Indian immigrants of recent origin are mainly into retail and garment business. It was not possible to visit the northern areas bordering USA, but I believe, there are old Sikh immigrants who have been largely assimilated with the local population. I did meet the representatives of two states, viz., Sonora and Sinaloa, seeking information on Sikh immigrants. They had promised to revert but no communication has so far been received. This area of the diaspora needs further study. Arjan Singh's life story is fascinating because of his enterprise with dignity and sensitivity. Satguru Singh is an epitome of determination in maintaining his values which many of us compromise at the first sign of adversity.

Arjan Singh Khalsa

He is a Dhillon from the village Kutianwala, Muktsar district. He did his matriculation from Khuban, B.A. from Chandigarh and M.A. from DAV College Jalandhar in 1974 at the age of 22. He worked briefly with LIC prior to his adventure overseas beginning in 1975. He had leftist leanings and was unhappy with the economic situation in India. His foreign travels started with Iran on a tourist visa via Kabul where no visa was needed. In Kabul, he spent four nights in the gurdwara, slept in the big hall, and listened to kirtan. He was travelling light

Plate 58: Mexico City. Arjan Singh, a Sikh immigrant from Punjab, now a follower of 3HO

but carried some books and, of course, his university degree certificates, etc. He had brought along US $400 in a toothpaste packet. RBI gave a stingy $10 (1 $ = Rs. 11 at the time). Although he had preconceived ideas of Muslims being untrustworthy, he found the Pathans to be surprisingly reliable and peace loving. Afghanistan was a poor country economically. He recollects that water for drinking was kept with resins in metal or glass vats. Green tea was always served. There were plenty of 'naans' to eat with 'chana' in the langar at the gurdwara. He met a group of 14–15 Sikhs who on arrival had cut their hair. Most of them had come through the help of agents for migrating to the West.

He left for Iran on a bus along with five other young men. It was a 24-hour journey with just a few stoppages for 'namaz'. Ladies had a separate section with heavy curtains. Arjan stayed overnight in a room at the border where he met a group of Punjabi young men returning from Greece. This country was a popular destination because it offered job opportunities as ship hands with prospects of jumping the ship in the target country. There were, however, dangers involved in these adventures, as one learnt that one out of 15 had been shot by the border guards. Arjan Singh found Iran to be prosperous and stayed there for ten days at the Amir Kabir Hotel. Iran was also a popular transit point for prospective migrants to the West. Some boys returning from Israel and Lebanon gave good reports of these countries. Some of them who could manage to get jobs as drivers, etc., stayed back. Arjan obtained visa for Turkey and started on the long road journey with a group of about ten young men. At the border, there were several representatives to help their clients. Arjan Singh did not stay in Istanbul but took a train via Bulgaria to Belgrade. After a day's stop in Belgrade, he took a bus to Austria and reached Vienna. Tourists did not need visa but a couple of his companions were refused entry as they had already visited that country. Arjan soon realized that Europe was expensive. He managed accommodation in a 'pension' called Turkish Hem in a dormitory. He was successful in getting a job with a newspaper printer. The deal was that they could take away newspaper copies in the morning to sell in lieu of wages for the night shift work.

This was Arjan's first European experience which he had been looking forward to. He managed to get admission in the Diplomatic Academy which entitled him to a one-year student visa. The Immigration Department was getting stricter in not allowing non-visa holders to work. Many illegals were being deported. Pressure of succeeding in a hurry was making him unhappy. Being a proud and sensitive person, he got the vibes that there wasn't sufficient social acceptance. And living amongst only the Indians was not satisfactory enough for him. He did not feel hampered or disadvantaged because of the turban except for pressure from his co-religionists, who would taunt the three turbaned Sikhs as 'Gianis'. Since acceptance at the level of the Whites was not possible, he started looking around for better options to migrate to. He was advised about migrating to Argentina where, he was told, citizenship was possible.

Obtaining visas for Brazil, Argentina and Peru he took an Aeroflot flight in February 1976 with a one-way ticket from Germany to Lima in Peru, as that was the cheapest fare available. He had $800 as savings. In Lima, he stayed for 15 days in the service quarters of the Indian Ambassador. Later a Sindhi businessman put him up for another 12 days. He also began learning Spanish. Arjan then took a bus to Quito (Ecuador) and from there to Colombia from where he flew to Panama where he was not allowed entry because he had only a one-way air ticket. He had to stay overnight in the Army barracks. Thereafter he continued his northward journey via San Jose, Costa Rica, El Salvador, Nicaragua, Guatemala, spending two nights in each city, visiting museums, etc. He finally entered Mexico on 30 March 1976. The first impressions were favourable. He got himself admitted for PhD in the university in Mexico City.

Initially, he stayed in a small hotel and attended the Spanish Language School. Shortly thereafter he managed to get a scholarship for six months. In the meantime he found the Yoga Ashram which had about ten people living there. He met Baba Ajit Singh, a local Mexican convert to Sikhism by Yogi Bhajan. He had an American wife. They accepted him and he started working for them. Yogi Bhajan came twice a year and he got an opportunity to be close to him. There would be an audience of 300-400 followers during his visits. Since university education was becoming expensive with hardly any income, he decided to become a 3HO Sikh Khalsa. He married in 1978 at 26, a Mexican Sikh (21 yrs) in a full 'Anand Karaj' ceremony blessed by Yogi Bhajan. About 400–500 people were present but, he said, sadly there were no relatives from India. His wife also named Arjan Kaur was studying Engineering but decided to give up studies and moved to the Sikh Centre in Toluca, the capital of Mexico State where about 20 turbaned Sikhs now live. They have a son who recently spent three years in Chandigarh where, besides other things, he learnt to play the tabla.

Discussing the popularity of Sikhism, Arjan Singh explained that it was difficult to define Sikh in the conventional manner. The 3HO believe a person to be a Sikh who wants to be a Shishu or a student of the Guru. He estimated that the number of Yogi Bhajan's followers to be more than 2,000. There are about 500 Yoga teachers alone and about 10 community leaders. There are about 5,000 students out of which some 3,000 would know actively about Sikhism. Many of them would also have Sikh names. The two Arjans run the local Sikh Centre. His wife is a Yoga teacher and their son is a student. Arjan Singh has of late got into textile and garments business which takes him to India regularly. He is also trying to promote health foods. He has a new business partner in Gurinder Singh, son of Harbans Singh of Delhi.

He feels happy and secure in Mexico. Having an intellectual bent of mind, he feels Mexico provides him with self-respect and fair opportunities. He is happy that he has a supportive wife and a son who is keen to follow good values.

Satguru Singh Khalsa

A handsome 32 years old Sikh drives in with his son in a 'Patka' to pick me up at the bus station in Xalapa, capital of Vera Cruz Province. Satguru's mother got divorced when he was 12 years old. He has an older sister who got married in 1993. One of Satguru's friends used to go for Yoga and one day he left behind a magazine. It was after several months that Satguru read the magazine and was totally taken up by Yogi Bhajan's description of a Baisakhi day in 1699 with Guru Gobind Singh Ji. At age 18, he decided to become a Khalsa. Naturally his mother was shocked as she had raised him as a devout Catholic. Being single, she had worked hard to bring up the two children on her meagre salary as a nurse. Because of keeping long hair he got into difficulty in the Technical School where he was specializing in tourism. As a mark of his protest, on his graduation day in 1994, he wrapped a turban around his head even though he did not know how to tie it. He got an opportunity to meet Yogi Bhajan in Guadalajara and was very impressed with his personality and commitment to the Sikh dharma. His friend Sadhana (already separated) whom he had met a year earlier, suggested that he go to Cancun where American tourists were less biased. Sadhana's sister Simran Kaur and her husband Satjeevan Singh had a gym in Cancun. They helped him get a job. Sadhana also came over to Cancun and they decided to live together and get married. While Sadhana came back to Xalapa to live with her mother, Satguru stayed back but soon moved back to Xalapa as they really did not like Cancun, a very commercial city. In Xalapa, Satguru started to work with her mother as an event manager, which involved working late hours. Sadhana encouraged him to go to Mexico City and meet other Sikhs.

He met Arjan Singh who was running the Sikh Centre. He

also met Pritampal Singh, a convert from Chile. Sadhana had a son, Satnam Singh, from a previous marriage and now they have two more sons, Simran and Ramhir. Satnam was six years old when they returned to Xalapa. They got him admitted to a private school but when seeking admission to the Secondary School, they faced severe hurdles because of wearing a 'Patka'. He had to approach the Human Rights Commission to get his son admission. Satnam is now well settled and in fact would be playing American Football for his school team. He is nick-named 'Traponse', a princess who has long hair after a local comic character. Simran is keen to visit Amritsar. They have to spend a lot of money as extra fees to send the younger son to a private school. In the meantime he met the Government Education Officer who was impressed with Satguru's courage and wanted to help him. He encouraged him to learn computers and now he has a job with the government.

Satguru has had a long chat with his teenage son who is committed to remain a Sikh. Sadhana is fully supportive. She wanted to keep a turban but found it difficult. Satguru has put no pressure on her either. Satguru does his 'paaths' and prayers regularly. Despite the challenges, their faith remains unshaken. A look at their photo shows how happy they are—and so very Indian.

Satguru told me that many people try to become Sikhs in Mexico but only a few have the will power to continue. When asked: 'Is it difficult to change one's name in Mexico?' He replied, 'Yes, it is very difficult but so is everything in Sikhi.' Amen.

Other 3HO Sikhs

Ramratan Singh: In Coatapec City near Xalapa, I met another Mexican Sikh family Ramratan Singh, his wife Harinam Kaur, son Ravi Singh (18) and daughter Jaygopal Kaur (16). They run a retail shop and a Yoga centre. Ramratan had read about 3HO through a Yoga magazine in Spain. He attended Summer Solicites in Mexico City. The couple have been married for 14 years and are getting total fulfilment through being a Sikh. They were happy to meet a Sikh from Punjab, the land of the Golden Temple.

Dyal Kaur Khalsa: She attends the National Autonomy University of Mexico (UNAM) and is writing a thesis on 'territoriality of Sikh Dharma in Mexico City'. When she was 15 years old, she went to a lifestyle camp and took part in 'Yoga and Sadhana'. There were 30 students out of which only seven were Sikhs. It was a struggle in the beginning but now she is totally satisfied and feels fulfilled.

Gurudas Singh Khalsa: His father is a businessman and mother is a nurse. He has two younger brothers and a sister. After college, he worked in the sugar industry but lost his job when the company closed down five years ago. Thereafter he worked at ad hoc jobs. In the meantime he got divorced. In 2000, he learnt about Yoga from a teacher in the South which made him move to the Sikh Centre in 2001 where he became a Sikh. He feels personal crisis was a major trigger. Now he works with Arjan Singh.

NEW SIKH IMMIGRANTS

In a book titled *India-Mexico: Similarities and Encounters Throughout History* by Eva A. Uchmany, and published by the Indian Council for Cultural Relations, March 2002 the author has the following to say:

> Besides the Mexican converts, there are relatively few Sikhs in and around Mexico City. These Sikhs are mainly into business specializing in garments or retailing. Jassie owns a resataurant, Koh e Noor. There are some other business people in Cancun, Guadalajara and other cities in addition to the old immigrants in the Northern Provinces. Most of the business men have come in 1990s.

Plates 59–60: Mexico City. (top) Sikh sangat at Jassi's Koh-e-Noor restaurant; (bottom) A large Sikh retail shop

Plates 61–62: Xalapa. (top) Gurusewak Singh, a 3HO follower with his family. (bottom) Gurusewak's younger son at home with photos of Sikh Gurus

Plate 63: Coatapec. Another 3HO shop

It would appear Nancy Craft of Delhi promoted by Narinder Pal Singh (Pali) was the fountainhead of many businesses, mainly garment exports. His elder brother, Surjit came to Guadalajara ten years ago. Nancy Craft had a large turnover running into several million dollars with establishments or associates in Tennerife, Brazil, Venezuela, Madrid, Panama, etc. Various people worked for Nancy Craft in Mexico and then branched out on their own. Some of the names that were mentioned were—Surjit, Chadha, Nancy, Sahiba, Bitu and Balwinder. Other names mentioned were Jassi, Kuku, Bakshi, Bagga, etc.

There are some professional expatriates, prominent amongst them being, Satinder Pal Singh who is with Shell Mexico. He provided useful introductions and help. Jassie of 'Koh e Noor' restaurant very generously hosted a dinner for the Sikh sangat so that I could meet them.

The immigrant Sikhs have constructed a gurdwara.

INDIA-MEXICO: SIMILARITIES AND ENCOUNTERS THROUGHOUT HISTORY

The above book (details mentioned earlier), has some interesting anecdotes about Sikhs in Mexico. I quote below some excerpts.

The more daring (Sikhs) climbed aboard any ship that crossed the Pacific Ocean and was bound for the west of the American union, as sailors and ship boys. They often preferred to disembark in the Mexican port of Manzanillo, and from there went to the United States of America. Some got lost on the way, and stayed in Mexico.

A great number of Sikhs were unable to go to the United States. According to Harold Jacoby, between the years 1920 and 1930, around 3,000 families of Indian origin entered the United States. The majority of them, mainly farmers from Punjab, arrived through the Mexican border, organized and helped by the Sikhs who were already settled in the border areas, usually in Mexicali.

Bruce La Brack's research confirms this process. In this way Mexico became the first stopover of the Sikhs in their clandestine journey towards the American Union. The older generations even settled in Mexico, constituting a point of passage between the different migratory waves, which in the 1920s and 1930s arrived in this part of the world in large numbers. The Sikhs first made their appearance in Mexico illegally. The majority of them disembarked at the port of Manzanillo and many others entered through the port of Salina Cruz. Some of them had tried their luck earlier in England and then set-off for Vera Cruz. It is probable, that before touching Mexican soil, they took off their turbans and shaved their beards, wanting to appear completely like the local people with whom they had many physical similarities.

The office of the Home Affairs Ministry in Mexicali, a Mexican border town with the United States, informed in 1923 the Ministry of Foreign Affairs on the existence and conduct of a number of men, all with the surname Singh, and residents in their locality. They were called honest and respectable people, of good conduct, very hardworking and dedicated to agriculture. It was pointed out that they had lived in the region for some time, although the years were not mentioned.

Isabel Duque's study of 25 cases of Indians settled in the country between the years 1920 and 1940 is interesting. Almost all of these migrants were Sikhs, natives of the cities of Ludhiana and Jalandhar in the Punjab. Forty-three per cent of them based themselves in Mexicali, and a little more or less than 14 per cent of them in Ciudad Obrego, Sonora; the rest dispersed. The majority of them were agriculturists and the rest were involved in other activities, such as trade. Fifty-three per cent said they professed the Catholic religion, although none of them had a Christian name. Only 4 per cent of them, approximately, dared to confess that they practised the Sikh religion. Only five of them were Hindus or Muslims. Of the 25 cases, studied 10 were married and the rest single.

THE SIKH EXPERIENCE IN SONORA

Of the above-mentioned Indians, the majority went to the United States, although some stayed on in Mexico. Others, after living for a while in the Imperial Valley of California, informed President Alvaro Obregon (ruled 1920–4) of their desire to settle in the State of Sonora. The president had a great interest in colonizing certain regions of the country, and opened its doors to some groups of foreigners. The Sikh agriculturists, through their lawyer Frank J. Barry, who was their representative before the Mexican authorities, pointed out that they were ready to colonize any number of acres with their compatriots whom they offered to bring from Punjab.

Ten years later, however, the new Governor of Sonora, Rodolfo Elias Callers, informed the Foreign Affairs Ministry about the settlement of a group of Indian nationals in the Yaki Valley, who were developing the region through their investments and the technical advances adopted by them in agriculture. This fact immediately drew the attention of the Mexican government, and the migratory status of those Sikhs began to be questioned. The result of the inquiry showed that the majority of them had not complied with the Mexican Federal Labour laws, whose article number 9 protected the Mexican worker. Indeed, the leaseholders of lands in the Yaki Valley were obliged to employ native Mexican workers for labour on their parcels. The Sikhs, nevertheless, farmers by profession, cultivated their land alone or in the company of their families as was the case of Dev(w)an Singh, who was forced to abandon his cotton harvest, or that of his brothers Dusand (probably Dasondha) and Brean (probably Beant) Singh, whose watermelon crop was confiscated on 23 May 1932.

Many of the Sikhs were mutually associated, like Alyer and Chanchal Singh, Lau and Karam Singh, Matan and Harbey Singh, Bontan and Sandhu Singh and, for this reason; they did not employ Mexican labourers. Consequently, the government confiscated their crops. However, those who employed one or two Mexican workers were also fined, like Tolok (probably Tarlok) Singh, as besides the Mexican labourers he employed in addition a cousin of his, who helped him in the farm work. Evidently, the employment of relatives from India was forbidden by the law. For his case the cotton crop of the partners Kartar Singh and Booton (Batan) Singh was seized, although they had given work to ten Mexican labourers, but they also used the help of four Indians. At the same time Batan Singh was fined for having dismissed one of his Mexican workers, supposedly without any justification. This was sufficient reason for the Inspector of Work, Luis Corrella, to make him pay the Mexican labourer 25 silver pesos for the days he had been without a job.

The most amazing case was that of Mann and Arjun Singh, who suffered great losses, as they were forced to leave 540 hectares of irrigated land, ready for the sowing of chick peas, whose total price would at that time equal $832,500. Besides this, 25 hectares of tomatoes valued at $83,250, as well as 100 hectares of cotton of the value of $34,965 were also confiscated from them—in sum, a total of $950,715. This amount did not include the loss of agricultural equipment, seeds, provisions, and neither the introduction of the irrigation system in the area and, even less, the total loss of all their personal goods. All this contributed to the migration of these farmers from the State of Sonora to Sinaloa and from there, once again to the United States. Of this group, Isabel Duque managed to locate one survivor. He is Gurmit Singh, resident of Culiacan, Sinaloa, and a native of Jalandhar in Punjab, where he was born in 1911. He arrived in Mexico in 1938, entering the country through Payo Obispo in Quintana Roo. The reason for his journey was his desire to visit his uncle, who lived in Mexico at that time. Gurmit Singh is a farmer and professes the Buddhist faith. He is married to Emma Cabanas with whom he has four sons, one of whom has a Punjabi name.

CHAPTER 10

Sikhs in Panama

INTRODUCTION

Sikh migration to Panama began with the construction of the Panama Canal by the Americans in early twentieth century. There is no evidence to suggest whether any Sikhs were involved in the earlier efforts to construct the canal by the French in the late nineteenth century. While some of the canal construction workers settled down in Panama, others returned to Punjab, while some moved on to other destinations in South America. There is at present a sizeable Sikh community in Panama with a very well run large gurdwara.

EARLY SIKH IMMIGRANTS: THE 'HINDOOS'

At the Mira Flores Locks Visitor Centre, in Panama Canal there is a large mural which has the following inscription:

CANAL HEROES—They came from many places and spoke different languages. Bringing with them nothing but their desire to work and their hopes, they came together to build the engineering feat that still marvels the world. Most came from Barbados, but also from Martinique, Guadeloupe, Trinidad and Jamaica. Spanish, Italians, Greeks, HINDUS (capitals mine—early Sikh immigrants were called Hindoos in USA also), Americans, Armenians, Cubans, Costa Ricans, Colombians and Panaminians also contributed to the effort. They managed to understand each other, started families, made fortunes and exalted the country.

In the mural, I could spot some workers with turbans, which I photographed. The story of the early Sikh Immigrants to Panama is connected with the construction of the Canal in 1904–14 by the US. There seems to be no evidence that Sikh workers were involved in the earlier effort to construct the canal in the nineteenth century by the French, which had to be abandoned later. I have come across references of some Indian labourers who had come at that time from the Caribbean Islands—possibly Indian indentured labourers, assume that they were non-Sikhs. The Central and South American Sikh migration is intertwined with Panama because of its strategic location. Panama has a substantial number of Sikhs or 'Singhs' with a Sikh ancestry. While many settled down, some of them returned, some permanently while others returned to go back again and still others migrated to other South American countries. There does not seem to be much recent immigration.

THE COUNTRY

The Spanish arrived in the Panama in the sixteenth century. Panama became a province of Colombia which gained independence in 1821. Colombia signed a treaty in the mid-nineteenth century permitting the USA to construct a railway to connect the two oceans and to defend it with military force. The idea of a canal had been broached as early as the sixteenth century. A serious attempt by the French in 1880 failed (ironically the same engineer who later successfully constructed the Suez Canal). The French effort resulted in the death of a large number of workers from malaria and yellow fever followed by bankruptcy for everyone involved.

A revolutionary junta declared Panama independent in 1903, with the overt support of the USA. The canal treaty granted the USA, rights in perpetuity over land on both sides of the canal. The treaty created friction between the two countries, because it was favourable to the USA at the expense of Panama and because Colombia refused to acknowledge Panama's independence. In 1921, the USA finally paid Colombia a large compensation. The USA began to build the canal in 1904, and ten years later, the first ship negotiated the engineering marvel. The US intervened in Panama's affairs repeatedly until 1936, when it relinquished its right to use troops outside the Canal zone. The two countries continued to argue over the canal contract until a new treaty was signed in 1977. Panama formally regained control of the canal in 1999. The canal is now being widened to allow passage of more traffic and larger ships

General Manuel Noriega took control of the country in 1984. Drug trafficking and money-laundering were his principal concerns during the 1980s. The 1989 USA invasion resulted in the arrest of Noriega and setting up of democratic rule there. Noriega has since been convicted and is currently serving a prison sentence in Florida.

The country is mostly known for its path breaking engineering feat of the Panama Canal joining the Atlantic and Pacific Oceans almost right in the middle. The country is fairly well developed economically and is a popular destination for older people from North America to settle down. The airport is a major transit point for South and Central America.

PANAMA CANAL

The Canal is both an engineering marvel and one of the most significant waterways in the world. Seeing a huge ship nudge its way through the narrow canal, with vast tracts of virgin jungle on both sides, is an unforgettable sight.

Stretching 80 km from Panama City on the Pacific coast to Colón on the Atlantic side, it provides passage for nearly 14,000 ocean-going vessels per year. The easiest and best way to visit the Canal is to go to the Mira Flores Locks, on the north-eastern fringe of Panama City, where a platform offers visitors a good view of the locks in operation. There is also a museum and a film about the Canal.

The Singhvi High Level Committee Report has the following to say:

Unofficial figures compiled by our Embassy in Panama would indicate that ethnic Indians number approximately 8,000 persons in this small country of 2.8 million inhabitants. If confirmed, this would mean that Panama has one of the largest concentrations of overseas Indians in this entire region, apart from the main Caribbean countries. On the other hand, official statistics provide a totally different picture, indicating the presence here of only 211 PIOs and 1953 NRIs! This statistical confusion is probably due to the fact that the official figures take into account only the relatively new arrivals. They may not have included the Indians who had first come to Panama during the construction of the Colon–Panama railroad in the 1840s. There are also several Indian families here that trace their origin to the first decades of the twentieth century.

The Indian diaspora in Panama consists mostly of Muslims from Gujarat State. They have been there for a long time. They often bring their male relative over from India to marry locally available Indian girls. They have built mosques and a school for their children. The Hindus in Panama are also mostly from the same state in India. They too have constructed a place of worship for themselves. Besides their temple, they have set up a cultural society that is called the Hindostana society of Panama. There is also a small Sikh community with its gurdwara.

The Indian diaspora in Panama has, over the years, established itself well and has been able to acquire some influence in the government. A few PIOs have occupied high positions in the government, including that of Vice-Minister and Director General of the National police. Many members of the community are running wholesale business and retail shops. At one time, the Panamanian road transport was in the hands of Indians settled here. Some PIOs companies are currently engaged in construction work. There are many Indian companies in the Colon Free Zone of Panama. They import Indian goods into the country, either directly or otherwise.

The community has adapted itself well to the living conditions in Panama by mixing with the local people and speaking their language. It does not have any specific demands or expectations from the government of India.

SIKH IMMIGRATION

When the US government began construction of the Canal a wave of immigrants came in, especially from the Punjab. As the completion of the Canal was in sight, restrictions were being introduced for immigrants from various nations including India. After the construciton of the canal in 1914, many immigrants took up jobs with the American United Fruit Company. Some Sikhs became peddlers called 'pheri' while others started driving locally assembled small pick-up vans called 'Cheevas'. Some of them went to other Latin American countries such as Brazil and Argentina. Others returned home either temporarily or permanently. There are some Sikhs presently working with the Canal in various positions either as Director, Pilot or in the IT Department.

THE GURDWARA

The gurdwara in Panama City was inaugrated on 13 April 1986 courtesy Rattan Singh Dhaliwal (who incidentally had donated the land) and other sangat, who had contributed generously to its construction. The gurdwara has a large hall on the first floor for *SGGS* and kirtan, the ground floor has a place for langar, a kitchen and an office. It was a quarter million dollar project. They ran short by about $50,000 which gap was filled by Prakash Singh and a Sindhi, Khemo Jhangi. The gurdwara now has fixed deposit in the bank and is financially sound. In an unusual arrangement, a Sindhi is the President of the gurdwara, an arrangement now well accepted.

Various Gurpurbs, Sangrands, Baisakhi and other occasions are celebrated here. Sunday service is followed by langar. On the day I visited the gurdwara, 100 people attended, and offerings added up to about $350. Only a handful of attendees wore turbans. There is a constitution of the gurdwara which is registered as 'La Sociedad Civica Guru Nanak Sahib', Apartado 6-497, Estafeta El Dorado, Panama, R. de P. Management

Plates 64–65: Panama. Gurdwara, outside view and *langar* being served

seems to be running the affairs professionally. A new granthi with his family lives on the premises much to the relief of the sangat as the earlier granthi had created problems and had to be sent back.

CASE STUDIES

Some of the interviews of the Sikhs there are detailed below. There are also write-ups on prominent Sikhs which have been taken from a book published by the Hindostana Society of Panama.

A Bengali Sikh Moves to Panama

Koreena's maternal grandfather Gursharan Singh Gill, when he was 28 years old, wanted to migrate to the USA. He set out from India around 1915 but when the ship docked *en route* in Panama, he decided to try out his luck in the country. As most others, he started with odd jobs, bought a 'Cheeva'—equivalent to the Punjabi 'Maruta'—and then on to buying and running an old bus and ultimately a flourishing transport (136 buses and a petrol station) business. He brought his wife Kartar Kaur (nee Randhawa) 5 years later. They had three children, sons Aziz (late) and Durbir and daughter Dalgir. Koreena's father Aziz Singh was the President of the Indian Society of Panama and ran a store called 'Casa Gill' trading in goods from Japan. Her grandparents and Koreena's mother got trapped in Japan during Second World War. Dalgir finished school and visited India a few times and got married to Rajpal Singh Bajwa, working in Indian Air Force, in 1959 and moved to India.

Post-retirement as Sq. Ldr. Koreena's father settled down in Calcutta (Hazra Road) where his parents had moved after Independence, from Sind. Koreena's mother Dalgir Gill Bajwa was the Hony Consul for Panama in Calcutta for ten years (1963–73). Rajpal visited Panama infrequently but Dalgir

Plates 66–67: Panama Canal. (top) Punjabi Sikh workers photo at the Indian Embassy; (bottom) Wall size mural at reception centre, Mila-Flores—Part view showing some workers with turbans

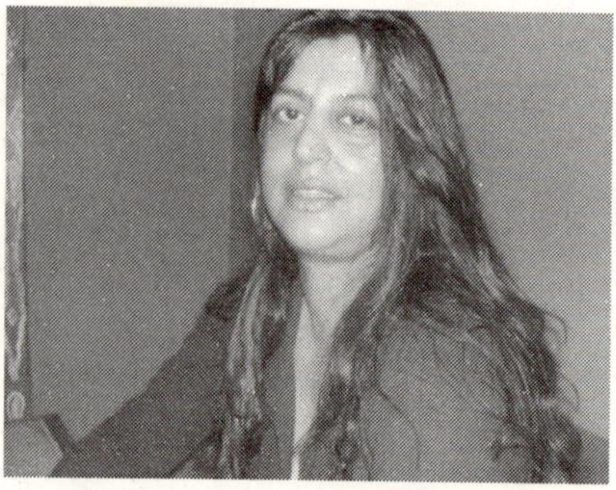

Plates 68–71: Panama (top) (L) Koreena Singh, Bengal born, (R) Julia Singh, Sikh immigrant's daughter; (middle) Balbir Singh, a Sikh professional locally born; (bottom) A part of Sikh *sangat* at the gurdwara

made several visits to Panama with her two daughters Koreena and Rajina. Dalgir moved to Panama in 1972 with her two daughters which involved Koreena finishing High School in Panama, and learning Spanish. As was in the blood, Koreena got into the aviation industry working for Brannif International as ground staff in 1981 and ending up in a senior position with Aero Continental in Colombia with postings in several other Central American countries till 2003. Her parents opened a restaurant 'Bajwa's Shamiana', in 1982 but her father passed away in 1988 (at 55 yrs) with her mother passing away five years later. Her father wore turban for some time in Panama but later cut his hair. Koreena married a Colombian in 1989 (civil ceremony in Miami, USA) after serious efforts to find a groom in India—a familiar story. The restaurant business continued but with new names and location each time, first as 'Calcutta' in 1991 and then as a Colombian restaurant, 'La Tienda de Cesar' and since 2005 as 'Masala'.

Prakash Singh

His father, Chanan Singh, came to Panama in 1952 and returned in 1973. Chanan's father Banta Singh had returned to Punjab in 1957 after staying in Panama for 37 years (migration *c.* 1920). He used to get pension from the Canal authorities. They belong to village Sakrulli, near Mahilpur.

Prakash came to Panama in 1962 when he was 18 years old. He visited India in 1966 when his uncle (father's brother) Chowdhury Gurmail Singh, was contesting election as an MLA on a Congress ticket. Prakash's wife lives in California, USA and works as a teacher. Their son works in a bank and daughter is a CPA—both are in USA. Their eldest son Avtar could not get a Green Card and lives with him in Panama. Prakash is into real estate and moneylending. His wedding in Delhi to Sushila as per Sikh rites was attended by Giani Zail Singh, the then President of India and Darbara Singh.

Surjit and Darshan Singh Dhaliwal

Their origins are from village Mansoorpur. Rattan Singh, their uncle left India around 1914–15, spending 1–2 years each in France and Cuba and then 5–6 years in Argentina with his elder brother Arjan Singh, before coming to Panama around 1924–5. He wanted to go back to Argentina because Panama was nowhere as prosperous as Argentina. But in the meanwhile he had given away all his money to his brother-in-law, so Rattan Singh settled in Panama by default. Surjit now owns the 2,000 hectares 'Sher-e-Punjab' farm, with about 800 cattle heads and 200 goats. A story worth admiring is as to how the turbaned Surjit and Darshan at 9 and 12 years of age respectively came to Panama on their own from Bombay via Genoa (one week stop-over) to be with their uncle Rattan. A unique journey in Sikh migration history. They are presently into real estate, finance and ranching business, having graduated from 'pheri'.

Julia Singh

She is the daughter of Balwant Singh whose father Viar Singh, came to Panama around 1915 (identity card issued in 1918). Initially he drove a 'Cheeva', and then graduated to driving a taxi, to show American tourists around. He married a 15-year old girl from Spain around 1926. Julia was born in 1928, the eldest of four boys and three girls. Julia has two daughters and a son. Balwant Singh never went to India but missed his country. According to Julia, he kept a photo of Guru Gobind Singh and did not allow his children to be baptized. He cooked 'rotis' and, more importantly, 'bakra' (goat) meat, which she fondly remembers and misses. Balwant wanted to send Julia to India for a visit and to get her married to a Sikh. She said, smiling ruefully, that she regrets not having done so. She knows many Singhs.

Balbir Singh

Born in village Udhowal, 3 km from Nakodar in Punjab, he came to Panama with his mother in 1958 when he was just five. His father was born in Panama in 1934 but went back to India in 1939 along with his grandfather, Kishen Singh. Grandfather returned to Panama in 1952 followed by his father Gurcharan Singh in 1956. Balbir has one brother and two sisters who were born in Panama. Kishen first came probably around 1920 but his brother Raula Singh Khehra came earlier with a group around 1910. Most of them worked in the Canal construction site but some started their own businesses in due course such as 'pheri' or 'cheeva' driving. While Balbir's father acquired a Panama passport in the late 1950s, his grandfather and mother Jit Kaur kept Indian passport. Balbir studied in Panama and now works with an automotive distribution company. According to Balbir, till the 1980s most buses were owned by Sikhs but several of them have since migrated to North America.

PROFILES OF SOME OTHER SIKHS

The following are taken from a book in Spanish published by the Indian Society.

Chain Singh

A native of Punjab arrived in Panama in the early decades of twentieth century with great enthusiasm and a strong desire to achieve professional success. Initially he worked in the construction industry and was involved in some major projects such as the stadium in Balboa, Howard Highway and some parts of Georges Hospital. He was successful in real estate and also marketed materials used in construction industry. He married Senora Anays Gomez Acevedo, a Panamanian national, and had four children all of whom became professionals—Chain

Plates 72–74: (top) Wedding picture of Darshan Singh Dhaliwal; (middle) Dhaliwal farm, Sher-e-Punjab; (bottom) Parkash Singh at Panama Canal Lock—Mira Flores

Singh Junior, Chemical Engineer; Carlos Singh, Pathologist; Enrique Singh, Civil Engineer; Robert Singh, Civil Engineer. Chain Singh enthusiastically participated in India's Independence Day celebrations in 1947 and was responsible for establishing the Hindustan Society of Panama. He was the second President of the Society in 1948 and was re-elected several times—in 1958, 1959, 1960, 1962 and 1963.

Randhawa Family

The senior Iqbal Singh Randhawa arrived in Panama in 1930 with great enthusiasm, expecting to do well in Panama. His wife Kirpal Kaur joined him in 1934. They headed a very solid family of the Indian community. They had four children: Gurmeet Kaur, Lakhbir, Jagdish and Balbir Singhs, all of whom provided several grandchildren for the Randhawas. They were very particular in providing good education to their children at the University of Panama which helped them become successful professionals. Iqbal was a very active person not in only in business but in community affairs as well. Independent India honoured Randhawa by appointing him the Honorary Consul in Panama. In this position, he built-up very healthy relations between India and Panama. He was President of the Hindustan Society for seven years. His chain of Oriental Stores was a great success.

Aziz Singh Gill

He was named Aziz meaning 'to be loved' by his parents a name which he fully deserved due to his meteoric rise and for his spiritual qualities. He studied first at the Pan-American Institute and later on graduated with honours from the University of Panama in journalism. His father Gursharan Singh Gill from Punjab arrived in Panama in 1924 and worked in the Panama Canal. He later started his own transport business, acquiring his first bus in 1929 to be followed by several more and to set up finally the Gill Transport Company. He was able to obtain special concession for transportation in the Canal Zone.

Gill Transport Company ultimately owned a fleet of 300 buses. The Gills had six children of whom only three survived. Aziz's real passion was the Hindustan Society which he headed for ten consecutive years. He contributed immensely to building relations between India and Panama and was successful in getting a street named 'Avenue of India' in Panama City. His death was a loss to the Indian community. He is survived by his son Gurziz who, is studying at the University, and by his wife Mrs. America Singh.

Rattan Singh

Originally from Punjab, Rattan Singh specialized in lending money. Amongst his clients were several professionals, educationists and other employees working at the American Military Base and at the Canal. As his business grew, he formed the 'Group Rattan Singh' with its headquarters in Santa Ana. After his brother Mengha Singh's death, he brought his brother's wife to Panama along with her two sons Surjit and Darshan. After their education the two nephews set up petrol stations and expanded the financial business as well. The Group is now a great success.

Nehal Singh Saturno

Nehal Singh's father, Amar Singh Mann, arrived in Panama in the 1930s along with other compatriots from Punjab. Most of them married locally and entered a variety of businesses in the Canal. Others moved to the interior of the country to carry out agriculture and cattle raising. In the 1950s Amar Singh Mann returned to India on the death of his brother and could not return to Panama because of political problems back home. His wife Ursula Saturno's father was Italian and mother

Spanish. Nehal was born in 1945 in Panama, and had his secondary education in Panama before going to Mexico to study Criminology. On return, he soon moved to the field of marketing and sales. He married Dalida Castillero, a teacher. They have three children: Antonio Miguel, a lawyer in Administration; Nanak, an industrial engineer; and Nehal II, a civil engineer. Nehal got to know recently that he has three (step) brothers in India. Nehal has been a member of the Board of Directors of the Trade Union for the Industries in Panama for more than 15 years. He was also a Governor of the Lions Club. At present he is one of the patrons of San Miguel Hospital of Arcangel.

NAME OF SOME EARLY IMMIGRANTS

As recounted by Prakash Singh in his house on 10 September 2006. (Names are followed by estimated year of arrival.)

Gurcharan Singh Gill (1920s), Iqbal Singh Randhawa (1920), Chainchal Singh Randhawa (1930s), Singhs Amar, Lota and Ujaggar (1920s returned after 30 years and came back in 1956), Santa Singh (mid-1920s, returned and came back in 1962), Baldev Singh Bhullar (1950), and many many others. Just shows that there was a lot of to and fro movement—they were evidently neither satisfied in Panama nor in India.

(*Note*: Exact dates are difficult to get as each person has an idea of approximate dates only.)

CHAPTER 11

Sikhs in Other Countries of South and Central America

As mentioned earlier, a peculiar feature of the Sikh migration to Latin America has been that the Sikhs kept moving (mainly by foot) from one country to another, over thousands of miles of tough terrain. It is my firm belief that there would have been some migrants who could not keep pace with the others due to the physical, mental or psychological pressure involved. They would have decided, howsoever, reluctantly, to stay back in the countries *en route*. Over the years, they would have lost touch with their other compatriots or people back home. Khushwant Singh, on his visit to Montevideo, came across a Sikh who had completely forgotten his mother-tongue, Punjabi. It would require a lot of effort to find such Sikhs in various countries but they can be located as most of them still have 'Singh' as their surname, which would help in scanning various records. Besides the countries visited, other countries like Peru, Colombia, Ecuador, and Chile, the Guyanas, especially British Guyana, and Surinam would have been other possible destinations for Sikh immigrants. The Sikh presence in Central America, Costa Rica, Guatemala, Salvador, Nicaragua and Honduras needs further investigation.

In some of the Latin American countries, the new immigrants faced severe hardships post-9/11 being mistakenly identified for their beard and turban with Osama bin Laden. Two examples in Peru and Chile are discussed below. The Sikh converts in Latin America have coped with such situations better than the immigrant Sikhs because they are better prepared mentally. In interviews of 3HO Sikhs in Mexico, La Paz and Sao Paulo, they never raised this issue.

The countries covered in this chapter were not visited by the author but information gathered is based on my correspondence with some of the immigrants and extensive website searches. The study of these countries provides still another dimension of Sikh migration.

URUGUAY

In an interesting write-up in the *Sikh Review*, Khushwant Singh details his encounter in Montevideo with an old Sikh immigrant who had forgotten Punjabi and Hindustani. This does indicate that there are the odd few Sikhs settled in other South American countries who are totally assimilated and have lost touch with Punjab and India. Khushwant Singh's letter in the *Sikh Review* published in vol. 53: 9 September 2005, no. 621 is worth reproducing:

Greetings from Latin America:

An interesting experience took place on my third day in the city (Montevideo). I was standing in the foyer of my hotel when a shortish wizened, old man, with only one eye, approached me and greeted me with 'Sat Sri Akal, signor!'

I answered his greeting and asked him in Punjabi if he was a Sikh. 'Si, signor', he replied in Spanish. To prove it he took out an old, battered British passport and pointed to the photograph in it: it was of a young Sikh in his early twenties with only one eye. He pointed to his chest and said in rustic Punjabi, naon (name) Chanchal Seongh (Singh), pay (peo, or father) Sohan Seon; Maoo (Mother) Gurdeep Kaur; Pind (Village) something or the other in district Lahore. Then he began to count ikk, do, tinn, chaar up to ten. Beyond these words he could neither speak nor understand what I said in Punjabi or English.

I asked my Spanish secretary to help me out. It was an incredible story.

Chanchal Singh had left Punjab as a young lad intending to settle in Canada. At that time he spoke no language other than Punjabi. The Canadian authorities refused to permit him to stay.

He escaped to the United States. He met the same fate there and was ordered to leave the country in a few days. He hitch-hiked his way southward through Mexico and Brazil. No country would have him till he reached Uruguay and got a job as a farm labourer. He married a Spanish labourer's daughter and had a large family by her. They were given both Sikh and Spanish Names: Dil Bagh Don Pedro Singh, Santi Carmelita Singh, and so on. Chanchal Singh, who spoke only Punjabi till he was twenty, could now not understand a word of it—fifty years had completely wiped it out of his memory.

I have found that it takes much less than fifty years to erase the memory of a language if one is not exposed to it orally or visually.

PRESENCE OF 3 HO

In my endeavour to collect further evidence on Sikhs in Uruguay, I came in contact with a small but active group of Sikhs who were the followers of Yogi Bhajan, who run an organization called the Sikh Dharma Bhaibandi Misión. Having visited my web site, they wrote:

Piare Veer Jee

Ke hal nee? For benefit of the Latin Sikh sangat, I have today uploaded an article, translated (not literal) and interpretation of you work in our blog with my own small contribution. After step to step upload and send for you the history of Sikh in Peru, Panama, Mexico, Cuba, Venezuela, Paraguay, Brazil, España, Portugal Y Uruguay. A great hug and meherbani for your inspirational work about our Sikh diaspora. Guru Fateh. HBS.

The next gurdwara is April 12 of 2008–11.00 hs. This is the Vaisakhi festival, the Khalsa Day. In our missionary home: Tahim 964 Esq. ARIEL–Sayagomontevideo-Uruguay; Tel: 3551299 Movil: 094597223. If you like collaborate with any seva, please inform before. Please invite all people of good will, Hindus, Cristianity, New, Muslim, etc. Guru fateh.

Bibi Ji Sarabjeet Kaur &
Bhai Ji Haribhajan Singh.

On their blog, they have translated Spanish extracts from my website on Argentina.

PERU

Peru is mentioned in various interviews and writings as a country through which early Sikh migrants transited. Whether any one settled down in Peru is unknown.

In my search to trace Sikhs in Peru, I followed the report of United Sikhs of 2005 and found a Sikh now settled in Delhi. I met Partap Singh and his family in 2006 at his family house where he introduced his wife Dolores dor Mercedes de Singh and his two children.

Partap Singh tried to settle in Lima but could not due to discrimination faced post-9/11. And this is despite the fact that he is married to a local lady. Because of Partap Singh's similarity with bin Laden he was literally hounded out of the country. Given below are two news items, one which appeared in *United Sikhs of North America* and another in the *Hindu* newspaper of India.

1. A *United Sikhs* report of 29 September 2005, had the following to say when Pratap Singh was in Lima.

Lima, Peru: Partap Singh moved to Peru nine years ago from Spain, where he had gone from India to study Spanish and work as a travel consultant. It did not matter that he and his wife Gurpeet Kaur were the only Sikh family in Lima. They were dedicated to keeping [alive] the culture and traditions of their beloved Sikhi. Partap Singh worked as a tourist guide and as an occasional translator. He also supplemented the family's income by conducting meditation classes. Their family was blessed first with a daughter, Manpreet Kaur and then a son, Vikram Singh.

Then September 11th changed their world. Turbans, beards and uncut hair were viewed with suspicion and fear. Partap Singh's employer said he looked too much like bin Laden and encouraged him to cut his hair and do away with his turban. While the family always intended for their children to attend school together, their son Vikram was refused entry into the first grade because of his patka and uncut hair. The school was adamant that their dress code required Vikram to have shorn and uncovered hair. The family had to enroll Vikram in another school a distance away, where he had to deal with problems stemming from his unique appearance. Putting both children into an expensive private school was out of the question after Partap Singh lost his job 'for looking like bin Laden' and due to his dedication to look and live as a Sikh.

Partap Singh's finances became dire. Doris Reynoso found Partap Singh's family living in a small one-room accommodation that served as both kitchen and bedroom for the family of four. The family was destitute with no money coming in and several months of rent unpaid. Hospital bills from his wife's surgery were unpaid. Partap Singh had found himself in this position despite repeated pleas to his community. There was no Sikh community (sangat) in Peru to turn to for support. 'The conditions became so bad that sometimes people threw stones at me and my family,' Partap Singh told *United Sikhs*.

Much like France, where Sikhs have been challenged about wearing turbans to school, this Sikh family has been the victim of intolerance because people equate a turban with terrorism. Children have been expelled from schools in France, gurdwaras have been defiled in Britain and the United States, and now, a family in Peru faces exile.

Partap Singh would love to remain in Peru to be the bearer of his Guru's message. But, Partap Singh says he believes he has no future left in Peru. The attitude towards his form will not change.

2. *The Hindu, 2 October 2005*

Chandigarh: Partap Singh moved to Peru nine years ago from Spain where he had gone from India to study Spanish and work as a travel consultant. His is the lone Sikh family in Lima. While Mr. Singh worked as tourist guide and occasional translator, his wife supplemented the family's income, conducting meditation classes. They have a daughter, Manpreet Kaur and son, Vikram Singh.

The 9/11 terrorist attack on the World Trade Center in New York changed their world. Mr. Singh's employer persuaded him to cut his hair and do away with the turban, as he 'resembled Osama bin Laden'.

The rest of the news is similar to the *United Sikhs* write-up.

Interview with Partap Singh, Delhi, 19 October 2006

The author met S. Partap Singh (Gill); Wife: Dolores dor Mercedes de Singh; children Manpreet Kaur Gill (10 yrs); Vikrampratap Singh (7 yrs).

Partap's father was from Lyallpur and was in the Army Engineering Corps. His father died five years ago. Pratap was born in 1955, and did his schooling in Delhi. His younger brother Didar is in Spain and his four sisters are in Delhi. He could not complete graduation and hence did a private course in Tourism. Partap also studied French at Alliance Francaise. He was acting as a guide to the inbound tourist groups visiting India. The Tourist Company (NF) invited him to visit France in 1982 where he worked part time. He took the opportunity to go to Barcelona on a student visa for six months to learn Spanish in the Aero Centro Language University. NF had a branch in Spain but he faced difficulty in getting job because of turban. Partap used to go for coffee in a seaside restaurant where he ran into Maria Theresa Coll, whose father used to play violin in Connaught Place in Delhi. She helped him get a job with her brother who was in travel business. He got to know some 3HO Sikhs. In 1985, he came to India as a travel guide with a tourist group of 101 persons. Partap tried to dabble in a few odd businesses but without much success. Someone suggested for him to go to South America where there could be better opportunities. So he decided to go to Peru. Initially he had difficulties in settling down. Peru is a low wage country and the only opportunity to make money was through some kind of business.

It was there that Partap met his wife Dolores who was spiritually very strong. They got married on 26 October 1997 with a lot of opposition from the priests, Dolores being a devout Catholic.

Their daughter was born on 4 August 1997. Dolores was an administrator in a leather factory. She has nine sisters. Partap Singh had to return to India with his family in 2005.

CHILE

In my searches for any Sikh in Chile, I developed a correspondence with a Sikh settled there. His name is Jatinder Pal

Singh settled in Santiago, and directing a firm named Importadora Guru Nanak. The following exchange of our letters gives a flavour of a Sikh's life in Chile.

First e-mail, Friday, 13 May 2005:

About the Sikhs in Chile: As far my information, I am the only Sikh living in Chile. There are some other persons (5–6 persons) whose last name is Singh but they are clean shaven. And there is another Sikh who has business in Santiago, but he comes only for 5–6 months to Chile. I brought my brother and my cousin two years back here in Chile, but they left because they had big problems after the 9/11 attack on USA I went to police for protection but they refused it and advised me to cut my hair. So, I went to court but nothing happened. I wrote some e-mails to SGPC about our problems, but you know they don't have time to listen the problems of Sikhs. Actually people here don't know about Sikhs and confuse them with the Mussalmans. So, till now I am struggling with these people. We had some physical fights also with local people. Here I'm sending my news with attached file which was published in the newspaper (see later).

Two times I had sent my news to *Daily Ajit*, Jalandhar. But they did not publish the same in their newspaper. This is the brief history of Sikhs in Chile.

J.P. SINGH
Importadora Guru Nanak,
U.L.A 32-C, SANTIAGO, Chile

In answer to my queries on some specific Sikhs in Chile advised to me by the Indian Embassy in Santiago, J.P. Singh clarified:

Davinder Pal Singh is my brother and Gagandeep Singh Dhamrait is my cousin. Jasminder Singh is that Sikh businessman and Mr. Jaswant Singh I don't know him. . .

At present Davinder is in Canada and Gagandeep is in England.

About the Sikhs in Argentina and Bolivia I don't have any contact with them.

And about my history of settling in Chile it is a long story, I will tell when you will come here.

A newspaper report published in Santiago—translated from Spanish, courtesy Puneet Mina, Jaipur.

The Third National, Friday, 22 October 2004

Jatinder Pal Singh says that on the streets of Santiago he was called the 'Tiger of Malaysia' by the people and after the Twin Tower attack the attitude of people changed towards him. He relates that wherever he goes they shout at him 'bin Laden' or 'Terrorist', in government offices, commercial centres or banks. He says he receives bad treatment everywhere.

The situation is same on any given day in the life of J.P. Singh, a trader of Indian nationality, when he walks through the streets of Santiago. As per the rules of his religion he wears a turban and a beard that he hasn't cut in his 29 years. People look at him and the problem starts—in metro, in market, in malls—they call him 'Laden' or add 'terrorist' to it sometimes, and such kind of comments. Initially it seemed funny but no more, claims the businessman. The truth is that what did not trouble him initially is turning out to be a nightmare, which started after the attack on the Twin Towers in September 2001. Before the attack they used to call him 'Sandokan' or 'Tiger of Malaysia' but now everything has changed. He says, 'they call me "Laden" but I hoped after some time they will forget, but now the problem is getting worse.'

J.P. Singh graduated in physics, maths, and computer from Guru Nank Dev University in India. J.P. says 'I have to confront racism and discrimination in Chile.' He affirms that he has received bad treatment in government offices, banks, malls, and marketplaces, even at the hands of the police.

The people seem to hate Muslims. Muslims are not the only ones who tie turban and have beard.

The situation since three weeks has worsened, when somebody tried to hit him. 'As I was climbing up to my shop a man hit me in the back, "Hey bin Laden, what are you doing here? I don't have a gun or else I would kill you right now".' I asked him what has happened, I am from India and have nothing to do with Laden. He answered 'you are a terrorist'. I said, 'You have gone mad.' He picked up a tube light which was lying in the street, broke it by hitting it against a tree and came to attack me. I defended myself with a stick that I was carrying and managed to save myself. He told me that I had killed thousands of people in the

United States and that I am a culprit, thus I should leave his country otherwise he is going to procure a gun and kill me.

Jatinder registered his complaint with the police and requested police protection that would allow him to live peacefully. Jatinder had reached Chile from Punjab, a northern state in India, at the foothills of the Himalayas, without knowing a word of Spanish but today he speaks flawless Spanish. He has a permanent address in Chile. He has an Indian products store in the commercial center in Santiago. 'I feel very bad. I am not a terrorist, I am a trader. Now if I go to a mall the guard announces "the Osama has arrived".'

Another incident is that he went to the airport to pick up his brother, also a traditional Sikh. The people when they saw them together said on their face 'Two Osamas'. A girl passing by made the same comment.

'I am tired and bored of all this. I have no patience left.' Now his response to such remarks are a few swear words like "bas . . . s" and they run away. They are cowards. On my face they say nothing, but when they pass by from afar they say all this.' Jatinder says he has been to Switzerland, US and Canada but there they do not see me the way they see me here.

VENEZUELA

There are a few Sikhs in Venezuela too—details are not available. One presence can be noted from the news item quoted below. The news item tells about human smuggling activities of some Sikhs. Niranjan Mann Singh mentioned, could be the same person as the one who helped Tuts buy a farm in Belize.

7 April 2005: 'US Charges Four in Extensive International Alien Smuggling Operation.' Immigration and Customs Enforcement, announced that Niranjan Maan Singh, also known as 'Jit Narinder Singh', and Ramesh Patel, who are alleged to have been leaders of an extensive international alien smuggling operation, were brought to New York last night to face criminal charges. After being deported from Venezuela, the pair was arrested in Miami, Florida. A grand jury in the Southern District of New York has indicted Singh, Patel, and two other defendants—Sunil Kewal Ramani and Gurdial Singh Pegany for conspiring to smuggle aliens into the United States for commercial gain and financial advantage. US Government Agents in New York and in the Dominican Republic have been investigating the alleged alien smuggling operation of Singh, Patel, Kewal Ramani and Pegany since 2003. In about November 2004, Singh advised that he was in the process of obtaining Venezuelan passports for smugglees because holders of Venezuelan passports are not required to possess a visa in order to enter the Dominican Republic. Singh allegedly discussed the various costs of smuggling his aliens into the United States. It is alleged that Singh subsequently sent two smugglees into the Dominican Republic in about January 2005. From there, the aliens were transported by ferry boat to Puerto Rico, where they subsequently took a commercial flight to John F. Kennedy International Airport in New York City ('JFK Airport'), according to the charges.

SURINAM

While surfing various websites, I came across correspondence by Charandeep Singh Dhanjal who is settled in Netherlands.

According to him, Sikh presence in Surinam, at least in recent years, is connected with Sikh immigration in the Netherlands. In an e-mail, he wrote:

> There are a lot of Sikhs living in the Netherlands today. The fact that Sikhs came here and married with a lot of Surinami women to get their passport was a rage among the Punjabi Sikhs who got here. Out of these marriages came a new generation of youth whose roots lies in Punjab as well as Surinam, a land that lies in South America. Many of these youths have 'pyaar' towards Sikhi and although many of them feel rooted to Surinam as well as Punjab they feel that they are Sikhs. Today there are even 1 or 2 gurdwaras in Surinam for the Sikhs.

A short history of the Sikhs in the Netherlands: I will use 'Punjabi' instead of 'Sikh' because the so-called Sikhs that came here were more Punjabi than Sikh. Ninety-nine per cent cut their hair and did things a true Guru ka Sikh would not do. Punjabis immigrated to the Netherlands back in the late 1970s. Many of the Punjabis that left Punjab in those days went straight to Canada or England. The Netherlands was then not a 'well known' country for migrating to the West as it is today. When the Punjabis came here they faced many problems. The biggest of them was to get a passport for which one had to wait for many years. Many didn't get their papers and eventually went back to Punjab or tried to enter other countries in Europe. However, the ones who stayed here used very tricky ways to get their papers. Most of them 'used' someone else's 'identity' to get a life of their own.

The Surinami People

When the British ruled most of the world in the eighteenth century, the Netherlands arranged a deal with the British to transport Indian citizens to Surinam to work. Many boats with people from Bihar and UP left India to start a new life in Surinam.

When Surinam became independent in 1975 most of the Hindustani people (Hindus, a few Muslims and a small group of Christians) saw that Surinam was doomed because the leaders lacked responsibilty. Out of desperation many of them left Surinam and immigrated to the Netherlands. Although they had lived for more than a century in a colony of the Netherlands, they faced many troubles on arrival. Not only racism but the cold winters and alien culture made life difficult for many of them. However, coming to the Netherlands gave them the opportunity to meet other Indians. On one side were the Punjabi Sikhs and on the other side the Hindustani Surinamis.

Strife between the Surinamis and the Punjabis

In the beginning, most Punjabi and Surinamis lived harmoneously. However, trouble began when Punjabis began to marry Surinami women. Where the Surinami women married out of 'pyaar' and to raise a family, many Punjabis only married to get their papers. This is really true as most of the marriages that took place in the 1980s broke up after three years. There is no research done but I personally think that 95 per cent of the marriages ended in a divorce. Unfortunately most Surinami women in the beginning did not know that the Punjabis were only fooling around with them. Later when many Punjabis left them and went back to get brides from Punjab, they understood how they had been tricked. Another element that played a big role was the financial factor. When the Surinami people came to the Netherlands they knew the Dutch language and the system. On the other hand, the Punjabis were illegal migrants and did not know how to build their life here. Many of them took up work in shops where they worked very hard for little money. Eventually they grew to hate each other.

The Second Generation

While a Punjabi husband of Surinami women was planning to leave his wife as soon as soon he got his papers, he did not care much if he had children with these women (their only goal was to get the papers, go back to Punjab, and marry Punjabi women and to start a new life in the Netherlands, though there are a handful of Punjabis who did not do so), the children of the Surinami/Punjabi people, who are youths today and are discovering their roots. There are many of them, however, who hate Punjabis but who can blame them? But this hatred is growing less as Sikhi is spreading more and more in the West and most of the Surinami/Punjabi children are looking for a new goal. Many of them are going to Punjab to rediscover their faith, language and culture. Many visit gurdwaras. Sikhi is spreading in mysterious ways. Whereas the so-called Sikhs from the 1980s left Sikhi aside and lived their lives like stupid fools, their children which they bore with women they didn't love, are feeling 'pyaar' for this truth on earth. Sikhi is slowly spreading in the minds of these people. The Sikh community is growing.

COSTA RICA

For Costa Rica my main information came from Arvinder Garcha who is settled in London but has some knowledge about Costa Rican Sikhs.

Arvinder Singh Garcha writes to me from London:

> One Indian restaurant in Costa Rica is owned by a Mr. Gill from Canada. He opens up restaurants all over Canada/USA/Central America. He lives in Canada but visits Costa Rica every month. He has a manager who looks after the Costa Rica restaurant. Apart from that, there are around 10 Sindhi families.
>
> Another Sikh guy who is married to a local woman, he is originally from USA but opened a restaurant in Costa Rica as well. I spoke to him before I went to Costa Rica and he asked me to bring him a 'kara'. When I arrived in Costa Rica his phone was out of order. I went to his restaurant which was closed down and there was no sign of him.

CONCLUSION

The above account of Sikhs in these five Latin America countries is fragmentary. But it also illustrates the difficulties in gathering data and information about smaller communities of Sikhs who are scattered across the globe. I hope these stories and information that I have outlined above will prompt Sikhs in those countries to share more information or encourage other Sikh scholars to undertake more organized studies.

CHAPTER 12

Americas: From North to South

'Maharaja—You have Parked Your Elephant in the Wrong Place'

Although this book is about Sikhs in South America, it is pertinent to include a chapter on my experiences as a Sikh in the USA from 1958–61. This is just the reverse of the story of most immigrants covered in this book, who wanted to migrate to the USA but were forced instead to go to South America because of barriers created through various legislative acts. It is also quite in contrast to what many travel agents do to the new age migrants by bringing them over to a South American country and consoling them by saying, 'This is America'—true, but how wrong!

The sub-title of this chapter relates to my getting a parking ticket once in Pennsylvania State University as a student on which was written 'Maharaja—You have Parked Your Elephant in the Wrong Place'. In those days, there were only a few Indians and turbaned Sikhs were a rarity. The Americans' view of India was a country of snake charmers and Maharajas. So a Sikh was either taken as a kind of Maharaja or a person who was so poor that he could not afford a shave. There is a somewhat similar experience later on when I was working in Austria and staying in the Directors' Guest House.

Because of my turban, a celebrity status was not uncommon. It is not to say there were not ticklish negative incidents but these were rare. There were frequent coverages in newspapers, magazines, and even TV interviews. Some of these scrap book collections have survived. This chapter is based on such newspaper clippings.

A SIKH IN THE USA FIFTY YEARS AGO

I went to the USA in 1958 to get my Masters degree in Engineering and thereafter gain work experience for about a year and a half before returning to India via Europe. The readers can compare this with the present-day situation and more importantly with the Sikh experiences in Latin America as outlined in the earlier chapters. Two very different scenarios, yet worth considering.

An Interesting Story

I left India after my B.Sc. (Engg) for the Pennsylvania State University as a Graduate Assistant. After my M.S., I joined Hanna Coal Company, Ohio, a Division of larger Consolidation Coal, as Efficiency Engineer. I returned to India in 1961. My experiences there are told through newspaper and magazine clippings and TV interviews. A Sikh was somewhat of a curiosity, to say the least. Americans were by and large generous, welcoming, and curious.

Introduction

Going 'Phoren' (Foreign) was a milestone in the 1950s not only for the person going abroad but for his family, neighbours, and friends. It was not uncommon to have the nameplate of a person ending with 'England Returned'. Going overseas was a newsworthy item. My own departure was duly covered by *The Onlooker*, the society fortnightly of the era. A tourist class ticket was well worth chasing by the sales staff of the Airlines and I was lavishly entertained by KLM on the lawns of the Imperial Hotel in New Delhi. Going abroad also meant flying for the first time. A lost baggage at Stockholm, which was a stop-over to meet a pen pal, was duly serviced by SAS Airlines. An Airlines representative took me personally to the best department store and bought for me shirts, a suit, shoes, etc. They were very apologetic for their inability to buy me a turban in Stockholm. They, however, agreed to fly the same to the USA if my family delivered the turbans to them in New Delhi. Those years, the aeroplanes had to stop for refueling enroute from Europe to USA. On arrival in New York, I was surprised that I could telephone my friend in the university from New York by just feeding coins and get connected 'pronto'. No booking of a trunk call.

My experiences were by and large pleasant ones. Everyone—from the Head of Department downwards was very helpful—My problem was their problem. The workplace, experiences were mostly positive but there was some resistance at times. Turban was a definite attention grabber not only with children but with mothers who would hush their child but could not resist giving side glances themselves. The general feel amongst the local students was that I must be rich to be able to travel overseas (foreign travel was a luxury even for Americans). Foreigners were not so much of a curiosity at the university campus. However, when travelling outside the campus, people were curious and wanted to meet and befriend the turban wearer. Newspapers found the turban newsworthy. I got invited by a nearby town to inaugurate a Bengali film as they thought I, with a turban, truly represented India—never mind whether I understood Bengali or not. In international business conferences and shows, I was treated as a VIP to be shaken hands with and photographed.

On taking up a job, I became even more of a curiosity because, unlike the university, there were very few foreigners and even less Indians, and no Sikhs there. Newspapers, church groups, schools, and professional clubs wanted me to speak to them about India, Sikhs, and my experiences in the USA. Many of my talks got coverage in the newspapers which is what this scrap-book is all about. In Wheeling, W.Va., I was invited one Sunday to speak on their weekly TV programme 'Downtown Personalities'. This was followed by a repeat appearance next Sunday to answer questions from the viewers.

Americans were generous in asking me to talk of my country and religion—even the church groups. They would want to pay me for my talks but I declined. They would, instead, present me with gifts (some are still with me). It felt good on seeing news headlines such as 'Indian Engineer says India needs time to solve its problems'. In retrospect, it really boosted my self-confidence. People's warm hospitality can be gauged from the fact that before I could order a drink in a bar, someone would be offering me one. There were some scary experiences too. The one I remember most vividly was in a night club when I was dancing close with a lady. This guy, no relation or friend of the lady, came menacingly to hit me and succeeded in pushing me. My host ran to the car to get his revolver to shoot the guy who had insulted his Indian friend. It took a lot of entreaties from his wife to cool down the situation. Of course, the offender was thrown out.

This chapter is a 'Thank You' note to all Americans for their hospitality and generosity. I have tried to return these kind gestures through my offering to help foreigners I meet in India.

From Punjab to the USA

I was born in Bharatpur, Rajasthan where my father was on deputation from Punjab with the Maharaja. At the time of India's independence I was studying at the Government Central Model School, in Lahore. My later schooling was in Punjab at Ferozepur, Ludhiana and finally Amritsar for matriculation. After F.Sc. from Punjab University College, Hoshiarpur, I obtained my Engineering degree from the Indian School of Mines, Dhanbad. Thereafter, in 1958, I went to the USA for higher studies. In February 1960, I moved to Ohio and West Virginia with Hanna Coal for work experience. The company offered to sponsor me for US citizenship but I opted to return in deference to the promise made to my parents—it needed a lot of convincing to my seniors in the company that I, indeed,

Plates 75–76: (top) Author as teenager; (bottom) Author's family photo in Batala before departure for USA in 1958

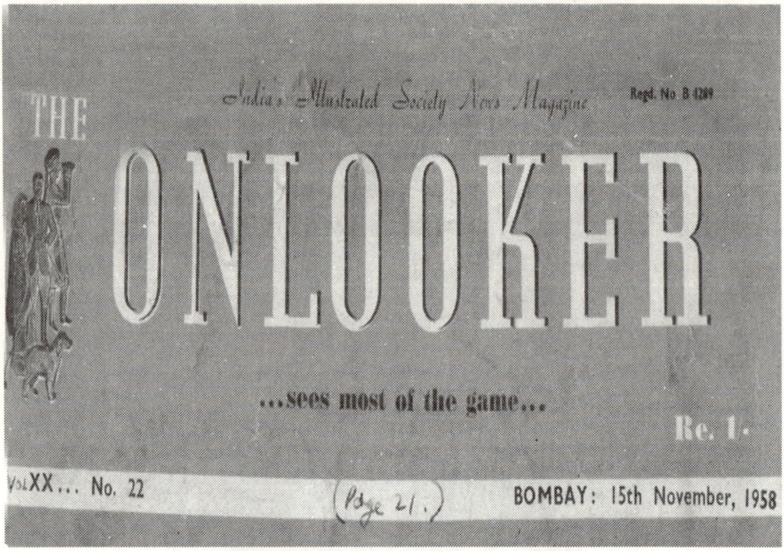

Mr. Sawaran Singh Kahlon, son of Sardar Lachhman Singh, retired Deputy Registrar, Co-op. Societies, Punjab left for the U.S.A. for higher studies in mining and was seen off by Lieutenant Harbhajan Singh, Mrs. Kuldip Hundal, his parents and Bonnie Hundal

Plate 77: A Society fortnightly magazine—Author's departure to USA for higher studies was announced liked USA but was returning due to other reasons. On my way back I visited Europe where I also had an opportunity for work experience in the mining industry in Austria.

Student Life

The Graduate Assistantship normally did not cover the summer vacation but the Mining Deptt. was helpful in giving me employment on special consideration. My job involved teaching on a half time basis. Teaching was somewhat daunting in the beginning but soon turned out to be fun. Student behaviour was at times annoying but I soon realized it wasn't personal. It was just the typical casual mannerism of Americans. But studies were a serious business due to the high tuition fee and other costs—only committed students joined the university. Life in the university town was fun. I had (coincidentally) the company of my senior, Madan Mohan Singh, from ISM, Dhanbad and Wasinder Mokha, my classmate for a year at Khalsa College, Amritsar. The students whom I taught were very understanding considering that I was from a relatively unknown and developing country. No discrimination was felt in renting accommodation. The faculty was also very supportive. In fact, they were encouraging enough to say that if I wanted to return to the US at any time, they would always have a position available for me—a very generous open offer. Assistantship did not pay much but was sufficient to live in a shared accommodation and to buy and run a car. During the Easter break, I went to Fort Lauderdale, Fl., a popular hang-out out for young students from all over USA during Easter holidays. It becomes a wild place for a few days; a street is cordoned off for dancing. Students rented out just one room in a hotel on the beach. Others slept on the beach but could use the hotel bathroom. There were enough outlets which offered unlimited food or beer at reasonable prices. Once when a hotel ran out of beer, students threw the chairs into the sea. Next day the restaurant hung up a banner apologiz-

Plate 78: Author in his office at Pennsylvania State University

CUES & NEWS

The University Christian Association at The Pennsylvania State University

Vol. II, No. 2 UNIVERSITY PARK, PA. October 19, 1958

Genevieve Biltz, Kozaburo Shimada, Swaran S. Kahlon, Betty Lorditch, Selbourne Mvusi, and Sally West enjoy participation in an International Fireside discussion. These programs meet twice a month on Monday evenings, usually in faculty homes. Subjects for the informal discussions are planned one meeting in advance according to the interests of those attending each time.

Plate 79: Pennsylvania State University—International students get-together ing and offering the same deal again. All was in good cheer—in true American spirit of the era.

There were over 200 international students including 40 Indians (4 Sikhs). The university had an International Students Deptt. to help them. Majority of the overseas students especially Indians were in Graduate School.

THANKSGIVING VISITS TO AMERICAN FAMILIES

Every year during the Thanksgiving break the International Students Office arranged for foreign students to stay with families in the small town of Pine Grove. What a gesture of hospitality! It was fun and in many cases the relationship with hosts developed into long-term friendships. My hosts (the Gensemers) were extremely affectionate and generous. They would travel long distances to celebrate my birthday. On my graduation day they came loaded with gifts. If I did not write to them for some time, they would telephone to check if everything was all right. They even sent me money for Easter holiday in Florida. They sent gifts to my sister in India. The latter created a piquant situation as the recipient had to pay heavy import duty (remember the era of penal duties). On hearing about it the Gensemers mailed dollar bills in an envelope, which she of course promptly returned in the same manner—all very illegal.

Curiosity Factor

Turban attracted a lot of attention, whether one stopped to get the car repaired or on a business visit. At times it was hilarious to see the small town people's reaction. At a restaurant while conversing in chaste English, we decided to have a little fun with the waitress. We started reading the menu upside down only to be told by her that the Americans read English the other way around. Simple folks! The waitress serving us would be questioned in detail by others as to who we

Mrs. Kurt Hortner (third from left) and Horace Hess (right), representing Pine Grove Women's Club and Rotary respectively, greet overseas students from Penn State University who are in Pine Grove for the holiday weekend. This traditional international good will venture of the two Pine Grove organizations is now in its fourth year. The guests are (left to right front) Singh Sandhu, India; Kazem Daneshi, Iran; Kaneko Minei, Okinawa; Teresita Blando, Philippines; Virginia Lattes-Deik, Chile; Hisako Matasubara, Japan; Mrs. Vincente Chi, China; (back row) Wasinder Mokha, India; Gopal Saksena, India; Nasimuddin Mufti, Pakistan; Abdul Kayoom Awan, Pakistan; Swarn Singh Kahlon, India; Ali Mohammad Saidi, Iran. Not pictured is the 14th visiting student, V. Gopala Krishna, India.

PINE GROVE HOST TO PSU OVERSEAS STUDENTS

This is the fourth consecutive year that the Thanksgiving week-national "flavor."

Men and women from nine different lands are guests of Pine Grove families. The group came to this county community from Penn State University.

Pine Grove Women's Club and Rotary sponsor the visitation yearly.

Today the PSU delegation toured Indian Head Breaker near Tremont and coal strippings.

Arriving early Wednesday evening, the visitors were met at Bethel by a Pine Grove delegation, then taken to homes of their hosts. They were given the opportunity to attend the community Thanksgiving service at Evangelical United Brethren Church, where Rev. Ralph Mehle, pastor of St. Paul's Evangelical Congregational Church, Pine Grove, delivered the sermon. Host pastor was Rev. N. I. Fake, with Rev. Roland Turnbach, St. Peter's United Church of Christ, assisting in the service.

Thanksgiving Day was spent for the most part in the homes of the host families, with the traditionally food-laden tables more than satisfying appetites. Watching parades and sports on television and some additional visiting were topped in the evening with an open house at Dr. Kurt Hertner's for the guests and their hosts.

Saturday will be devoted to individually - planned activities of the hosts, with a group supper at 6 p.m. in St. John's Lutheran Church. A social gathering will follow, or the Penn State University group will have the opportunity of attending a basketball game at Pine Grove Area Joint High School.

Sunday will conclude the visitation, with church services in the morning, dinner and departure for Penn State at 2:45 p.m.

Guests from PSU are: Teresita Blando of the Philippines who is a graduate assistant in speech; Kazem Daneshi of Iran; Ali Mohammad Saidi, Iran, a graduate student in the field of petroleum; Abdul Kayoom Awan, Pakistan, freshman in applied arts; Hisako Matsubara, Japan, graduate student in the arts; Nasimuddin Mufti, Pakistan, nuclear scientists; V. Gopala Krishna, India, a graduate student in chemistry. Swarn Singh Kahlon, India, graduate assistant in physics; Wasinder Mokha, India, a sophmore, civil engineering; Singh Sandhu, India; Virginia Lattes-Deik, Chile, a graduate in home economics; Mrs. Vincente Chi, China, a special in home economics; Kaneko Minei, Okinawa, a graduate in home economics.

Plate 80: Thanksgiving: Visit by international students to American families' homes for stay

The Latrobe Bulletin

"THE FAMILY NEWSPAPER—PRINTS THE NEWS THAT IS FIT TO PRINT"

VOL. LVII, No. 157 ESTABLISHED 1902 LATROBE, PA., TUESDAY, JUNE 23, 1959

THE WEATHER

Sight-See Here

EXCHANGE STUDENTS from India, Swarn Singh Kahlon (left) and Madan Mohan Singh, who are studying mining at the Pennsylvania State University, view the sights in Latrobe while awaiting repairs to their automobile. They visited coal mines in the Johnstown district yesterday, stayed here overnight and planned to go to Youngwood this afternoon to inspect a coal mine. (Bulletin Photo)

Page-1

Plate 81: Turban was newsworthy even if we had stopped in a town to get car repaired

MINING engineering

Vol. 11 NO. 2 FEBRUARY 1959

PITTSBURGH HOLDS 13th OFF-THE-RECORD MEETING

The distinguished visitors seen below left added an international flavor to the festivities, and the mass of conventioneers below enjoyed a breather after the technical sessions, courtesy of the many Pittsburgh industries. H. R. Loxterman was chairman of the Suppliers Committee that gave the party.

Plate 82: Attending professional conferences—foreign students were warmly welcomed

were. Our behaviour would be reported in the minutest of detail. Children would come to shake hands, going back feeling very pleased after that. Everywhere I visited, people went out of their way to be helpful and friendly.

PROFESSIONAL VISITS

Summer job provided useful visits to mines which in turn helped build contacts in the industry. During one such visit to Ohio, I was offered a job. Although in India, Sikhs are exempt from wearing safety helmet, I decided to comply with the local laws. My professor wanted me to take up research on explosives which I declined as I felt it would be of no use in the Indian job market on return. Instead, I did my research on coal cut-

Indiana Evening Gazette

A Local Page For Local People

Volume 59.—No. 139. Indiana, Pennsylvania, Wednesday, January 28, 1959.

FOREIGN STUDENTS CONDUCT TIME STUDY—Three Penn State University foreign graduate students and one undergraduate student, along with their professor, are conducting time study surveys this week in local mines of the Rochester and Pittsburgh Coal Co. They are pictured as they completed their shift in Kent No. 10 Mine yesterday afternoon. Dr. Boris Kochawowsky, center, is shown looking over one of the time study reports. Looking on from the left are two students from India, S. S. Kahlon, extreme left, and M. M. Singh. On the extreme right is Y. C. Kim from Korea. The other student, Rodger Brooks, is a senior at Penn State.

(Gazette photo by Sipos)

Plate 83: Field visits to mines were important enough for newspapers to report ting machines which did away with explosives. As fate would have it, on my return, I joined ICI, a British multinational, in their Explosives Division. Fate is supreme!

HE WALKS AT NITE!

At the Mining Show in Cleveland, Ohio, I was quite a star attraction as a Sikh. All display booths would want a photo opportunity with the turbaned guy, including the 'Coal Beauty Queen'. There was interest by mining equipment manufacturers to sell their machines to India and to set-up local manufacture. India was of interest to the Americans but was considered a difficult market due to State/Public ownership of the mining industry. But all Americans were unanimous that India, one day, would be a large market. This cartoon (Plate 84) was drawn by an artist in the Cleveland Mining Show. The caption speaks of how intrigued they were of a turban.

Plate 84: Turban was intriguing enough for an artist to sketch a cartoon at the Cleveland Mining Show

FAR REACHING CHARM—Miss Claire Ann Carney, 1958 Pennsylvania Coal Queen, capped her reign as queen of the State Coal Show at Carmichaels with an official visit to the American Mining Congress in Cleveland last week. Miss Carney, with her charm and personality, was a big hit with exhibitors and coal company representatives from throughout the nation. Her visit even took on an international flavor, as shown above, when she chatted with Swarn Singh Kahlon, a student of mining engineering at Penn State University under a scholarship from the government of India. Miss Carney and her mother were accompanied by Mr. and Mrs. William E. Gabler, of Mapletown, and her trip was sponsored by the King Coal Association of Carmichaels. Mr. Gabler snapped the above picture.

Plate 85: Author with the Pennsylvania Coal Beauty Queen, Ann Carney at the State Coal Show

The Mining Society

Newsletter

Penn State AIME Student Chapter

Swarn Singh Kahlon, graduate student from India, will be the recipient of a master's degree in Mining Engineering from Penn State in January. Swarn is 22 years of age, single, and a very likable person.

Before coming to Penn State, Mr. Kahlon received an extensive education in India culminated by a B. S. degree in Mining in 1958 from Bihar University, and an A.I.S.M. diploma from The India School of Mines. All degrees and honors that he received were in the first division which is the highest division in all of India.

Considering Mr. Kahlon's tender years, he has certainly obtained a vast experience in the field of mining. As an apprentice mining engineer in India for eleven months, Mr. Kahlon has been associated with both coal and hard rock. In coal, Mr. Kahlon has had experience working with shallow and deep mines up to 1500 feet, low and high coal up to 23 feet thick, and with pillar recovery with hydraulic stowing. Finally, working with the extraction and preparation of mica sheets in India mines, and with the control of high rock pressures and temperatures in the 10,000-foot-deep Kolar Gold Mines, has given Mr. Kahlon a well-rounded experience in India.

At Penn State he has been a graduate assistant with the thin seam project of the Commonwealth of Pennsylvania for three months and has been for 14 months concerned with basic research in slate properties and mining, effectiveness of rotary drills, and teaching a mine surveying course.

With such an impressive background in his chosen field, Swarn Singh Kahlon can certainly look forward to a successful career in mining. He would like to secure a job with a mining company in the United States for several years before returning to India.

Plate 86: University Newsletter promoting author for a possible job with the US industry

Hanna Coal Company, Ohio

During the summer research field visit in 1959, I met the Senior Vice-President of Hanna Coal, and was offered a position on graduation. However, no written offer was forthcoming. With graduation day fast approaching on 31 January 1960, I made a somewhat desperate call to the V.P. His prompt reply was, 'Of course, we have a job for you—just come over.' So the very next day after graduation, I drove to St Clairsville, Ohio, and met the V.P. in the late afternoon. As a starter, the V.P. asked me if I wanted to rise in life, to which my obvious reply was, 'Of course, yes'. The V.P. advised me that in that case I should forget that I have any degree and start learning the mining practices from the bottom. There was a background to this advice, about which I learnt later. The V.P. had no formal degree in Engineering, and so was the case with many other senior mine managers. However, the company was well known in the industry for its super efficiency. Some of the largest and specialized equipment of the American mining industry were first introduced at Hanna Coal. This included transportation of coal as a fluid through pipes to ships several hundred miles away at the port, the largest opencast shovel, the highest OMS (output per man shift). And I was to work as 'Efficiency Engineer' in such an environ. The V.P. called the General Manager of Ireland Mine in W.Va, to tell him that I was to work there. By the time I reached the mine several miles away it was dark and snowing heavily. I was told to report at 7.00 a.m. the next morning at the pithead for going underground with the shift manager. No one offered assistance on where to stay nor did I ask for help. I was no more a pampered foreign student in the University but in the rough and tumble of industry. So I booked myself in a motel in Moundsville, a town 15 miles away. I had to buy a lunch box as I was expected to stay eight hours underground.

On reporting to duty next morning, it was dark and still snowing. I was assigned to a foreman for studying a continuous mining machine, a latest acquisition by the company. This machine cuts the coal like a shaving machine in vertical and horizontal movements. As the coal is cut the mine tunnel roof can fall down. The workplace was really scary, dusty and noisy. At the front end of the mine, it was like a real war zone. My assignment was to evaluate the effectiveness of the machine through time and motion study and suggest ways for maximising its efficiency. (In India we were still mining coal using manual pick mining.) The foreman had a gang of four people. No one talked to me except during lunch break sitting on the dirty mine floor next to the machine. On coming out of the mine while taking the community shower, the ice was gradually broken after a couple of days. Soon afterwards, I got invited for a drink at the Moundsville bar. It was tough going for a Master's Degree holder but I stuck on. In the meantime I moved to a mobile home which could be rented on a weekly basis.

After about two weeks, I was told to report to the VP of the company. On arrival, I was asked straightaway by the VP, if I would like to become a US citizen. The company was willing to sponsor me for the same. Evidently they had been monitoring my attitude and competence, etc. Imagine the VP's disappointment when I turned down the offer. He appeared very hurt.

Work Experience with Hanna Coal

Arising out of my promise to my parents I decided to return to India. My employers really could not understand this approach to career and life. The VP thereafter offered me to work for the allowed 18-month period (student visa requirement) to gain experience in the areas of my choice. This gave me an opportunity to rotate around in different departments and mines. I was invited to the VP's house for a pool side party. An experience worth recounting is of being sent to another mine. As I entered the Manager's office, he said to me in a somewhat hostile manner 'Are you the VP's man who has come to teach me how to run my mine'? Indeed, the mine was industry famous in operational efficiency on all counts. He asked me to go down the mine with a foreman. Here was the cruncher! I refused and sat down in the chair which had not even been offered to me. I told the Manager that since we seem to have a problem, there was no point in my going down the mine. Somewhat stumped by my stance, we got talking. Within a few days both of us became buddies—the criterion being that when a major baseball game was on, he would ask me not to go underground but to stay back to watch the game with him on his office TV.

On looking back, I realize that hardly any of the employees had ever invited me to their homes—a life far different from my student days. However, many other people, organizations, schools, etc., were keen to meet me and learn about India and the Sikhs. There was a fair bit of coverage about me in the newspapers, starting with the *Moundsville Daily*, whose editor and his son became good friends. Soon after joining the company, Hanna Coal's in-house magazine had my full page photo on the cover. So within the company, I got known to the employees and their families. Professional organizations like Rotary, Kiwanis, Junior Women's Club, etc., invited me to speak to their members. Various Church groups, e.g. Methodist, Presbyterian, United Council of Church Women and Unitarians invited me to give lectures. Some schools also wanted me to interact with their students. The most memorable was to speak to a Sunday Church Group, age group 5–8 years old. It was so nice to interact with them with their innocent questions. The touching part was that after the talk each child came to me, one by one, to say 'Thank You', and more importantly, to say 'May God Bless You'. Those words from young and beautiful children remain ever fresh in my memory. I feel truly blessed.

SPEAKING TO VARIOUS GROUPS

Typical questions at these gatherings used to be:

What are the basic tenets of the Sikh religion? Details about my family?. How long were my hair and turban? Would I marry an American? Do people in India sleep in the streets? etc.

On the political side, there were queries about India and Indians' attitude towards Britain and USSR.

The following, an excerpt from my speech in 1960 would illustrate the general interest in India at the time of the Cold War and India's tilt towards Russia:

Freedom brought its complicated problems to India and the Nation needs time to develop a stable economy. The average Indian has no grudge against the British. They left in a very cordial atmosphere. There are as many British there as in the past. He expressed the need for American aid. In speaking of Russia, he said, we are not against Russia but against the political system there. The nation needs private investment to raise its living standard, now regarded as one of the poorest in the world.

No wonder the local librarian was rather intrigued that I was the largest borrower of books on India. I had to learn about my country in these three years to answer the variety of questions thrown at me. I made some good friends who ensured that I was well looked after socially and otherwise. Moundsville turned out to be too small a place for me and my possible social interests. So I decided to shift to a service apartment in a larger town 30 miles away at Wheeling, W. Virginia. I could develope better social circle there, including intimate relationship with an elegant couple, the Seabrights. I met them frequently and became a part of their household and circle of friends.

It was with a heavy heart that I left for Europe in 1961, where I planned *en-route* to visit, UK, France, Spain, Italy, Greece, and Egypt. I also got an opportunity to work in Austria for a couple of months. But that is another story.

Next few pages cover news clippings on my speaking and other activities.

Plate 87: Hanna Coal Company magazine–Front cover

MARSHALL COUNTY'S ONLY DAILY NEWSPAPER

MOUNDSVILLE DAILY

ECHO'S 69TH YEAR NO. 80 DAILY'S 64TH YEAR NO. 272 MOUNDSVILLE, WEST VIRGINIA 715 Lafayette avenue, Second-class mail privileges authorized at Mounds

Sikh From India To Work Here At Hanna

SWARN SINGH KAHLON (at left) came into the Echo last evening with Julius Olzer, safety director of Ireland mine, seeking a place where he can live the next 18 months while he is working for Hanna Coal, and here they are going over the Echo "for rent" ads.

Mr. Kahlon graduated Sunday with master of science in mining engineering at Penn State University, and will be working as a regular employee of Hanna at Ireland and their Ohio-side mines in the engineering department for the next 18 months; then he will go back to India to direct mining there.

He is a very interesting, courteous person who willingly answers questions about his people. He belongs to the Sikhs, long known as fierce warriors, who are four percent of the population of India.

Their religious faith is between that of the Hindus and the Moslems. They worship one God as do the Moslems; but unlike them they hold women in equal position ("No religious service is complete without a woman present," he said.)

Every Sikh bears the middle name "Singh" which means "Lion." They never cut their beards; and those who look closely at him will find that he has his, too, but it is wrapped in a hair net and bound back up his cheeks, looking much like a chin strap on a helmet.

His turban makes him distinctive as he goes about town. While in India the Sikh miners do not wear miner's hats, here he makes this concession to Western industrial rules, and removes the turban when he in in a "hard hat" area.

Already one of the Hanna people in St. Clairsville has asked him to speak before a group there.

Page 1.

Plate 88: Author with Company Personnel Manager searching for accommodation

Bellaire

Indian Engineer Kiwanis Speaker

Swarn Kahlon Singh, Indian engineer who is in this country for training with Hanna Coal Co., will be the guest speaker at the Tuesday noon meeting of the Bellaire Kiwanis Club in the City Restaurant.

He will be presented by co-hosts John Phetzing and Lester Pinsky, and his topic will be "India As It Is". Dr. John Foster, club president, will be in charge of the session.

RTINS FERRY, O. — TIMES-LEADER — BELLAIRE, O.

WEDNESDAY, MAY 4, 1960

Engineer Says India Needs Time To Whip Its Problems

India needs time to solve its complicated industrial, social and economic problems, and thus must tread the neutral path between Russia and the free nations, Swarn Kahlon Singh, Indian engineer, said Tuesday in a talk at the Bellaire Kiwanis Club meeting in the City Restaurant.

Presented by co-hosts Lester Pinsky and John Phetzing, Kahlon, who presently is observing mining engineering at Hanna Coal Co. operations, gave a brief history of India, citing the fact that the country has been at the mercy of invaders for most of its 4,000 years of recorded history.

Given independence by the British in 1947, India was partitioned into two nations, India and Pakistan, which erupted into a bloody battle, and the many refugees coming into India from Pakistan added to India's problems, Kahlon said. Under the guidance of Nehru, the crisis was passed.

However, freedom brought its complicated problems to India, and the nation needs time to develop a stable economy, Kahlon said. For that reason, it can ill afford war or disturbance, and with Russia on its borders, must travel a neutral path between the communists and the free world. However, Kahlon said, India's ties are much closer to America than to Russia, and he noted that within the past five years, America investments in India have risen by 200 per cent.

The nation needs private investment to raise its living standard, now regarded as one of the poorest in the world. To raise that standard, he said, it has been necessary to adopt certain phases of socialism, and at present the government is attempting to force the return of 15 per cent of the national income into production. Only five per cent now goes into production, he explained.

India's attempts at birth control have been based on a government plan to ease the food situation, Kahlon said, but the attempt is not working too well

Plate 89: Kiwanis Club, Ballaire: Author's talk being promoted and reported in newspaper

Sprecken(ing) Deutsch-- Or How Now Brown Cow

They're not whistling. They're not chirping. They're not cooing. And they're certainly not singing. Then what could they be doing? Actually, they're locked-in a bitter-end struggle with the German language and the correct pronunciation thereof. All are members of a ten-week class in elementary German being given at the YWCA under the direction of Elizabeth Bernhardt, a professor of languages at Wheeling College. Supposedly all five are struggling with the same German word, or vowel — or sound — but it would appear that not all of them are making the same kind of noise. But, after all, it's only the first class for them in the language of Goethe, Heine and the Katzenjammer Kids. Just wait until they get to those juicy 30-letter compound words the Germans gargle! And how, you ask, does a mere male get into the YWCA? Sign up for the class in elementary German! Tuition is only $9.50 and you'll be able to order sauerbraten mit potato dumplings in its native tongue.

SWARN S. KAHLON
1031 National Rd.

MOLLY McDONIE
Boggs Run

HELEN SUSAN DURKIS
1401 Chapline St.

MRS. JOSEPH T. BELGRADE
9 Birch Ave.

MARY JANE SONNEFELD
5 Pleasant Dr.

Plate 90: Author—learning German language at the YWCA

Published In Ohio, First With Latest About Ohio People

The Times-Leader

Eastern Ohio's Best Home Newspaper

FINAL

Punjab Native Y-Teen Speaker

Plate 91: Author with High School students

Plate 92: Speaking to Church women

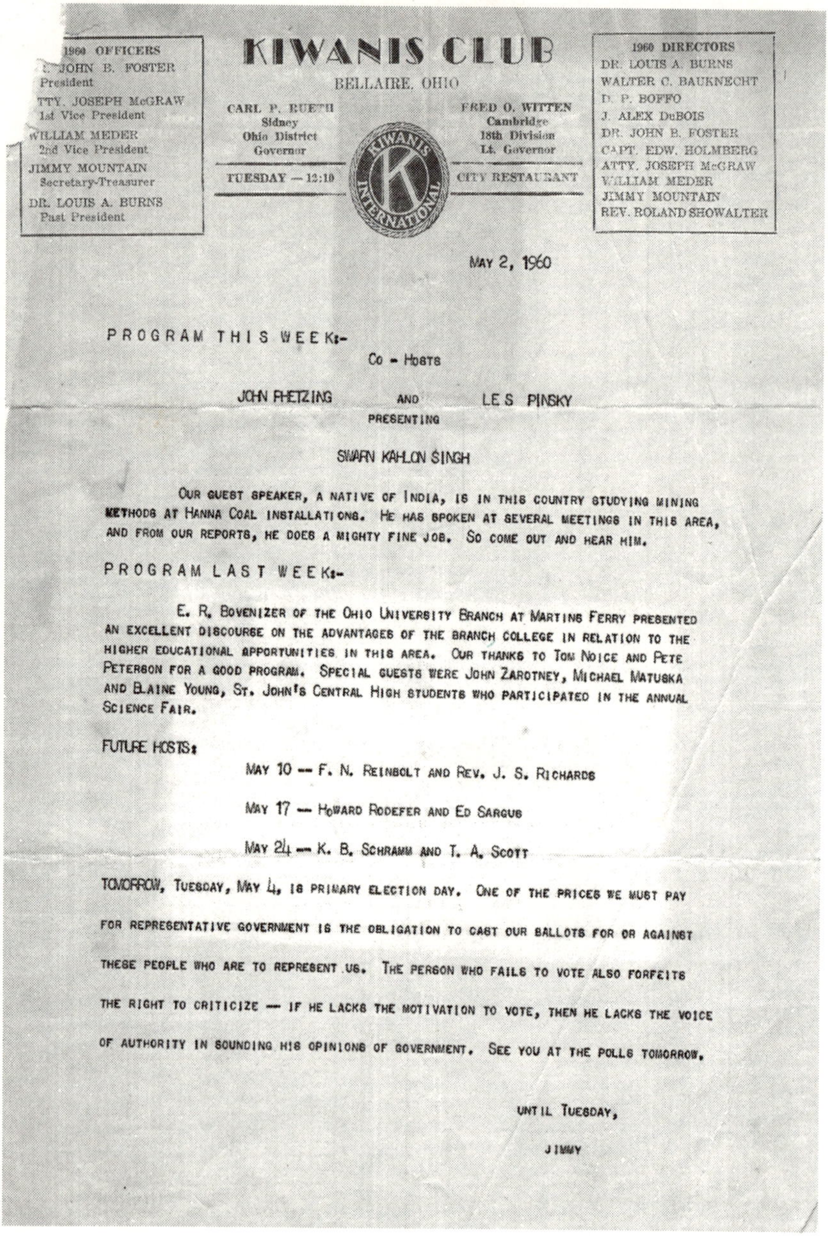

1960 OFFICERS
. JOHN B. FOSTER
President
TTY. JOSEPH McGRAW
1st Vice President
WILLIAM MEDER
2nd Vice President
JIMMY MOUNTAIN
Secretary-Treasurer
DR. LOUIS A. BURNS
Past President

KIWANIS CLUB
BELLAIRE, OHIO

CARL P. RUETH
Sidney
Ohio District
Governor

FRED O. WITTEN
Cambridge
18th Division
Lt. Governor

TUESDAY — 12:10 — CITY RESTAURANT

1960 DIRECTORS
DR. LOUIS A. BURNS
WALTER C. BAUKNECHT
D. P. BOFFO
J. ALEX DuBOIS
DR. JOHN B. FOSTER
CAPT. EDW. HOLMBERG
ATTY. JOSEPH McGRAW
WILLIAM MEDER
JIMMY MOUNTAIN
REV. ROLAND SHOWALTER

MAY 2, 1960

PROGRAM THIS WEEK:-

CO - HOSTS

JOHN PHETZING AND LES PINSKY

PRESENTING

SWARN KAHLON SINGH

OUR GUEST SPEAKER, A NATIVE OF INDIA, IS IN THIS COUNTRY STUDYING MINING METHODS AT HANNA COAL INSTALLATIONS. HE HAS SPOKEN AT SEVERAL MEETINGS IN THIS AREA, AND FROM OUR REPORTS, HE DOES A MIGHTY FINE JOB. SO COME OUT AND HEAR HIM.

PROGRAM LAST WEEK:-

E. R. BOVENIZER OF THE OHIO UNIVERSITY BRANCH AT MARTINS FERRY PRESENTED AN EXCELLENT DISCOURSE ON THE ADVANTAGES OF THE BRANCH COLLEGE IN RELATION TO THE HIGHER EDUCATIONAL APPORTUNITIES IN THIS AREA. OUR THANKS TO TOM NOICE AND PETE PETERSON FOR A GOOD PROGRAM. SPECIAL GUESTS WERE JOHN ZAROTNEY, MICHAEL MATUSKA AND ELAINE YOUNG, ST. JOHN'S CENTRAL HIGH STUDENTS WHO PARTICIPATED IN THE ANNUAL SCIENCE FAIR.

FUTURE HOSTS:

MAY 10 — F. N. REINBOLT AND REV. J. S. RICHARDS

MAY 17 — HOWARD RODEFER AND ED SARGUS

MAY 24 — K. B. SCHRAMM AND T. A. SCOTT

TOMORROW, TUESDAY, MAY 4, IS PRIMARY ELECTION DAY. ONE OF THE PRICES WE MUST PAY FOR REPRESENTATIVE GOVERNMENT IS THE OBLIGATION TO CAST OUR BALLOTS FOR OR AGAINST THESE PEOPLE WHO ARE TO REPRESENT US. THE PERSON WHO FAILS TO VOTE ALSO FORFEITS THE RIGHT TO CRITICIZE — IF HE LACKS THE MOTIVATION TO VOTE, THEN HE LACKS THE VOICE OF AUTHORITY IN SOUNDING HIS OPINIONS OF GOVERNMENT. SEE YOU AT THE POLLS TOMORROW.

UNTIL TUESDAY,

JIMMY

Plate 93: Kiwanis Club inviting members to hear author's talk

Unitarians Will Hear Indian Sikh

Swarn Singh Kahlon, a Sikh from India, will speak on the various aspects of life in India during this Sunday evening's meeting of the United Fellowship of Wheeling.

The meeting will be held at the Windsor Hotel starting at 8:30 p.m.

Kahlon will discuss India's religion, the people's attitudes towards western customs and other phases of life in that country.

Kahlon's talk will be in the form of an interview conducted by Sam Shaw of the Moundsville Echo. Questions will be welcomed from the floor.

Sunday's speaker has a master's degree in mining engineering from Penn State U. and is working at the Hanna Coal Co. for 18 months prior to his return to India. April 10, 1960

Junior Woman's Club To Hear Speaker From India

Swarn Singh Kahlon, a native of Amsitsar, Punjab, India, will be guest speaker when the Shadyside Junior Woman's Club has its April meeting Tuesday, the 19th, at 8 p.m. in the multi-purpose room of the high school. The speaker will be introduced by program leader, Mrs. Richard Campbell. Mr. Kahlon recently completed graduate studies at Penn State College and for the ensuing 18 months will be associated with the Hanna Coal Company. He will speak on "Women of India." Mrs. Daniel George will give the devotions.

Also on the program will be a group of students from the public speaking class at the high school and their instructor, Rudy Mumley. Janet Boyer, vocal music instructor at the Shadyside public schools, will present the high school ensemble in two numbers for which she will play the accompaniment.

Mrs. Jack Berger, president, is reminding members to bring "Clothes For Save The Childrens' Federation." An invitation has been extended the Martins Ferry Junior Woman's Club to attend.

Mrs. Walter Ambler is chairman of the hospitality committee and is being assisted by Mmes. Philip Andes, Richard Jerico, Remo Malpiedi, Kenneth Marling and Marvin Roscoe.

ped off a block from the gate, with the impressive car out of the sight of other youngsters

Swarn S. Kahlon T[o] Speak At Methodis[t] W.S.C.S. Meeting

Swarn S. Kahlon, Indian Sik[h], a native of India currently workin[g] in the United States, will be th[e] guest speaker fo the W.S.C.S [of t]he First Methodist Church o[n] Wednesday, April 20, at 8:00.

The program will be a questi[on] and answer affair with Mr. W. [...] McColloch serving as moderator.

Mr. Kahlon is employed by [the] Hanna Coal Co. and is residing [in] the Wheeling area. He expects t[o] return to his native India aft[er] some study and work in the fie[ld] of engineering.

Plate 94: Calling organization members to hear author talk on India and Sikhs ville Daily Echo, Moundsville, W. Va.

FRIDAY, MARCH 4, 1960

JOTS

We've enjoyed a couple of fascinating evenings lately, both of them at the home of Mr. and Mrs. Dan Bihler on Third street.

The other affair was last night. It combined a birthday dinner for Alexandra Shaw, with a get-together with the Sikh, Swarn Singh Kahlon, who is an engineer at Hanna's Ireland mine.

We of course plied him with many questions about his country's politics, his people, his dress, his religion. He asked us about American ways.

We were amazed to find he knows more Cha-Cha dance steps than anyone else present; and he enjoys Dixieland jazz. Young Danny took him down to the recreation room and showed him how to play his outfit of drums.

Here is a young man who never had anything to do with snow before last summer, nor knew how to drive— and now he is faced with driving his car over slick roads that would test the skill of those who done it for years. He lives in Wheeling out the pike next to Wickham's. So the Bihlers had him stay overnight rather than risk that trip to Wheeling and back at dawn today.

* * *

Mr. Kahlon is an unusually inteligent and mannerly ambassador of his people. This writer will be interviewing him at the Unitarian discussion group meeting in Wheeling's Windsor hotel on next Palm Sunday evening at 8:30, April 10; the meeting is open to the public.

November Meeting of The R.E. [illegible] Sunday School Class of First Methodist Church.

Thursday, Nov. 17th at 6:30 PM, to be held in Church basement with the [illegible] Circle ladies serving us.

Swarn Sing Kahlon of India, and a mining Engineer with Hanna Coal Co. will speak to us.

Music by Negro Bridgeport Mens Chorus.

Other guests with us on this night will be the Men from South Bellaire, Shadyside, West Bellaire Methodist Churches,

The price; $1.50 will come close to bring it. Support the President and his comittee, be there.

Indian Sikh To Address Class

The Bykota class of the First Christian church will meet at 7:30 p. m., Thursday, Feb 25th, at the home of Rev. and Mrs. Charles Brooks. The hosts and hostesses will be Mr. and Mrs. Carl Wayne and Mr. and Mrs. David Borkett. Mr. and Mrs. William Cullum are program chairmen.

The guest speaker will be Swarn Kahlon, Sikh of India.

Off To Australia

Mr. S. S. Kahlon, Explosives Sales Manager, B. R. O. left India by air for Australia on 27th August, for a 6 week visit to Sydney, Melbourne, Brisbane, Rockhampton, Adelaide and Whyalla.

Mr. Kahlon's visit includes a study of the Australian Explosives market with particular reference to their practice in selling techniques sales promotion and publicity, market research, transport, storage and handling. In addition Mr. Kahlon will also make a study of the organizational set up, including distribution of explosives through dealers.

Plate 95: Newspapers reporting on author's talks at various fora

MOUNDSVILLE DAILY
MARSHALL COUNTY'S ONLY DAILY NEWSPAPER
ECHO'S 69TH YEAR NO. 157 DAILY 65TH YEAR NO. 43 MOUNDSVILLE, WEST VIRGINIA 715 Lafayette avenue, Second-class mail privileges authorized at M

Sikh Addressed Presbyterian Meeting

SIKH SWARN SINGH KAHLON of India, who is in the States and employed at Ireland Mine, is shown at the social time following the meeting of the Presbyterian Woman's association, Tuesday evening.

He is with a group composed of Rev. Richard Jones, at left, and Mr. and Mrs. Lionel Sarff (he is also with Ireland Mine, and is behind Rev. Jones).

Mr Kahlon told of his Sikh religion, and gave various historical date concerning India, and information on current conditions there.

Also on the program was the Opus Music club, which rendered "I Believe' and "This is My Country". Mrs. Millie Fromhart was director and Mrs. William Nesbitt accompanist. Mrs. Philip Hodgman and Rev. Jones had the devotional.

Mrs,. Betty Bradon conducted the business which began the evening. She annouhced the state meeting for Davis and Elkins college June 1-3 and the Council of Church Women May luncheon for this Friday.

Reports were made on the sick, of which there are more than usual. Among them are Mrs. Frank Peters and Mrs. A. R. Day who have returned from hospitals Mrs. George Schaub, now in the hospital, and Mrs Ella Richardson now able to be out. Several others are also in nursing homes and at home.

A social time followed, with Mrs Don Adams and her committee in charge. The table rooms were lovely with vari-colored lilacs, in addition to the Sunday church flowers.

The evening was arranged by Miss Jean Moore, Mrs. Mabel Walton and Miss Evelyn Toland.

Mrs. Ernest White announced that the June program will feature a Christian Education film, "Meet Bill Hyder", a talk by Mrs. Claude Eans, and a solo by Mrs. Genevieve Peters.

A number of visitors were present Tuesday from outside the church, and among women of the church who do not ordinarily attend the association.

Plate 96: Speaking to Presbyterian Church group

BRIDGEPORT

R-O-T-A-R-Y S-P-O-K-E-S

Jan. 12, 1961

F. W. Richardson, pres.
Daniel Giffin, v. pres.
John Cowl, secretary
Glen Zimmerman, treas.
ken Burley, program chr.
Directors:
Art Conaway
R. J. Boccabella
Eugene Remenar

ATTENDANCE--Prez Gabby is quite concerned over the attendance, or rather lack of it, as the club slipped several notches in December. It's a new year so let's get these absentees on the ball.

PROGRAM--Today's speaker is Swarn Simgh Kahlon of India. He is a time study engineer with Hanna Coal Co. Mr. Kahlon was an honor student in mine engineering in India and received his master's degree in mine engineering at Penn Stat University a year ago.

PROJECTS--Recently, the club discussed the possibility of undertaking a project. As someone mentioned, very few people know there's a Rotary Club in Bridgeport. It would be grand if some enterprising membercould come up with a solid idea.

HOLE-IN-TWO--Rem was approaching the tee when he eyed the next hole and said, "Well, I should make this with a long drive and a putt." However, his drive trickled only a few feet off the tee, whereupon his caddy voiced, "Now for a helluva putt!"

Incidentally, HAPPY NEW YEAR!!

WELCOME--Since the last bulletin was published (can't remember that far back) several new members have joined the club, so a hearty welcome to Ed Jr., Paul, and Bcb, Bridgeport's only smiling Irishman.

PROGRAMS--Fellas, Rotarian Ken has done an excellent job of supplying us with interesting programs, but nevertheless needs the support of the members. Remember, when it's your turn for a program, don't let him down.

---SERVICE ABOVE SELF---

Plate 97: St. Clairsville PTA meeting—author's talk on 'Education in India and United States'

Plate 98: TV interview, Wheeling, W.Va—Downtown Personalities, a weekly programme

MARTINS FERRY, O. — TIMES-LEADER — BELLAIRE, O.

St. Clairsville PTA Will Meet

ST. CLAIRSVILLE — St. Clairsville P-T.A. will hold its first regular meeting of the year tonight at 8 in the multi-purpose room of the Elementary school building.

Members will have the opportunity to meet the newly hired teachers at this meeting.

Swarn Kahlon, mining engineer from India, will be the guest speaker. His subject will be "Education in India and United States. Mr. Kahlon is visiting the Hanna Coal Co.

A social hour and refreshments will follow the business session.

Plate 99: Rotary Club announcing author's talk

Plate 100–103: Various facets during author's 3-year stay in USA

CHAPTER 13

Conclusions

First, an important finding—I have been able to establish through my travels and talks with Latin Americans and correspondence with Sikh scholars that Sikhs started migrating to Latin America around the same time as they were entering Canada and the USA. That is to say, in the last decade of the nineteenth century. It is usually assumed that migration to Latin America is a later phenomenon.

Sikh migration is an important feature of the Indian diaspora. The two most significant features have been its pioneering nature and the global spread. The migration continues and the illegal element has become unacceptably predominant—a totally different pioneering mode. On percentage basis, the Sikh diaspora to its total population is the largest when compared to other Indian diasporas even though Punjab has the disadvantage of being land locked. This has had a major impact on the Sikh community in various aspects including religious practices. It is going to impact the Sikh community still further. The Sikh diaspora has been well studied by Sikhs, other Indians and more increasingly, foreign scholars. But the countries where the Sikh presence is small has so far been neglected. This study makes a beginning in filling that gap, at least in one major geographical area. The study is based on extensive interviews covering over 75 persons in eight countries. A unique feature is the interview of immigrants' extended families in Punjab villages and some of the returnees who have now decided to settle in Punjab.

A fundamental issue which emerges from Latin American Sikhs is what can only be called 'dilemma of small communities'. As all these countries have a small number of Sikhs who are widely scattered, they face unique problems of retaining the Sikh culture and religion. Moreover, because of the small numbers involved, there is further uncertainty about their ultimate goals. Some are trying to settle in countries where there are more Sikhs—California and a few other states of the USA and Canada are the obvious choices.

A related issue to this 'small numbers symptom' is the late building of gurdwaras. As building a gurdwara requires sufficient number of Sikhs with resources at one locality, most of the gurdwaras in Latin America are of recent origin—almost all have been constructed in the last three decades. Gurdwara is a great institution which helps bind the community. Deprived of a central place for religious life, it must have been extraordinarily difficult for these Sikhs to retain Sikhi or inculcate the same in the new generation. Even other kinds of adjustments were more acute because of the small numbers involved, including maintaining contact with Punjab. One cannot begin to fathom the kind of hardships these Sikhs must have faced in the earlier stages of their settlement. Therefore, it is not surprising that some of them opted to take off their turbans and marry local women. Those thus married of course were set on a path of assimilation in the host society.

The early migrants invariably helped relatives back home through money remittances and chain migration of relatives and village mates. Many came in groups but some came alone. They tried to keep their turbans in the beginning but most of them gave it up in due course. Since it was not expedient to get a wife from Punjab, many of them married locally. Some who were married in Punjab also had to settle for local partners. This resulted in them getting assimilated, particularly the second and third generations. So now we have many Singhs who do not know the background for calling themselves a Singh. Those who had Punjabi wives were better equipped to maintain their cultural and religious identities. Also, in countries where new migrants kept coming, there has been more connectivity with Punjab and Sikh ethos. Interestingly despite being married locally, many in the first generation gave their children Sikh names.

Another issue was conspicuous by its absence. In most Sikh diaspora studies there is almost an over-play of caste distinctions. Even if these are relevant for some countries, the evidence from Latin America presents a contrast. In many of the Sikh locations which I visited and the talks that followed, there was hardly any mention of caste. Even though I asked specific questions about this issue, there was no particularly strong view about it among the immigrants. Is it the case then that caste considerations become prominent only as immigrants cross a certain number, or alternatively, as their families join them?

During my sojourn I had several kinds of feelings for these long distance Sikhs. Some of them never returned to their homeland in Punjab. It must have been a tough choice. Many became 'twice migrants' by moving on to mainly North America, especially the younger set who are able to manage immigration to these more prosperous countries. 'Singh' is still a valuable brand image for honesty, diligence, and adaptability. The work being done by Yogi Harbhajan's 3HO in propagating Sikhism across whole of South America is to be commended. The devotion to the Sikh religion by the converts is really admirable. Carrying the *SGGS*, which is not a small book like the Bible or the *Gita*, by the early migrants, is an example of true devotion.

The immigrants in these countries are isolated but feel more so as the mainstream Sikh community has done little to connect with them. A visit of a turbaned Sikh is eagerly looked forward to. I am still intrigued as to how more than 100 years ago these so-called illiterate peasants of Punjab could get to know of such far-off lands as Argentina and find their way to these destinations. They travelled via the Pacific, and Indian Ocean and South Africa and via the Mediterranean and Atlantic Ocean. They must have changed ships enroute at strange ports. Did they not want to stop in these ports and not proceed further due to physical or mental exhaustion? Originally, Sikh immigrants' priority destination was North America but soon they felt comfortable in other localities too. However, the El Dorado, especially for the younger generation, is still the USA and Canada.

It was almost magical to see sign-boards of commercial establishments within a totally alien landscape with names of Sikh Gurus or Khalsa or Sikh. How tormenting it must have been, the process of giving up Sikh symbols including the turban. Their marriages to local ladies must have been a challenge but probably such alliances made the daily life in these strange lands somewhat easier. How they conveyed and shared their nostalgia of homeland Punjab is difficult to imagine.

The process of settling down, choosing various professions from agriculture, transportation, labour in farms and industrial establishments to retail trading must have been difficult. The subsequent generations qualifying themselves for various professions is commendable. How they had to innovate when facing various challenges and challenges were aplenty! How they coped with the local environ of language, food, social mores, religion, and other customs has to be appreciated considering that almost all of them had come from a rural background with no exposure to the outside world. What it must have been waking up every morning to a new challenge can be left to just speculation. Injustices done to the immigrants, e.g. in Mexico's Northern Province settlers is history but difficult to accept. All these are important factors needing comment and study.

When asked which were the most memorable experiences and the not-so-nice ones, I had to really start thinking. The most satisfying moments were perhaps meeting some of the second or third generation Singhs whose Sikh fathers or grandfathers had married locally. For them to meet a Sikh with a turban from Punjab (who appeared to them to be relatively well off when all they had was an image of India as a country of poor people) was a unique experience. Their love or nostalgia flowed back to me. *These were beautiful men and women who exuded affection*. Argentina was especially memorable and so was my meeting with Walter Sansara Singh in Brazil. The dramatic entrance of Sham Kaur (Gisela) in full Sikh regalia into the hotel in La Paz and meeting Satguru Singh Khalsa and his family in Xalapa, Mexico were wonderful experiences.

The behaviour of Cuban immigration and custom departments was of course annoying. About the touristy part, flying above the Andes Mountains, seeing Lake Titicaca at 13,000 ft, Panama Canal, Rio de Janeiro (even though Copacabana beach was deserted due to inclement weather) were some other highlights. A few uncertain moments were airline-related for the very first travel to Buenos Aires via Sao Paulo and immigration authorities at land border between Belize and Mexico. The fear of walking around or taking a public transport in Rio for possible mugging or being robbed was drilled in by the hotel people. Hotels were generally good and reasonably priced with wifi facilities, etc. People were by and large welcoming and even more helpful to those in a turban, I felt.

The problem of the Sikh immigrants after 9/11 attack was their similarity in physical appearance with Osama bin Laden. A couple of incidents with me gave me an inkling of the problem which these settlers must be facing. On the other hand, my experience of USA fifty years ago is reflected in a way through the euphoria shown towards the recent turbaned 'Peanut King' in Argentina.

Several letters and e-mails, especially from young people who have surfed my website, www.sikhglobalvillage.com, have been extremly satisfying. I am overwhelmed with the interest which seems to exist about knowing, meeting, and studying the Sikhs in these countries.

I should also add that although this book covers only Sikhs in Latin America, I have been to many other countries with smaller Sikh populations. I would like to bring out a sister volume to this book covering these visits.

For migration to British colonies, the Sikhs could expect protection of the Indian state which was not available while migrating to Latin America. This must have made some difference to their experiences from those of migration to the British colonies.

I suggest a tip for researchers—to establish contacts which is quite a problem in countries where Sikh presence is small, to stand wearing a turban, on the main square of the town, chances are that the word will be around and Sikhs will locate you!

WHO IS A SIKH?

This question is not being raised for the first time. There are different definitions by the SGPC, the census authorities, common understanding, etc. These have been changing and evolving over the years. A broader view, of course, could be to accept anyone who says he or she is a Sikh or is born of Sikh parent/s and include all converts. Is the definition on birth only confined to the first generation Sikhs and not the subsequent ones, if they have not married a Sikh?

However, the problem is with regard to the SGPC definition which impinges on who is to manage the affairs of the Sikh Sangat at large. According to the 'Rehat Maryada' (the Sikh code of conduct and conventions), a Sikh is defined as 'any human being who faithfully believes in One Immortal Being; the ten Gurus, from Guru Nanak Dev to Sri Guru Gobind Singh; the *Sri Guru Granth Sahib*; the utterances and teachings of the ten Gurus and the baptism bequeathed by the tenth Guru; and one who does not owe allegiance to any other religion'. The Wikipaedia helpfully adds: 'The most common symbol of all Sikhs, because of its simplicity, is uncut hair (including beards for men) and turbans.'

Under the Indian Census Act, however, anyone can declare that he or she is a Sikh. Earlier on during time of the British Raj there were certain definitions of a Sikh for census purposes which at one stage included a person who does not smoke, etc. A study of the Sikh population numbers as per census over the decades (since nineteenth century), shows ups and downs, some of which cannot be explained by natural growth or otherwise but might be attributed to definition change of 'who is a Sikh'.

For the purpose of my study anyone who says he or she is a Sikh, howsoever distant, is my subject of interest. The story of the Singh fascinate me especially when they are in small numbers, away from their origin.

SIKH POPULATION

According to Government census of 2001, the total population in India was 1,028,737,436 out of which 19,215,730 persons declared their religion as Sikhs which accounts for 1.9 per cent of total Indian population. The Sikh population of Punjab accounts for more than 75 per cent of the total Sikh population in the country. For the sake of comparison, the percentages for other religions are: Hindus 80.5, Muslims 13.4, Christians 2.3, Sikhs 1.9, Buddhists 0.8, Jains 0.4, others 0.6, No religious affiliation 0.1. Out of total population, Sikhs account for in Punjab (60 per cent), Chandigarh (16.1 per cent), Haryana (5.5 per cent), Delhi (4.0 per cent), Uttarakhand (2.5 per cent) and Jammu & Kashmir (2.0 per cent). As an interesting statistic, according to SikhWomen.com, the world population profile (as a percentage of total world population) of various religions percentage-wise is Christians 32.7, Muslims 19.7, Hindus 13.3, Buddhists 5.8, Sikhs 0.4, Jews 0.2, other religions 13.0, non-religious 12.4, atheists 2.5 (2002 est.).

It is interesting to note the trends in Sikh population both before and after Independence. Grewal (1994) in his book *The Sikhs of the Punjab*, makes some interesting observations.

> Sikh population increased from 2 million in 1881 to over 4 million in 1913. In 1911, when the total population of the province (Punjab) was actually 2 per cent less than in 1901, the Sikh population increased by more than 37 per cent. The early census operators were instructed to return only those Sikhs as 'Sikh' who wore kesh and refrained from smoking. In 1911 for the first time all those persons were returned as

Sikhs who thought of themselves as 'Sikh', whether 'Keshdharis' or 'Sehajdharis'. Increase in the number of Sikhs was generally attributed to the policy of the British to give preference to Sikhs in many branches of government service as well as in the army. Another cause of increase in the number of Sikhs was thought to be conversions due to concern for religious reform among the educated Sikhs. There is no doubt that many persons were influenced directly by *parchar* or the propagation of reform. Many more, however, were affected by the growing consciousness of a distinct identity. A change of sentiment on the part of the Sikh community had led many persons recording themselves as Sikhs who were formerly content to be regarded as Hindus.

SIKHS AND TURBAN ISSUE

I draw upon my experience of travel and recall some of the issues faced by Latin American Sikhs. In this context, I also take an overall view of the Sikh diaspora, while pointing towards some specific issues faced by Latin American Sikhs. I raise questions of Sikh culture, issue of Sikh identity, role of turban as a Sikh symbol, and gurdwaras as builders of Sikh religiosity. Finally, considering the physical distance of Latin America from Punjab, the issue of linkages between these far-flung Sikhs and their homeland is also discussed.

I am raising some fundamental questions about the role of Sikh institutions especially of the SGPC. In setting out such an agenda it could help the Sikh diaspora and the Sikhs in Latin America. If my remarks are somewhat emotional, it is only to show the need and urgency of solutions and hope the readers understand my aims and best intentions. On a personal note, I should add here, that having lived all my working life in Kolkata and Mumbai and moving relatively recently to Chandigarh (where I feel like an immigrant), I have observed more interest in Sikhi outside its homeland, i.e. Punjab.

So let me start with a general statement that Sikhs overseas are doing a commendable job under very difficult circumstances. The issues that I raise arise from my personal impressions through travel among the Sikh communities settled in South and Central American and other countries.

On the religious front there are concerns within the community on the 'Rehat Maryada', focusing on the fading presence of the turban. This is true not only with immigrants abroad, which to some extent is understandable. There is a bigger malaise in Punjab. It is now a common sight to see a Sikh family on a scooter with a turbaned father and cut-hair son on the pillion. I think it was Gurcharan Singh Tohra, President of SGPC who lamented on going back to his village, that he did not recognize the place with so few turbans. At a cultural event by a troupe from Malaysia in Chandigarh's Tagore Theatre, the accompanying minister remarked in his introductory speech that he was expecting more turbans in the theatre or in the city. So it is a noticeable development and probably is just the beginning of denudation of the external symbols of the Sikhs. The difficulties faced because of external symbols are a major issue with the Sikh community overseas.

There are other minor issues which are debated such as: whether 'langar' can be had seated on a table and chair in the gurdwara, whether Sikh marriage ceremony can be performed at home and not in a gurdwara, performance of *kirtan* in gurdwaras in unconventional ways such as only with guitar or instruments other than the harmonium and *tabla*, use of English in sermons or gurdwara functions. The role of *granthis* in gurdwaras, their training and upgradation of skills has also been a matter of concern for many Sikhs. The role of women as *sevadars* in Golden Temple and other gurdwaras need to be resolved. It is necessary if our claim that Sikh religion treats the two sexes equally is to have credibility. The withering away of Punjabi language usage both in writing and conversation is a matter of grave concern. The trend amongst the so-called upwardly mobile Sikhs is to speak English and not Punjabi even amongst themselves. This is more so in Chandigarh and Punjab.

The politicization of the apex body of Sikhs has become

counterproductive. The role of SGPC has been under criticism for lack of any positive efforts by them to spread Sikhi, and Punjabi in any meaningful way. The focus of this august body is on insignificant and frivolous issues rather than on major and grave issues facing the community. There may not be a consensus on the way forward but someone has to take a lead to make a beginning in finding solutions. At least there is a need to recognize them and build a general consensus.

The 5‘k’s, as external symbols of a Sikh, generate the most intense internal debate and external concern. As I.J. Singh in his book *Sikhs and Sikhism: A View With a Bias* (2004), says,

> To serve well, symbols must remain visible. In many religions and with many followers, sometimes they are hidden or unobtrusively displayed. Sikh symbols too can be easily concealed—all except the long, unshorn hair. Sikhs have somehow created a hierarchy of their symbols; the long unshorn hair has come to occupy first. A Sikh feels this as a gift of his guru. This is wholly consistent with the philosophic significance of a Sikh, and I venture to say that no matter how Sikhs change and what demands are placed upon them, as long as there are those who call themselves Sikhs, there will be long-haired Sikhs in the form that Guru Gobind Singh gave them. The dictum on the interdependence of form and function is significant and worthy of our attention.

However, questions are being increasingly raised on the essentiality of turban and beard, etc., as part of the Sikh community. There is also the stark fact that more and more Sikhs are not keeping *kesh*. The pressure would build-up still further in years to come. The reasons are several, the more significant being:

1. Migration from India and the problem of assimilation in societies where wearing turban creates difficulties. It is more so where Sikhs are small in number. Sikhs in Argentina, Bolivia, etc., have almost totally abandoned the turban.
2. There is no denying that non-keeping of *kesh* among Sikh children is becoming a norm in Punjab and the rest of India. Acceptance into mainstream Indian society is con-

sidered more important and the turban, the visible symbol, is allowed to go for their children.

3. There is general questioning about religion and religious symbols with increasing globalization and Westernization. The negative influence of TV demanding conformity, fashion, etc., are also invoked as some other reasons.
4. The issue of other 5 'k's such as 'kirpan', etc., is not favourably viewed as unfortunately the use of kirpans in internal gurdwara fights has done a great damage to this symbol.

In a documentary titled 'Roots of Love' by Harjot Gill (2011) telecast by Doordarshan TV in India, I had quoted that in a judgement of 30 May 2009, Punjab and Haryana High Court has concluded that 'uncut hair' are an essential feature for being categorized as Sikh (in the case of Gurleen Kaur *versus* State of Punjab).

There are possibly several more points which could be raised and debated. Notwithstanding all these concerns, it cannot be denied that the brand image of a Sikh is a turban and beard, which is under pressure. As anyone who has studied corporate identity would know, the brand has a tangible value which is built over long time and is even included in the balance sheet. Are the Sikhs going to let their brand image go?

Do we have an alternative plan—or like in many instance, we have only criticism but no solutions? No one can argue or deny that turban is a rallying point of the community and the faith. Another important point for the branded Sikhs (if I may use this term) is that they cannot fight for their rights to wear turban, if the community and gurdwara leaders or representatives do not themselves wear turban. Consider the plight of a turbaned Sikh to be represented by a non-turbaned Sikh on say the turban issue. Unless, of course, the non-turbaned Sikhs are saying that the turbaned Sikhs should follow their wisdom to cut hair, the earlier-the-better. It would give them more comfort and reduce their guilt complex.

There is further erosion of religious identity as various Sikh religious forums, the SGPC and others are not working to promote the 5 'k's in a situation which demands a sophisticated approach. The Sikh priests do not command respect. Even if they are not 'literate', the least they can do is to 'appear pious and be truly *seva* oriented'. Finally, we should remember that 'Faith' cannot be put to stand 'Logic'. To me 'Turban' is nostalgic and has an emotional bond with the community and the religion. It is an integral part of my association with my folks and home state. This nostalgia cannot be denied but whether it must be perpetrated at any cost, especially among overseas communities such as Latin American Sikhs, I cannot answer.

I must also share my worry about the future of our faith. A threat to Sikhism has been and is, that some Hindus do not recognize Sikhism as being different from Hinduism. They claim that Sikhism is just one of the many forms of their religion—more so the Hindus of north India. Generally one does not come across a Bengali, south Indian, Gujarati or a Maharashtrian raising this insinuation. For this reason, Sikhs fear they will not be able to maintain their distinct religious identity and will be absorbed into Hinduism. In this respect, it is interesting to quote I.J. Singh who says: 'John Kenneth Galbraith is correct in his somewhat facetious observations that anything that goes to India or develops there eventually gets Hinduized'. Galbraith was talking of industry, but it is equally true of religions.

Sikhism too has lost some of its lustre of its pristine purity by its constant brushing with Hinduism. If Sikhism has not been absorbed into the Hindu fold entirely, it is not for want of trying by Hinduism, but due to two reasons: (a) its distinct philosophy which is at odds with and bluntly scornful of many Hindu practices, and (b) the distinct external symbols of Sikhism which sets the Sikhs apart in appearance and behaviour. I think that the rot in Sikhism had set in, but has been checked somewhat temporarily by the trauma of the 1984 tragedy. In many ways, those events have forced many Sikhs to reexamine community values and self-worth.

PUNJAB-CENTRICITY

Let us begin with the position of Punjab in the minds of those who have left it more or less forever. This is what I have termed 'Punjab-centricity' among overseas Sikhs. It implies that for overseas Sikhs that Punjab is their 'homeland'. Punjab occupies their mind a lot. They are concerned about Punjab and it will continue to be part of their mental and social world. It is understandable. All the Gurus were born in Punjab except one. The major historical developments of the religion took place in Punjab. Even as the last two Gurus spent considerable time outside the state and had followers there, most historical shrines are located in Punjab. As mentioned earlier, 75 per cent of Sikhs of India live in what is now of course a truncated Punjab.

It is natural and logical that Sikhs and Punjab are linked and thought of as integral to each other. It is not surprising that the Sikhs have been able to claim successfully the regional and territorial identity despite a large presence of Hindus in the present Punjab and a majority Muslim population in the erstwhile pre-partition Punjab. It does not matter how removed they are from Punjab or by generational differences or distance; events in Punjab affect overseas Sikhs in many ways. Punjab as a cradle of Sikhism, indeed of the Sikh civilization, is the reference point by which they continue to define themselves.

As born in Punjab or related to it through generational gaps, there are a number of issues which have been of concern to overseas Sikhs about their homeland. One should start with two of most tragic events of the twentieth century; first was the partition of Punjab that affected overseas Sikh communities. The second was the June 1984 tragedy (Operation Blue Star). While partition was something that was forced upon them by a colonial state, the 1984 tragedy was a creation of India's leaders. The 'glow of freedom' promised by the Nehru regime of a new India to the Sikh *qaum* did not fructify. In the post-1947 era Punjab was further reduced in size. In 1966, large parts of it were shaved off to carve out a new state of Haryana while the more beautiful hilly areas were transferred to Himachal Pradesh, leaving only the plains region as the new Punjab. The reorganization left many issues unresolved which keep spoiling the relationship between Haryana and Punjab and has led to a not-so-hidden hostility by the two neighbouring states towards Punjabis and mostly Sikhs.

The desecration and destruction of parts of the Golden Temple complex is something no Sikh shall ever forget. The event will remain a sad memory for the community for all times to come. The attendant events of this tragedy, i.e. Indian Prime Minister Indira Gandhi's assassination, and the subsequent riots and killings of thousands of Sikhs in Delhi and other parts of India are now part of Sikh history and memory. It is very well to advise Sikhs not to talk about the 1984 tragedy and ask that they should 'move on'. True, but the same people cannot even forget about the Ravana and Sita episode of Hindu history which took place several thousand years ago. How are Sikhs expected to forget so recent a history?

After Maharaja Ranjit Singh's reign, Sikhs could and did pick themselves up from the defeat through preferential recruitment to the army and police by the British. The census of the era show a major increase in Sikh population compared to other religious groups because declaring to be a Sikh became advantageous. Opening of the Canal Colonies of Lyallpur, Montgomery, and Sargodha and the like towards the end of nineteenth century helped raise the standard of living of thousands of Jat Sikh families. However, this was nullified by the migration of refugees after the creation of Pakistan on 14 August 1947. The Green Revolution of the 1960s brought about another dose of prosperity followed by NRI remittances by the Sikh migrants abroad. The movement for Punjabi Suba and thereafter of Khalistan are non-issues now, but they have done their damage in various ways.

Punjab has over the last couple of decades lost out to other states in economic, industrial, social, and services fronts. Even in legal out-migration, Punjabis are being left behind by other communities, especially south Indians in IT-related industries and Gujaratis in trade and industry. In sports and athletics, once a monopoly of the Sikhs, they are slipping back rapidly. It is not just the abandonment of turban but the entire Sikh pride, which is at stake. Once, not long ago, Punjabis and Sikhs were admired for their leadership role in agriculture and rural resurgence. The Punjabi farmer was a by-word for rural prosperity and innovation—no longer so. The Punjabi farmer has gone down the scale, while it is the farmers from other states of India who are spearheading development and rural transformation.

Punjab needs alternative avenues of economic growth. There is hardly any industry in the state. Once the Sikh technician, be a mason, plumber, carpenter, machineman, mechanic, electrician or factory worker, was known for his expertise, honesty and professionalism. No more. Punjab needs to revive, expand, and upgrade its ITI's to churn out specialist skilled workers. There is plenty of demand today and it will expand in future years. Let this be our specialization for which we are better equipped. On the other hand, we need to jump start, even though we are late, on information technology and internet skills. The Punjab government can take a lead in providing broadband connectivity to all the villages. It will bring about a sea change in the countryside of the state. Government can provide all the services, land records, filing of FIRs, etc., on the net. It would save the farmers' time of visiting tehsils and police stations. Only a revolutionary step change in thinking can help Punjab gain lost ground and take the lead once again. It is possible.

It is the frustration from rampant unemployment among

rural Sikh youth that has given rise to this obsession of going abroad at any cost. The state has to create jobs for the semi-literate rural youth because agriculture has become un-remunerative. Earlier, large recruitment of Sikhs into the army was a major outlet, but the Indian Government's policies towards recruitment have dramatically curtailed this avenue of employment. Another popular profession, that of transport; i.e. trucks and taxis, is being increasingly captured by others. The closing of these two traditional avenues of employment has meant the Sikh youth are seeking migration out of India as their only way of survival. Rural life is in crisis with acute power shortage, receding water level, and diminishing return from traditional crops. So with all these issues, what can bind the new generation of Sikhs to their land? Although there is much talk of the need for a new kind of Green Revolution but who is going to bring it about? These challenges seem to be beyond the calibre of contemporary political leadership of Punjab.

On the social front, serious issues have arisen such as drug addiction, female foeticide, etc. The phenomenon of *deras* with caste confrontation on one hand and indulgence in extravagant weddings and the dowry scourge on the other have sullied the image of Sikhs and Punjabis.The properties and other assets of Sikh NRIs have become targets of unscrupulous usurpers. Some of the visiting Sikh immigrants, who visit Punjab for nostalgic reasons, experience exploitation from relatives and neighbours.

For the last few decades, Sikhs and Punjab have no new idea of how to bring in prosperity to the state and the community. How to rally the Sikhs for the next challenges which would be more economic and social? This would need, not emotional or sentimental sloganeering, but intellectual and well thought out response. Punjab is in the grip of a crisis. Intellectuals in the community need to do some serious thinking. There is an urgent need to bring back the leadership, reinvent the competitive edge in areas of future potential such as computer literacy even though it seems already late. On the migration front the state needs to make arrangements on a bilateral basis with some countries that have vast agricultural lands needing development. The Bolivian type experience which failed needs to be made successful. The recent conference organized by the Central Minister of State, Ministry of External Affairs, Preneet Kaur in Patiala inviting African envoys to develop this theme needs an active follow up.

While Sikhs have done a good job to survive, they need a strategy to thrive. A focused approach is needed. Nothing less than a total revamp at a political, social and religious level is required.

One is happy to see a Sikh becoming the prime minister. The Sikh turban is now more known and accepted globally. With Manmohan Singh as the P.M. and Montek Singh Ahluwalia as his colleague, the stigma on Sikhs being non-intellectual, has been to a great extent diluted—one does not hear that often Sikh jokes now.

THE SIKH DIASPORA CONTRIBUTION

The Sikh Diaspora is engaged in some innovative ventures of reproduction of *Sikhi* and Punjabi language. When travelling in the Far East, I was particularly impressed with many gurdwaras undertaking measures for religious education. Thus in Singapore gurdwaras I was impressed by the work done by persons like Prof. Bhajan Singh. Sikh children there have access to CDs on the 'Gurus', 'family relationships' with interesting title like, 'Why Khalsa was Created'. These CDs are tastefully produced and set in melodious music making them very attractive to the younger generation of Sikhs. In many other countries there is strong awareness that our valuable traditions need to be adapted for the new world of internet and websites.

Similarly, almost all overseas gurdwaras hand out the script of the *shabads* being sung in Punjabi and Roman script making young Sikhs' participation possible. No longer they can complain they cannot understand what is going on in the gurdwaras! The display on large screens of the *shabads* being recited along with their translations into English, has brought a new dimension of participation of young Sikhs into community life.

During my visit to the new Southall Gurdwara, I was impressed by the general cleanliness and overall efficiency of the langar department. One could eat sitting on the floor, chairs or just standing and I got the impression that those persons serving the langar (and among them the majority were ladies as usual), showed a dedication and gentle gratitude—it was overall a remarkable experience. It suggested they were enjoying while serving—that is Sikhi to me.

I have seen many well-meaning Sikhs in the diaspora perhaps more than in Punjab proportionately, who are conveying the true Sikh message in an attractive and convincing manner. I should also clear my feeling on the 3HO and Yogi Harbhajan Singh's legacy abroad. There is some controversy surrounding him within the community. Instead of pointing an accusatory finger we should look within ourselves. I am convinced that the Yogi has given a morale boost to Sikhism through these converts. During the course of my travels, I had time to interview several followers of the Yogi in Brazil, Bolivia, and Mexico. There is much to be admired amongst them, though there might be some points of criticism too. The *Guru Granth Sahib* is available in Spanish language and for this 3HO has to be thanked. Should not the Sikhs welcome an addition to their numbers?

Some of the issues I have outlined should be addressed by the SGPC. Unfortunatly the SGPC has not been able to develop any meaningful relationship with the Sikh diaspora. The present set up of SGPC is totally inadequate to handle sensitive and important issues that a global Sikh faces both at individual and group level. SGPC does not command international respect nor does it has the capacity to articulate the Sikh concerns wherever and whenever they arise in any part of the globe from time to time.

Then there is basic work which is neglected by the SGPC. It has not prepared a list of overseas gurdwaras. Its website has nothing on overseas Sikhs—and rather in poor taste, all it contains is how to donate! It should get a country by country directory of gurdwaras and Sikh societies. Such basic reference works would mean better communication. And in era of internet communication, to undertake this task is fairly easy. The efforts of individuals in this area are to be commended.

Another major issue facing the Sikh community in Punjab is the extent of illegal migration abroad. *The Tribune*, and other daily papers of Punjab, periodically report how hundreds of Punjabi youths are lodged in jails in various countries on grounds that they have arrived there illegally. Besides well-known destinations, it is said countries like Sri Lanka, Algeria, Ukraine, Mali, Sudan, Malaysia, Thailand, Pakistan, Turkey, Morocco, Italy and Russia too have Punjabi prisoners on this account. According to the President of the Lok Bhalai Party, Balwant Singh Ramuwalia (*The Tribune*, 20 April 2007), there are an estimated 30,000 Punjabi youths in various jails across the world. Several hundreds have been killed while crossing the border from one country to another. 'According to statistics with the Regional Passport Office at Jalandhar, over one lakh residents from six districts of Jalandhar, Nawanshahr, Gurdaspur, Amritsar, Kapurthala and Hoshiarpur have either been deported or are facing deportation proceedings in different countries for travelling without valid travel documents over the last six years.' Most cases of deportation were referred by Indian embassies in Germany, Italy, the UAE, US and UK. In a new trend this 'cross-over brigade' is getting younger by the day. Some of the 40 immigrants, who performed the vanishing trick in New Zealand after entering the country as part of the pre-World Youth Day celebrations were as young as 16. Educational tours seem to have become a new avenue for illegal migration. Six students from Punjab, recently went on an educational tour to Germany and disappeared. Earlier, another group of six students, including two from Jalandhar, along with a woman teacher from Hoshiarpur district, went missing during a trip to NASA.

Will the proposed Punjab Prevention of Human Trafficking Act curtail the flight of these *kabootars*, and tighten the grip on the fraudulent agents?

MORE WORK NEEDED

Finally, more work needs to be done by scholars for a detailed study of the Sikh diaspora in these countries. The author fervently hopes that this challenge would be taken up by various Sikh Chairs in the Western world and others specializing in diaspora studies.

I would suggest that the Government of Punjab ought to have a special interest in the study of Sikh and Punjabi diaspora. I had put up a proposal for the study of Punjabi diaspora on the lines of the Singhvi High Level Commission and had even offered to do this in many countries at my own cost. Regrettably there was no response from the Punjab government.

Special discriminatory requirements for getting a visa for Sikhs visiting Ecuador need to be removed by approaching the Government of Ecuador by our Ministry of External Affairs. A small but important point regarding the issue of ID cards and driving licenses in many countries requiring Sikhs to take off the turban, needs attention from the Government of India.

APPENDIX 1

Methodology, Fieldwork and Interviews

1. SOME METHODOLOGY ISSUES

(A) Punjabi-Sikh-Singh

My initial plan was to have a broader canvas of studying the Punjabis. An issue regarding the Pakistani Punjabi cropped up as it was felt that their exclusion would be somewhat unfair. I have come across studies of Tamil and Bengali diasporas, wherein Sri Lankan or Bangladeshi migrants have been included in the study. It was therefore decided to confine the study to Sikhs, which made the subject more focused. In any case, it so happens, that a vast majority of immigrants in these countries except perhaps Panama (which has a large Gujarati and Sindhi community) were Sikhs. Amongst Punjabi migrants, Sikhs formed a major chunk. Defining a Sikh is not easy because there are various definitions by scholars, SGPC and government bodies. The issue of defining a Sikh can become an emotional issue. It was decided to include all persons of Sikh parentage at any level and those who had some affinity with Sikhism and Sikhs, now or in the past. It was decided not to get too much concerned with the number count as the idea was to introduce to the readers the historical and other aspects of the migrant stories.

(B) Non-availability of Secondary Data

Hardly any secondary data is available. Appendix 10 taken from High Level Committee Report of December 2001 by Government of India gives a broad picture of the Indian migration to Latin America. Besides desk survey of published literature, news items, articles and books, an extensive use of the internet was made to ferret out whatever information that could be gleaned. Internet searches were of some help but in most cases such leads did not fructify into concrete information. In some cases even marriage websites were tried with the cooperation of my lady secretary, but somewhat un-successfully. Indian restaurants, gurdwaras and even mosques were tried with hardly any useful leads. Only limited success was forthcoming. It was a great help that earlier migrants still use 'Singh' as their surname which made scanning of records including telephone directories somewhat easy.

(C) Response from Indian Embassies

Contact was also made with the Indian embassies abroad. Some help was forthcoming but the embassies have their own limitations. They generally do not go out proactively to look for 'Persons of Indian Origin' as defined by the Government of India but tend to confine themselves to those who either visit the embassies or those who invite the officials for some purpose—commercial or social. In these countries most of the Sikh migrants have got totally assimilated and hence the embassies do not have detailed information on PIOs. It can be noticed that the Government of India's High Level Committee, with large resources at their command, have not been able to get as much detailed information as my study would indicate.

(D) Overseas Visits and Field Interviews

While most of immigrants and their siblings were willing to be interviewed, some migrants were not agreeable to meet me but these were exceptions. With illegal immigrants such an attitude was understandable and expected. Annexed is a copy of the interview format which was intended to be used. But almost always the interviews had to be conducted in a very informal setting and with serious time limitation—a formal interview set-up was totally missing. Immigrants were more interested in social tete-a-tete as they had usually not met a turbaned Sikh from Punjab for a long time. In each country, the time available was a meagre 3–7 days and in many countries, visiting places other than the capital meant spending considerable time on internal travel.

A book on Panama's important immigrants and another on India–Mexico had some interesting references to Punjabis and

Sikhs. A few newspaper clippings were collected during my field visits.

(E) Punjab Villages

Visits were also made to some of the villages in Punjab from where the migrants had originally left. This was a useful experience. One met some 'returnees' from these countries, specially Argentina and Bolivia, who are now settled back in Punjab, to their comfort or otherwise.

(F) Some Challenges

The project was a personal study for which both time and money resources had to be mustered. It turned out to be an expensive but very satisfying venture!

The most difficult part was to locate the first few contacts in each country. From one or two initial contacts, some idea could be gleaned as to places needed to be visited and persons to be met. However, the real story unfolded only upon arrival. Pre-arrival contacts being limited, one had to improvise at all times to meet as many immigrants as feasible. One got more leads from whosoever one met and stories got developed like in the *Panchatantra*. The logistics of contacting persons on arrival and setting up meetings was a challenge.

Language was another barrier, both for interviewing people and for study of the limited documents and published literature. Spanish being the language of Latin America except in Brazil, where Portuguese is spoken.

Travel was not only expensive but had annoying elements such as getting visas as a tourist. Up to now I had travelled on business visas, which was relatively simple and easy because of the business contacts. However, getting a 'Tourist' visa met with general suspicion and disbelief, Latin American countries not being a popular destination with the Indian tourists. Because of the illegal migration, there seemed to be some kind of a racket expecting monetary incentive at embassies especially at the first level of contact employing Indian staff. Many Latin American countries require references to their Home Ministries for tourist visa clearance, which is time-consuming. Ecuador has a special requirement of 'Indian Police and Medical Clearance' for all Indian visitors. All Sikhs, even citizens of other countries, need visa—an act of discrimination no doubt. Travel to these far-off countries is not on the routine radar of travel agents in India and the information available with them is somewhat rudimentary. Visa issuing embassies require confirmed tickets and hotel reservations at the time of putting in the visa application. Considerable time and financial resources are needed to just get started. Let's face it, 'No one wants the Indians'. He must struggle at each step. This experience, however, did give me a glimpse of the plight of migrants who travelled with no language skills and meagre money in their pocket and with nothing to fall back on. This study is, in a small measure, a salute to these heroes.

2. FORMAT OF FIELD INTERVIEWS

(*Courtesy Saritha Selvan U.K.*)

General Introduction

Interviewer to explain to respondent the aim of the interview. It must be made clear to the respondent that information gathered during the interview may be used in the research paper, but names will be kept confidential, if desired by the interviewee.

Warm Up

Respondent must be made comfortable and told that the research was not judging the findings to be right or wrong. These are opinions and views and everyone is free to have their own views.

I. Original Immigrants

Q: According to the respondent, when did the first immigrants come to the country? (Interviewer *to include name of country accordingly*) In the respondent's view:

Q: When did they first come?

Q: Why did they choose to come to this country?
Q: What according to the respondent could have been their other choices?

II. Background

(The questions below are best asked in 3rd person)

Q: Who were they?
Q: What do you think made them take this decision?
Q: Do you think their families supported their decision? (*This question will lead to answers to how actually the respondents family reacts*)
Q: Was it a family decision? (*At times we do hear of people making sudden spontaneous decisions*)

III. Settling Down

Q: When they came here what did they do for a living?
Q: Had they planned their occupation before hand?
Q: Were they largely skilled people?
Q: Were they willing to take on any project?
Q: What according to you would have been the most difficult for these migrants? (*Probe: Language barrier, Acceptance, Jobs, Financial, etc.*)
Q: Did they ever face problems with maintaining Sikh symbols, e.g. turban, etc.
Q: Did they ever feel the need to take off the turban? (*Interviewer to ask this question if the respondent is wearing the turban. In case respondent is not wearing the turban, then ask:*)
Q: Why do you not wear a turban? Is it social pressure? Image issue? Difficult for society to accept you with a turban?

IV. Concerns

Q: Do you think the immigrants ever missed their homeland (Punjab)?
Q: Did you ever miss it?
Q: What were the views on returning back to India?
Q: Was it an option?

Q: Did the children ever go back (*Curiosity/To meet family*)?
Q: Did they feel like ever visiting India?
Q: Do they at times feel that they may have missed out? (*Probe: On what aspects—religion, culture, festivals, etc.*)

V. Second Generations

Q: How did their children adjust?
Q: What values were imparted to them?
Q: What religion do they follow?
Q: What festivals do they celebrate?
Q: How rooted are they?
Q: If you were to choose for the second generation, what value would you like them to hold on to? (*Probe: Certain Symbols, Religious Beliefs, Ethical, and Social*)

V. The followers (Later immigrants)

Q: Who came next?
Q: Were they the relatives of the first set of migrants?
Q: Were they marriage partners?
Q: Do you think news of their (i.e. the first migrants) success spread back home?
Q: What jobs/businesses have they taken up/set up?

VI. Onward to other destinations

Q: Do they/you have any plans to move out?
Q: If so, why? And where to?
Q: Do they/you have a final destination in mind? For example, USA or Canada?

VII. Ties with homeland and village

Q: How much of a link do you have with your homeland or village?
Q: How do you maintain these links?
Q: Is there constant contact with family in their respective villages?
Q: Do they ever visit? If so, how often? If not, why not?

Q: Do the people back home need any support or assistance (*Probe: Monetary, Old relatives, etc.*)

VIII. Current Profile of Respondent
(Interviewer to bring respondent back to the 'todays' world)

Q: How do you feel today? Do you think you have achieved all that you wanted?

Q: If you were to relive your past what changes would you make?

Q: Do you have any regrets?

Q: When you just arrived, there may have been difficult times, financial, emotional (*as have left family back home, etc.*). How do you find your situation now? (*Interviewer to gauge level of prosperity*).

Q: Have you made friends?, Do you take part/interest in local political issues?

IX. Social commitments

Q: Would you consider yourself active in the Punjabi/Sikh community?

Q: How often do you (*probe: respondent, family, children*) visit the gurdwara?

Q: Do you celebrate Sikh/Punjabi festivals?

Q: Are there any religious or community associations/groups that have regular meetings?

X. Future prospects & issues

Q: Many people work abroad, but when they retire they like to come back to their villages, what is your view on this? (*Probe*)

Q: Do you plan to stay on or do you have any plans on relocating to India.

XI. Interviewer to ask to see if possible the following

Photographs, documents, letters, old pamphlets, newsletters, notices, diaries, newspaper clippings, magazine write-ups:

Thank you: Interviewer to thank the respondent

3. LETTER SENT TO VARIOUS SIKHS AND OTHERS IN ARGENTINA IN SPANISH

Querido / a Sardar Sahib / Sardani Sahib,

Sat siri akal. He estado leyendo acerca de un pequeo grupo de inmigrantes Sikh en Argentina y estoy muy interesado en conocerlos y tal vez en escribir sobre ustedes como ejmplo de un emprendimiento Sikh. He tenido la suerte de conocer a una muy agradable y colaboradora joven ingeniera, Eugenia, proveniente de Buenos Aires. Actualmente ella está trabajando en Chandigarh y estaría volviendo a Argentina más adelante, en el presente año. Con el objeto de ayudarme ella accedió a contactarse con ustedes y con los otros inmigrantes Sikh a su regreso. Yo tengo planeado visitar la Argentina los primeros meses del año 2003 y conocer a la mayor cantidad posibles de los integrantes de la comunidad Sikh. Estaría interesado en conocer a varias generaciones de los primeros inmigrantes para trazar su árbol genealógico y los cambios sociales, económicos y culturales que son una parte integral del proceso inmigratorio en cualquier región. Me gustaría pedirles algo de ayuda y saber nsi podrían encontrarse con Eugenia y conmigo más adelante.

Necesitaría conocer la siguiente información de ustedes:

1. Nombre de los poblados, ciudad en Punjab de donde sean sus ancestros, familiares o amigos. Nombres, direcciones, teléfonos, fax, e-mail, etc de algún allegado o familiar que aún viva en el Punjab. Cualquier pequeña información o detalle que puedan darnos será bienvenida.
2. Nombre, dirección, teléfono, fax, e-mail de inmigrantes Sikh, sus hijos, familiares o amigos que estén en Argenina; especialmente aquellos con los que podamos comunicarnos mediante el correo electrónico.
3. Cualquier escrito o publicación sobre los inmigrantes Sikh en la Argentina.
4. Cualquier tipo de información acerca de inmigrantes Sikh en otros países sud o centroamericanos.

La razón por la que les pedimos esta información de sus hogares en Punjab es porque Eugenia y yo visitaremos sus poblados para hablar con personas que pudieran darnos información sobre sus antepasados. Nosotros también sacaremos fotografías de sus hogares natales y Eugenia o yo se las llevaremos a ustedes. Si existe algo más que ustedes quisieran del Punjab por favor siéntanse libres de avisarnos. Recientemente me ha llegado un ejemplar del Japji Sahib en castellano y estaría complacido en darles una copia del mismo.

Les estaré agradecido por recibir vuestras respuestas ya que me ayudarán a progresar en este proyecto, que es un emprendimiento puramente personal y no comercial.

Algunas palabras sobre mi: Soy ingeniero con un master en USA y he trabajado para una la sucursal en India de una compañía química multinacional de origen británico por treinta años antes de comprar una de sus subsidiarias. Nuestro centro de operaciones está principalmente en Bombay pero mi esposa Livleen y yo nos hemos mudado recientemente a Chandigarh aunque sigo visitando Bombay cuando es necesario. Tenemos un hijo, Gurtaj, que opera nuestra compañía desde Bombay y está casado con una joven europea. Nuestra hija, Mini, está asentada en San Francisco, USA.

Me despido esperando noticias vuestras.

Swarn Singh Kahlon

Ahora, algunas palabras de mi propia cosecha, es decir de la 'traductora'. Mi nombre completo es Maria Eugenia Cervantes Bolaño y egresé de la universidad de ingeniería mecánica el año pasado. He tenido la magnífica oportunidad de conseguir una pasantía en India por seis meses, que ya está llegando a su fin y la gran suerte de conocer a personas tan maravillosas como Swarn y Livleen.
Estoy muy entusiasmada con este proyecto y espero poder conocerlos pronto!

Eugenia

APPENDIX 2

Passports of Old Immigrants

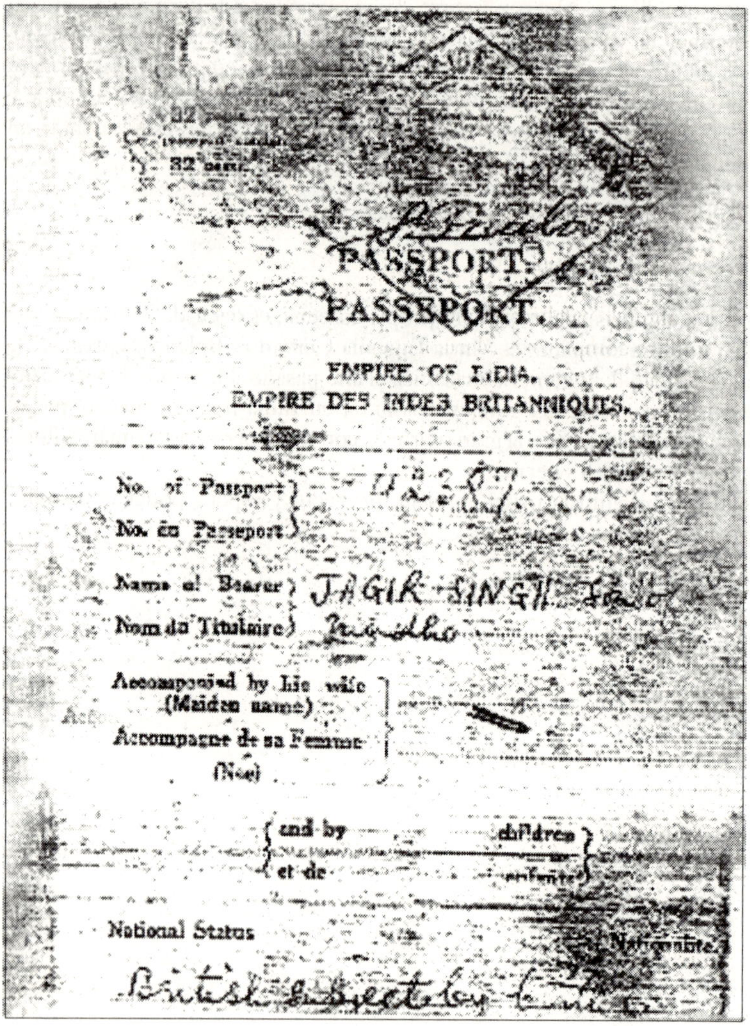

PASSPORT.

PASSEPORT.

EMPIRE OF INDIA.

EMPIRE DES INDES BRITANNIQUES.

No. of Passport }

No. du Passeport }

Name of Bearer } JAGIR SINGH

Nom du Titulaire } Madho

Accompanied by his wife (Maiden name)

Accompagné de sa Femme (Née)

and by children

et de enfants

National Status

Nationalité

British Subject by

A.1: Passport of Jagir Singh Madho—A British Subject

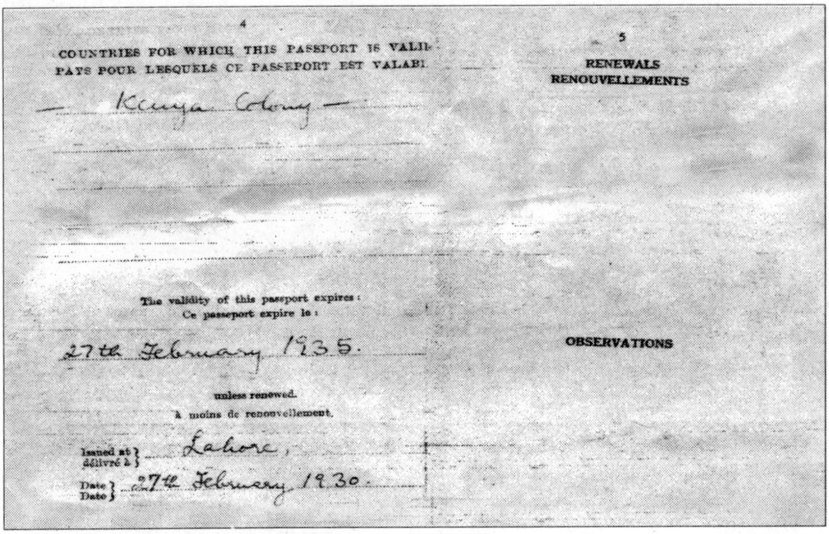

4

COUNTRIES FOR WHICH THIS PASSPORT IS VALID
PAYS POUR LESQUELS CE PASSEPORT EST VALABLE

Kenya Colony

The validity of this passport expires:
Ce passeport expire le:

27th February 1935.

unless renewed.
à moins de renouvellement.

Issued at / délivré à: Lahore,
Date / Date: 27th February 1930.

5

RENEWALS
RENOUVELLEMENTS

OBSERVATIONS

A.2: Passport of Jagir Singh Madho—Issued at Lahore on 27-2-1930, valid for travel to Kenya (he presumably changed his mind to travel to South America instead)

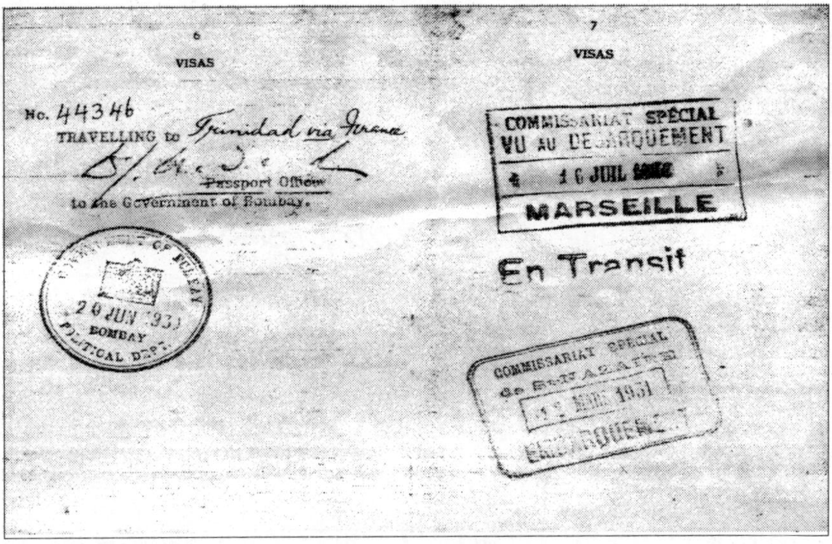

6

VISAS

No. 44346
TRAVELLING to Trinidad via France
Passport Officer
to the Government of Bombay.

20 JUN 1931
BOMBAY
POLITICAL DEPT.

7

VISAS

COMMISSARIAT SPÉCIAL
VU AU DÉBARQUEMENT
16 JUIL
MARSEILLE

En Transit

COMMISSARIAT SPÉCIAL
1931

A.3: Passport of Jagir Singh Madho—Endorsement of 20-6-1931 for travel to Trinidad via France. Transit stamp of Marseille 16-7-1931. Another stamp of 1931 not clear

A.4: Passport of Jagir Singh Madho—Another endorsement for travel to Cayman 8-8-1931, in transit to Brazil. Another stamp of British Guinea. One more stamp not clear

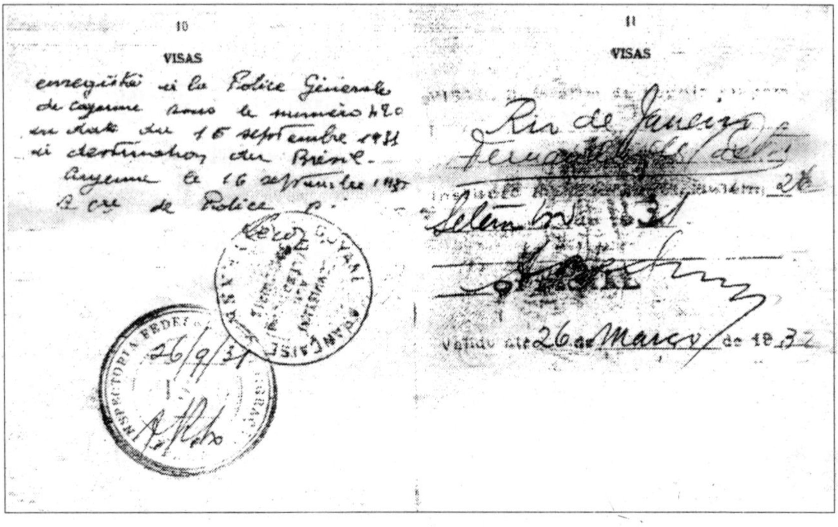

A.5: Passport of Jagir Singh Madho—Arrival in Cayman 16-9-1931. Gets a 6 month visa on 16-9-1931 for travel to Rio de Janeiro, Brazil from where he presumably crossed over to Argentina

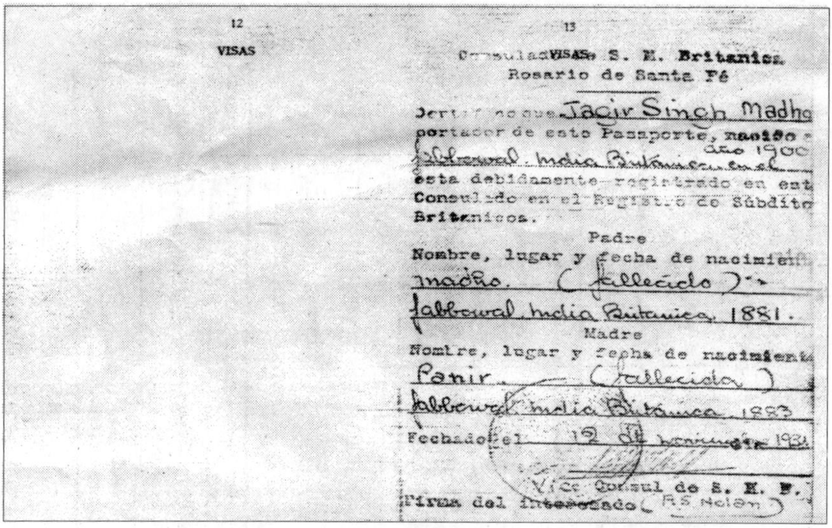

12 VISAS

13

Consulado de S. M. Britanica
Rosario de Santa Fé

Certifico que Jagir Singh Madho
portador de este Passaporte, nacido año 1900
Jabbowal, India Britanica en el
esta debidamente registrado en este
Consulado en el Registro de Súbditos
Britanicos.

Padre
Nombre, lugar y fecha de nacimiento
Madho. (fallecido)
Jabbowal, India Britanica, 1881.

Madre
Nombre, lugar y fecha de nacimiento
Panir. (fallecida)
Jabbowal, India Britanica, 1883

Fechado el 12 de noviembre 1931

Vice Consul de S. M. B.

Firma del interesado (R S Nolan)

A.6: Passport of Jagir Singh Madho—Father's name—Madho, Mother's name–Panir

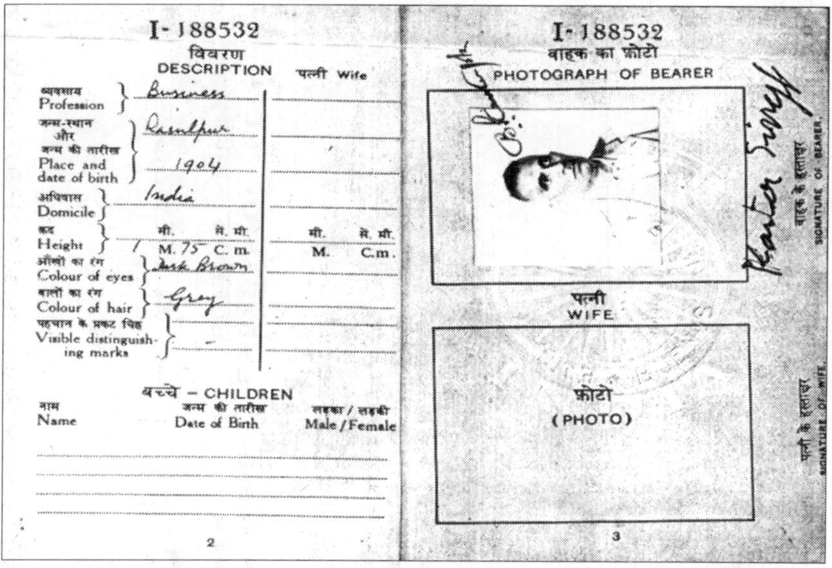

I- 188532
विवरण
DESCRIPTION पत्नी Wife

		पत्नी Wife
व्यवसाय Profession	Business	
जन्म-स्थान और जन्म की तारीख Place and date of birth	Rasulpur 1904	
अधिवास Domicile	India	
कद Height	मी. 1 M. 75 सें.मी. C.m.	मी. M. सें.मी. C.m.
आँखों का रंग Colour of eyes	Dark Brown	
बालों का रंग Colour of hair	Grey	
पहचान के प्रकट चिह्न Visible distinguishing marks	–	

बच्चे – CHILDREN

नाम Name	जन्म की तारीख Date of Birth	लड़का / लड़की Male/Female

2

I- 188532
वाहक का फ़ोटो
PHOTOGRAPH OF BEARER

वाहक के हस्ताक्षर SIGNATURE OF BEARER: Kartar Singh

पत्नी WIFE

फ़ोटो (PHOTO)

पत्नी के हस्ताक्षर SIGNATURE OF WIFE

3

B.1: Passport of Kartar Singh—village Rasulpur (Tehsil Jagraon, Distt. Ludhiana). Profession—Business. Born 1904, grey hair, 1.75 metres tall. (Evidently educated as he could sign nicely)

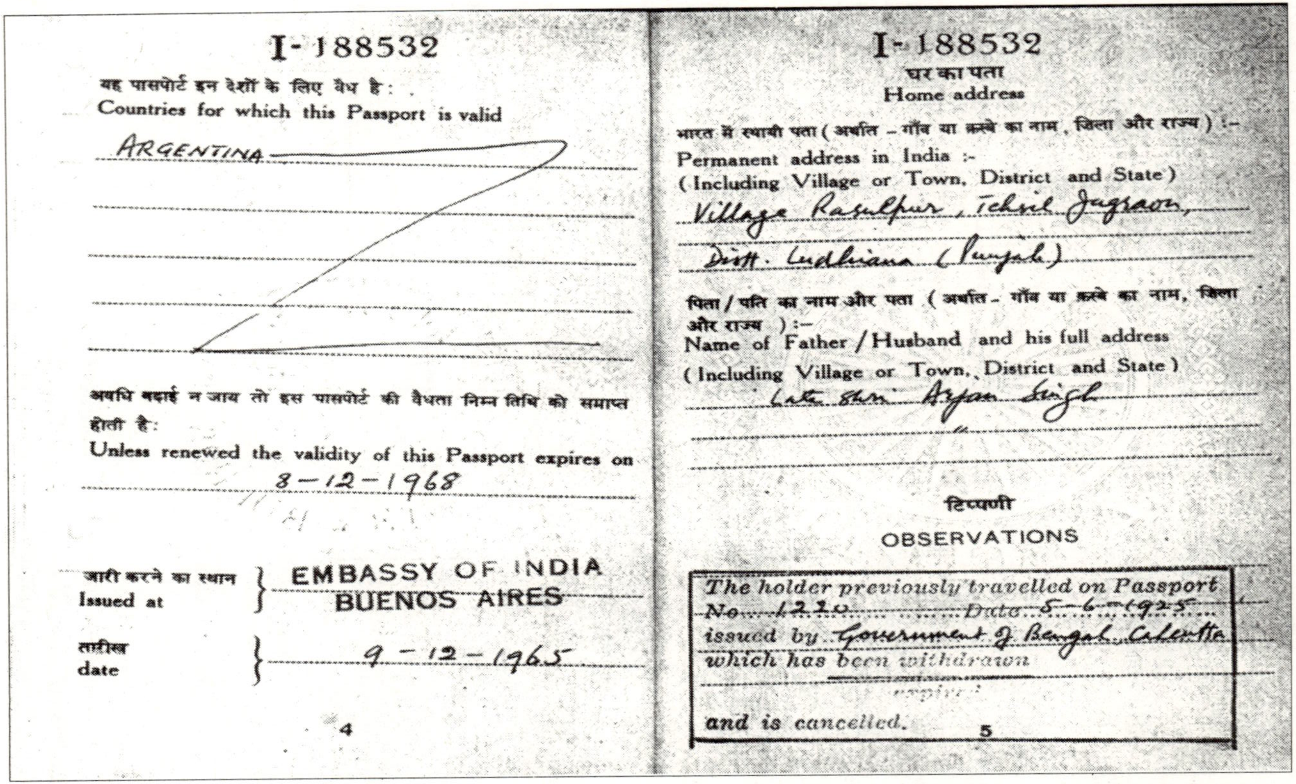
I-188532

यह पासपोर्ट इन देशों के लिए वैध है :
Countries for which this Passport is valid

ARGENTINA

अवधि बढ़ाई न जाय तो इस पासपोर्ट की वैधता निम्न तिथि को समाप्त होती है:
Unless renewed the validity of this Passport expires on
8-12-1968

जारी करने का स्थान
Issued at } EMBASSY OF INDIA BUENOS AIRES

तारीख
date } 9-12-1965

4

I-188532
घर का पता
Home address

भारत में स्थायी पता (अर्थात – गाँव या क़स्बे का नाम, ज़िला और राज्य) :–
Permanent address in India :-
(Including Village or Town, District and State)
Village Rasulpur, Tehsil Jagraon,
Distt. Ludhiana (Punjab)

पिता / पति का नाम और पता (अर्थात – गाँव या क़स्बे का नाम, ज़िला और राज्य) :–
Name of Father / Husband and his full address
(Including Village or Town, District and State)
Late Shri Arjan Singh

टिप्पणी
OBSERVATIONS

The holder previously travelled on Passport No. 1220 Date 5-6-1925 issued by Government of Bengal, Calcutta which has been withdrawn expired and is cancelled.

5

B.2: Passport of Kartar Singh—issued 9-12-1965 valid for 3 yrs for travel to Argentina. Father's name Late Arjan Singh. Holder previously travelled on Passport no. 1220 dated 5-6-1925, isued by the Government of Bengal, Calcutta. (Shows he travelled from Calcutta in 1925)

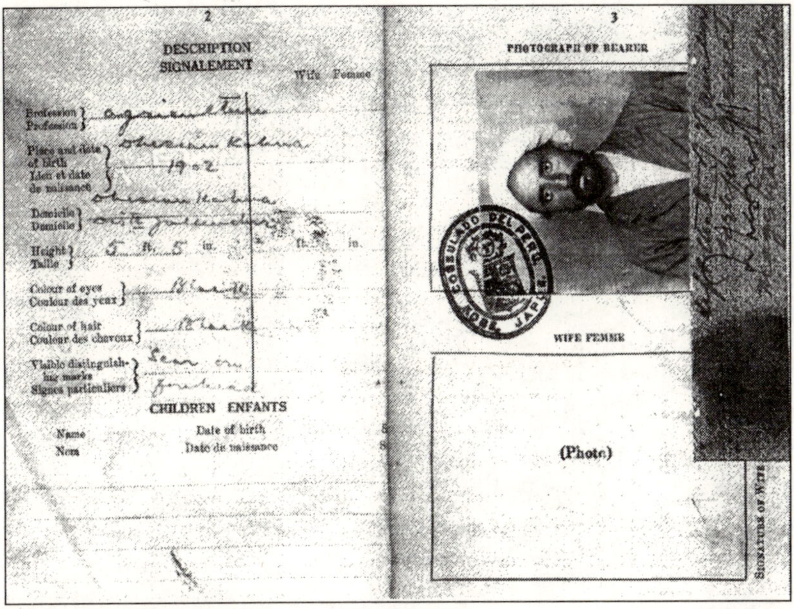

2

DESCRIPTION
SIGNALEMENT

Wife Femme

Profession / Profession

Place and date of birth / Lieu et date de naissance

Domicile / Domicile

Height / Taille — 5 ft. 5 in. — ft. in.

Colour of eyes / Couleur des yeux

Colour of hair / Couleur des cheveux

Visible distinguishing marks / Signes particuliers

CHILDREN ENFANTS

Name / Nom — Date of birth / Date de naissance

3

PHOTOGRAPH OF BEARER

WIFE FEMME

(Photo)

SIGNATURE OF WIFE

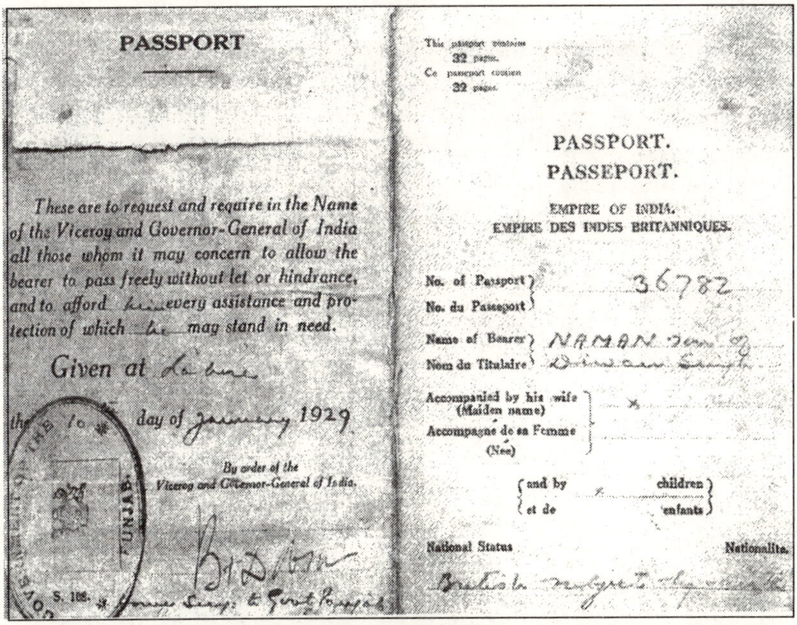

PASSPORT

These are to request and require in the Name of the Viceroy and Governor-General of India all those whom it may concern to allow the bearer to pass freely without let or hindrance, and to afford every assistance and protection of which may stand in need.

Given at

the 10 day of 1929

By order of the Viceroy and Governor-General of India.

S. 186.

This passport contains 32 pages.
Ce passeport contient 32 pages.

PASSPORT.
PASSEPORT.

EMPIRE OF INDIA.
EMPIRE DES INDES BRITANNIQUES.

No. of Passport / No. du Passeport — 36782

Name of Bearer / Nom du Titulaire — NAMAN

Accompanied by his wife (Maiden name) / Accompagné de sa Femme (Née)

and by children / et de enfants

National Status — Nationalité

C.1 & 2: Passport of Naman s/o Diwan issued at Lahore 10-1-1929. Date of birth 1902. Profession—Agriculture, ht 5 ft-5 in. Stamp on photo appears of Japan

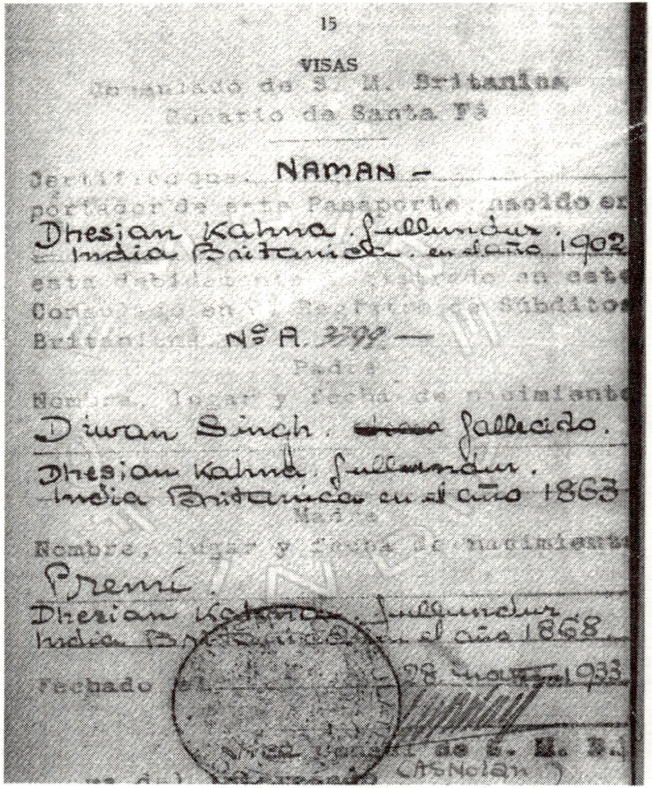

15

VISAS

Consulado de S. M. Britanica
Rosario de Santa Fé

NAMAN —
Dhesian Kahma. Jullundur
India Britanica en el año 1902
Nº A. 3799 —
Padre
Diwan Singh. fallecido.
Dhesian Kahma. Jullundur.
India Britanica en el año 1863
Madre
Nombre, lugar y fecha de nacimiento
Premi.
Dhesian Kahma. Jullundur
India Britanica en el año 1868
Fechado el 28 marzo 1933

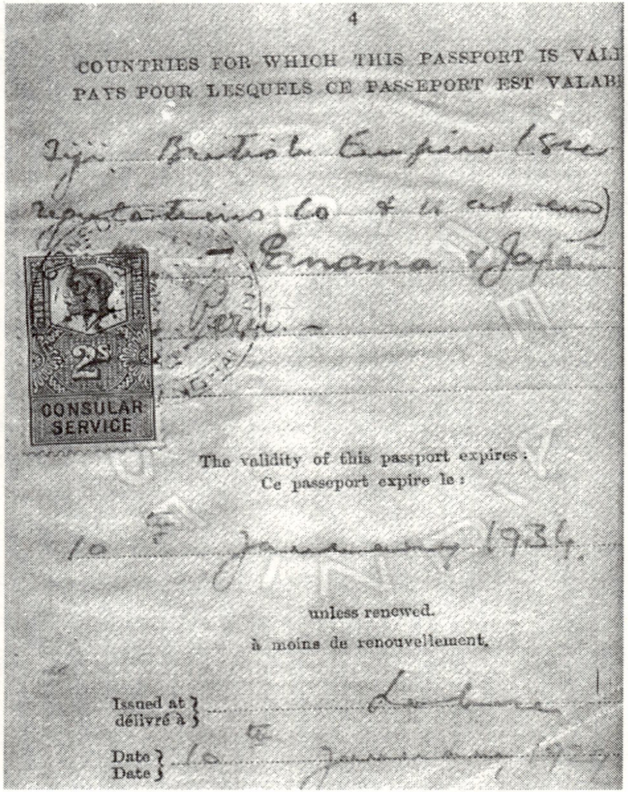

4

COUNTRIES FOR WHICH THIS PASSPORT IS VALI
PAYS POUR LESQUELS CE PASSEPORT EST VALAB

The validity of this passport expires:
Ce passeport expire le:

10 January 1934.

unless renewed.
à moins de renouvellement.

Issued at / délivré à
Date / Date 10

C.3 & 4: Passport of Naman of Dhesian Kahma, Jullundhur—for travel to Fiji, Panama, Japan and Peru. Evidently not clear where he was heading. Travelled from India via Pacific not Atlantic

APPENDIX 3A

Newspaper Articles on Sikhs in Argentina

Please note in old photos, all Sikhs have turbans which are totally missing in recent photos.

Feb 16 10 03:12p Raj and Mini +1.415.647.7920 p.1

The Hindostanic Inmigration in the Republic of Argentina

by - Dr Jacobino Sierra

DR. OF MEDICINE SIERRA E IGLESIAS JOBINO P
MITRE 203
SAN PEDRO de Jujuy, 4500
Tel. (~~0388~~)(03 884) 420494

LA INMIGRACION HINDOSTANICA EN LA REPUBLICA ARGENTINA

Fué realizada por los siks(sik significa discípulo),también se los denomina sijs o sikhs,pertenecen a una secta religiosa que practica la religión llamada Sikhismo,que habitaba en el Noroeste de la India y Norte de Pakistán,en el antiguo Punjab.Se los considera de raza indoaria.(Fig.Nª 1,Fig.Nª 2 y Fig.Nª 3).

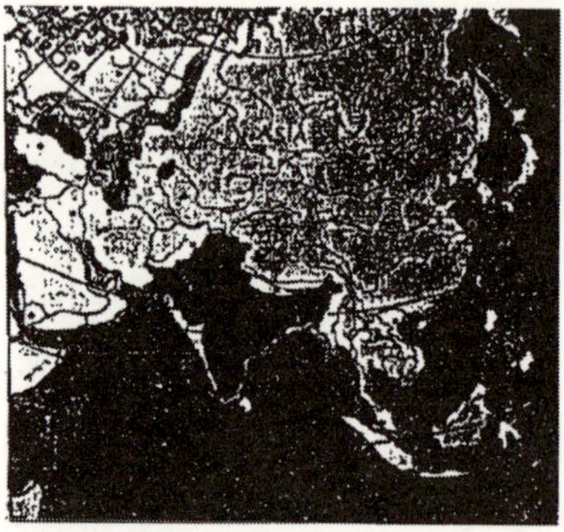

Fig. Nª 1.Ubicación de la Península Hindostánica(Pakistán, India y Bangladesh)en el Continente Asiático.

Fig. Nª 2.El antiguo Punjab comprendía territorios de India y Pakistán y abarcabala región de los cinco grandes ríos afluentes del Río Indo.

al comercio mayorista de venta de granos y comestibles en general. De sus descendientes algunos cumplen actividades comerciales de venta de alimentos al por mayor, los hay empresarios de transporte, empleados calificados, maestros normales, profesores de enseñanza secundaria, profesionales universitarios.

Todos los siks en la Argentina llevan el apellido Singh, esto es debido a que es costumbre entre ellos agregarse Singh, nombre que perteneció al Gurú Govind Rai Singh, como segundo nombre y no usar su apellido salvo en contadas ocasiones, por lo cual en nuestro país el nombre Singh ha reemplazado el apellido en todos ellos.

Si bien la inmigración hindostánica fué pequeña en su número, en comparación con las de otras nacionalidades, ha sido un núcleo muy activo y trabajador, respetuoso de las leyes y tradiciones de su país de adopción, que dejó una descendencia laboriosa y pujante que honra a la República Argentina.

En 1982 se constituyó en Centro Hindoargentino con sede en la ciudad de San Pedro de Jujuy. (Fig. Nº 5).

Fig. Nº 5. Hindues y sus descendientes festejando un aniversario de la independencia de la India en San Pedro de Jujuy.

lgunos nombres de inmigrantes siks:
hakar, Rakha, Chanan, Surjit, Santan, Guardial, Sukhvinder, Gurdava, Visa, Karta-a, Dhan, Naman, Mali, Bhana, Piara, Kamar, Charan, Balour, Kuldip, Atma.

lgunos apellidos de inmigrantes siks:
haliwal, Grewal, Sidhu, Brar, Bassi, Rai, Gil, Dhilon, Dhangal, Dhinjal.

de la primera contienda,que eran de propiedad de inglesas.

Durante los años 1932/33 los siks alcanzaron su máximo número en el país, llegando a ser alrededor de 400,distribuídos aproximadamente así:Prov.de Jujuy,80 en Ingenio La Esperanza (San Pedro de Jujuy),30 en Ingenio Ledesma(hoy Libertador Gral.San Martín),10 en Ingenio Río Grande(la Mendieta) e igual número en la Capital;Prov.de Salta,30 en la ciudad Capital y otros tantos repartidos entre las localidades de Tartagal,Orán y Rosario de la Frontera;Prov.de Tucumán,50 a 60 trabajaron entre San Miguel de Tucumán y los ingenios azucareros;Prov. Santa Fe,50 a 60 se emplearon en los talleres ferroviarios en Rosario;Prov.de Córdoba,cerca de un centenar se estableció en la Capital;algunos otros se ocuparon en los FF.CC.Roca,San Martín y Belgrano.(Fig.Nº 4).

Fig.Nº 4.Hindúes en el Ingenio La Esperanza(Prov.de Jujuy).
Década del veinte.

a mayoría de los siks realizaron trabajos rurales como los que practica-
an en su tierra,otros se ocuparon como maquinistas,serenos,empleados en
errocarriles,también fueron vendedores al menudeo y ambulantes.

omo consecuencia de la independencia de la India del dominio inglés,mu-
hos regresaron a su patria,otros fallecieron con el correr del tiempo,
on lo cual el grupo originario quedó en el presente reducido a alrededor
e 60,distribuídos aproximadamente de este modo:San Pedro de Jujuy(12),Ro-
ario de la Frontera (30),Santa Fe (10),Capital Federal (10).

la actualidad ninguno tiene las actividades del comienzo, se dedican

Si bien el idioma oficial de la India es el hindi, desde 1949 entre los dialectos reconocidos por la Constitución figura el penjabi, lengua que hablan en 1984 la creencia sik fué aceptada como religión separada.

En la actualidad la mayoría vive en el Estado de Punjab Oriental, pero los hay distribuídos por todo el país, en especial en los estados vecinos al Punjab Oriental, como Haryana, Uttar Pradesh, Jamu y Kasmir, Rajasthan, Delhi y Maharashtra; hay también un grupo grande en Bengala (Calcuta). Fuera de la India comunidades siks de importancia se desarrollan en Canadá, Sud Africa, Gran Bretaña, EE.UU. y Sudeste asiático (Singapur y Hong Kong).

La inmigración hindostánica a nuestro país, que se hizo solamente con hombres, fué discontínua, por grupos, que vinieron en épocas diferentes.

Alrededor de 1910 llegaron los primeros siks a la Argentina, como la mayoría de los inmigrantes arribados a nuestra tierra, lo hicieron en busca de mejores horizontes económicos, también hubo los que se habían visto precisados a dejar su patria por cuestiones políticas, por oposición a la dominación extranjera.

Habían oído hablar en su tierra de América, que confundían con Norteamérica, sin saber que en América había otros paises. Se embarcaban generalmente por el puerto de Bombay, sobre el Mar Arábico. situado como a 1500 Km. de su lugar de orígen. Así llegaron a EE.UU. donde a la mayoría no se les permitió desembarcar, los buques al seguir su itinerario los dejaron en las Antillas, ros a través del Canal de Panamá alcanzaron Perú y atravesando Bolivia, mino que realizaron en gran parte a pie, salvo el Lago Titicaca, arribaron la Argentina por La Quiaca. Para otros, tal vez la mayoría, el destino fué puerto de Buenos Aires y por el F.C.C.N.A. (hoy Belgrano) llegaron a las iones central y noroeste del país, hubo luego quienes alcanzaron el puerto de Rosario en la Prov. de Santa Fe y también a pie llegaron a las Prov. de umán, Salta y Jujuy.

primeros en arribar se contactaron con sus familiares y amigos y así se nsificó su radicación.

nte la primera guerra mundial muchos siks fueron utilizados por el eito inglés como soldados de ultramar y como ayudantes en el transporte ateriales, esto les dió un más amplio conocimiento del mundo; pasada la enda el ejército británico les proveyó de certificados de buena con-, donde los recomendaba para que fueran empleados por compañías ingle- or eso los encontramos en ingenios azucareros y ferrocarriles después niendo a cinco representantes de las distintas castas y bebiendo con ellos el caldo uno a continuación de otro, en dos oportunidades, significando con esto que no había separación de los hombres en castas, y que el sik forma parte de una gran comunidad. Recordemos que el vedismo dividía la población en castas, y que prohibía al individuo de una casta beber en el mismo vaso con el de una casta diferente.

Govind Rai Singh construyó el Templo Sagrado, de techo de oro, centro de la religión, en la ciudad de Amrisart, dentro del lago de la inmortalidad, lago rodeado de una gran vereda donde se levantaron también otros templos menores dedicados a Gurúes sobresalientes; así mismo tuvo la necesidad de darle a la secta un carácter guerrero, ya que le tocó actuar durante el período del Gran Mogol Aurangzeb, donde fueron objeto de encarnizadas persecuciones, estableciendo que el sik devoto debía dejarse crecer la barba y el cabello, colocándose en éste un turbante para protegerlo, como así usar pantalón y capa o manto azules, sable y brazalete de metal, también prohibió el alcohol y el tabaco.

Con el tiempo se formó una comunidad que conservó una independencia política hasta ser sometidos, tras cruenta lucha, por el ejército inglés en 1849, entrando entonces a formar parte de la India Inglesa.

Fueron los mejores soldados de las tropas británicas de la India y hoy también del nuevo ejército de su patria, del que forman el 15 %, donde los siks son quince millones, en un país que cuenta con setecientos veinte millones de habitantes. Ocupan una parte muy importante de los cargos políticos, el actual Presidente de la República de la India es un sik.

Desde su origen los siks habitaron las llanuras del Río Indo, pero desde la separación de la India de Pakistán, la frontera está alejada de este curso de agua, su antigua capital Lahore quedó en territorio pakistaní y debieron fundar una nueva llamada Chandigart.

Se dedican a la agricultura, siendo sus principales cultivos: trigo, cebada, maíz, centeno, legumbres y caña de azúcar. Son vegetarianos pero no les está prohibido por religión comer carne; activos trabajadores soportan con resignación los malos trances, el sufrimiento dentro de la religión es una lógica, la familia es patriarcal, no existiendo marcada diferencia económica entre ellos, pero forman parte de una clase media en constante ascenso; deciden los acontecimientos políticos más importantes por asamblea pública, el consejo de los ancianos es tenido muy en cuenta, en general son lon-

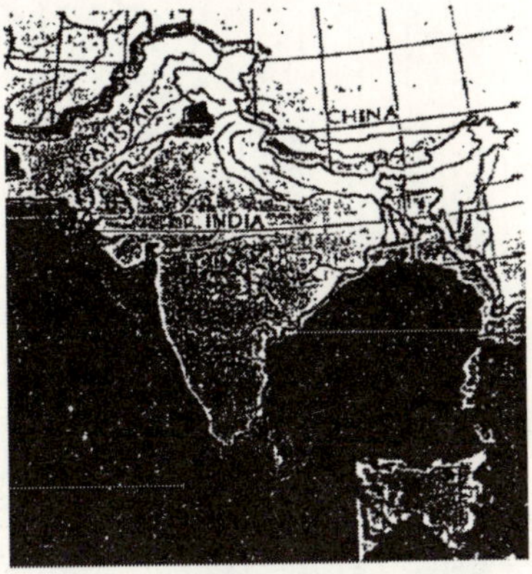

Fig.Nª 3.El actual Estado de Punjab Oriental dentro de la República de la India.

SIKHISMO O NANEKISMO

Es una religión comparativamente joven,fundada alrededor del año 1500,por el reformista religioso Nanak o Nanek(1469-1538)en el antíguo Punjab(llamado también Panyab,Penyab,Penjab,Punjabi,y que en su lengua significa País de los Cinco Ríos),tomando elementos de las antíguas religiones regionales (hinduismo e islamismo),pero dándole una individualidad propia.Recibió él y sus sucesores el nombre de Gurú(en sánscrito significa mestro para predicar la religión),al Gurú se lo considera representante de Dios en la Tierra,a la muerte pasa a ser una divinidad.La religión es monoteista,creen en Dios como ser supremo,universal,todopoderoso y verdadero;no aceptan la reencarnación,ya que consíderan que con la muerte desaparece el indivíduo, a sus adeptos les está prohibido adorar imágenes,acostumbran cremar los cadáveres.

Los acontecimientos más destacados en la vida de un sik,nacimiento,bautismo,casamiento,muerte y las principales festividades,giran en torno a la vida religiosa,la que constituye el núcleo central de su existencia,convirtiéndose en el móvil de todas sus actividades;la religión insiste en la futilidad de los ritos y ensalza la humildad y sinceridad.

Los sucesores de Nanak predicaron sus doctrinas en letra y espíritu.

En el siglo XVII,el décimo Gurú Govind Rai Singh realizó algunas reformas, reunió las enseñanzas del fundador en un libro sagrado llamado Granth Sahib(sublime libro),cuya lectura y rezos se usan en las ceremonias religiosas.También instituyó el bautismo con un caldo azucarado(néctar),reu-

APPENDIX 3B

Newspaper article on Sikhs: 'Los Gauchos Hindues'

(English translation in the text under the chapter 'Sikhs in Argentina'

LOS GAUCHOS HINDUES

Son doce familias sikh. En Ciudad Güemes, Salta, se debaten entre costumbres ancestrales y argentinas

Sonia Mónica (7) y Franco Alberto (5). Más argentinos que sikh.

Los mayores apenas hablan el castellano, los menores apenas hablan el hindú. Preparan empanadas salteñas, pero con pollo para no romper la prohibición de comer carne vacuna. Son una extraña mezcla de costumbres indias y argentinas.

Mil novecientos veinticuatro. Estado de Punjab, India. Bark Singh no había podido dormir en toda la noche. Cada segundo que pasaba le parecía único e interminable. Con los primeros rayos del sol se levantó, lavó su cara, y leyó una vez más algunos párrafos del Guru Garanth Sahib, el libro religioso de los sikh. Luego desayunó en silencio, observando a su mujer y a sus hijos como si fuese la última vez.

Y en cierta medida, no estaba muy lejos de la verdad. Tuvieron que pasar muchos años hasta que volviese a ver esos mismos rostros.

Poco después de aquel desayuno, Bark Singh tomó un tren que lo condujo hacia el puerto donde un barco lo estaba esperando con rumbo a Cuba. Tres años estuvo en la isla y volvió a emigrar hacia el extremo sur del continente americano. Lo recibió un país cuyo nombre apenas podía pronunciar y del que sólo sabía que era pródigo en tierras muy similares a las de su Punjab natal. Agricultor había sido y agricultor quería ser. Bark Singh, de tez oscura, túnica larga, turbante y una barba interminable, miró la tierra nueva y pensó: "Esto es lo que estaba buscando". Corría 1927 y había llegado a la provincia de Salta. Allí se quedó hasta el día de su muerte, cincuenta y siete años después.

Bark no fue el primer indio

36 SIETE DIAS

En la Argentina hay ciento treinta indios y ciento setenta descendientes, ubicados en la provincias de Salta, Tucumán y Jujuy.

en venir a la Argentina, pero llegó a ser uno de los más antiguos y prestigiosos. Tuvo una finca en Ojo de Agua, cerca de la frontera salteña con Jujuy, que hoy pertenece a sus descendientes. Se había especializado sobre todo en el cultivo de tabaco, de la variedad Virginia, siendo tan buena la calidad que parte de la producción era destinada a la exportación. Cierta vez, incluso, un gobernador, luego de varias décadas, lo felicitó por el trabajo que había realizado.

"Mi padre amaba esta tierra –recuerda hoy su hijo Bikram, 67–, decía que era el mejor país del mundo. Tuvieron que pasar cincuenta años para que se decidiese volvera a Punjab a visitar familiares, y no se demoró mucho en regresar.

Cuando murió, a los 85 años, todavía estaba vital. Hacía solo sus compras y su aseo y mantenía ciertas actividades. Le gustaba ir con los evangelistas porque decía que había muchos puntos en común entre las dos religiones, como eso de no fumar, no beber, etcétera. Al punto que hasta el día de su muerte mantuvo las dos religiones. Siempre decía que al morir había que hacer lo que dijesen los evangelistas. Y así se hizo."

Bikram Singh es actualmente el patriarca de la familia y el más anciano de los que viven en Ciudad Güemes. Su padre lo había hecho venir en 1963, cuando tenía 44 años, ya que en estas tierras no contaba con herederos. A los tres años volvió a la India y regresó nuevamente en 1969. En 1973 hizo venir a su mujer Gurdes Kaur y sus dos hijos varones. Pocos años después llegaron sus dos hijas, con lo que se completó la familia.

Los comienzos para Bikram fueron algo duros. "A los pocos días de venir quería regresar a mi tierra. No conocía a nadie acá, no entendía la lengua ni las costumbres de los habitantes del lugar. Y encima me aburría y extrañaba a mi familia. Pero acá estaba, con un trabajo y la perspectiva de tener tierras propias con el correr del tiempo. Mientras en mi país, a miles de kilómetros, la situación era más difícil. Luego la Argentina empezó a gustarme."

Los Singh fueron agricultores hasta 1978, en que juntamente con las otras familias indias de la región decidieron arrendar sus tierras y mudarse a Ciudad Güemes para dedicarse al comercio. El campo les brindó la posibilidad de crecer económicamente y ganar seguridad, pero las nuevas generaciones reclamaban una actividad más tranquila y cercana a la ciudad, donde podrían encarar nuevos negocios y sus hijos iniciar sus estudios. La gran mayoría de las diez o doce familias indias de Ciudad Güemes actualmente se dedican al rubro alimentación. También los Singh, que tienen un almacén y una panadería.

"Yo también soy sikh, pero ya tengo las costumbres de los de acá"

Con la mudanza y el paso del tiempo la vida se les fue haciendo más sedentaria y las costumbres cambiaron de a poco. Bikram se jubiló por la Caja de Autónomos y hoy se dedica a descansar. Por la mañana lee algo de religión, hace las compras para su mujer, camina un poco, pasea en bicicleta y conversa con los vecinos. "Con los argentinos nos llevamos bien, siempre fueron respetuosos con nosotros. Aquí tengo muchos amigos, ellos me invitan a comer y yo los invito a ellos." Su yerno,

Bikram Singh y su mujer Gurdes Kaur, los bastiones de la tradición sikh.

¿Quiénes son los sikh?

Con sus catorce millones de miembros, los sikh componen apenas el dos por ciento de la población de la India, pero tienen una notable influencia en el comercio, la milicia y el transporte. Cobraron fama mundial en 1984, cuando algunos de sus integrantes asesinaron a la primera ministra Indira Gandhi.

La religión sikh nació a fines del siglo XV por iniciativa de Guru Nanak, quien buscó un camino intermedio para acabar con las disputas entre hindúes y musulmanes. Los sikh creen en un solo Dios pero repudian el sistema de castas. No fuman, no beben alcohol ni se cortan el pelo o la barba en señal de pureza.

Entre otras cosas, en su país reclaman que Amritsar sea declarada ciudad santa, que no se venda tabaco, alcohol ni carne en los alrededores del templo Dorado y que se permita a los sikh viajar en avión con el kirpan (el puñal sagrado).

La mayoría de los indios de Ciudad Güemes fueron agricultores hasta hace unos años y hoy se dedican al comercio en el rubro alimentación.

Los sikh no fuman, no beben alcohol ni se cortan el pelo o la barba.

Jasvir Kaur (28), maneja los negocios familiares.

Cada tanto se reúnen algunos miembros de la colectividad en la "capilla" que tienen en su casa. Bikram lee algunas oraciones y el resto reza a su alrededor. Finalmente reparten un dulce preparado con harina, azúcar y manteca en partes iguales. La cocinera es Gurdes Kaur (57),su mujer, quien como en cualquier familia occidental es la "dueña y señora" de la casa.

Gurdes invierte buena parte del tiempo tratando de preparar comida india pese a que no siempre consigue los elementos necesarios. De la Argentina prefiere las cosas dulces, aunque cada tanto hace empanadas salteñas pero con pollo, ya que la carne de vaca está prohibida para los sikh.

El mayor de sus hijos hace un par de años se fue a vivir a Inglaterra donde existe una colectividad hindú muy importante desde los tiempos en que la India era una colonia del imperio. El resto de los hijos permanece en Salta. Rajinder (31), la mayor, consiguió marido por "correo" desde la Argentina. Aunque tal método pueda resultar extraño aquí, para ellos es una manera de resolver la obtención de pareja en una colectividad tan pequeña. Entonces escribió y mandó su foto para que algunos familiares se encargasen de buscar la persona adecuada. Finalmente apareció Jasvir Kaur, quien también envió su foto. Entonces el matrimonio se concretó y actualmente ambos tienen dos hijos argentinos con nombres locales: Sonia Mónica (7) y Franco Alberto (5).

Rajinder atiende la panadería de *Nueva Delhi*, en donde cotidianamente tienen la oportunidad de contactarse con argentinos. "La gente es muy buena aquí, nos llevamos muy bien –explica–. A veces,cuando llegan los clientes,escuchan música de la India y nos empiezan a preguntar cosas. Sobre todo les interesa saber cómo se vive allá."

Satnam Singh, el menor de los hijos, nació en la India hace 19 años,pero vino aquí cuando tenía 5. "Yo también soy sikh, pero tengo las costumbres de los de acá –dice–. En la India es normal que uno tenga la barba larga,pero aquí me sentiría incómodo. A mi padre no le molesta que me afeite, pero sí que fume o que tome alcohol. A veces también como carne." Satnam hizo todos los estudios en la Argentina y rompiendo la tradición familiar de ser agricultores –que por otra parte fue abandonada cuando se mudaron a la ciudad– piensa estudiar medicina para ejercer en Salta. "Y si es posible acá, en Güemes."

Habla el castellano con cierto acento, pero mejor que cualquiera de sus familiares mayores. Sus mejores amigos son argentinos y con ellos se divierte. Habitualmente juega al fútbol y sonríe cuando dice con cierto orgullo: "¡No sé si soy bueno como los argentinos,pero al menos nunca me sacan de titular!" Su madre no se opone a que converse con chicas argentinas, pero sí a que la relación pueda ir más allá. "No me gustaría que se case con una argentina –reconoce–. Yo no entiendo bien el castellano y no podría conversar con ella. Además,allá las mujeres no se cortan el pelo, no tienen vicios, nada..."

De juegos, de películas e indios que sólo hablan castellano

Los hindúes de Ciudad de Güemes no suelen reunirse en fiestas ni para jugar, aunque es frecuente que se visiten los fines de semana y conversen sobre la marcha de sus asuntos. En ocasiones también miran en video las películas que algún viajero trajo de la India.

Pero saben que tarde o temprano sus costumbres dejarán lugar a las locales –ya hay un indio que se casó con una argentina–. Los más chicos, como Sonia Mónica y Franco Alberto, entienden la lengua de sus padres pero no la hablan y sí el castellano.

Bikram, por su parte, pese a ser el mayor y supuestamente el bastión de la tradición, permanece inalterable frente a todos estos cambios. Tal vez se podría pensar que frente al cambio de los menores pudiese reaccionar con una reafirmación de sus propios valores. Quizá desea pasar sus últimos años en su país natal, donde residen sus fuentes. Pero él no se deja engañar por todo esto. "Claro que me gustaría volver a la India, pero a pasear no más. No para vivir. Allá está muy duro, hay guerra civil... Si aquí tengo para comer y beber, ¿para qué voy a querer ir a otro lado?"

Gustavo Javier Wrobel
Fotos: Alfredo Calascione

APPENDIX 4

Excerpts from Gadari Baba's Books

DIARY GADRI BABA HARJAP SINGH BY GURMEET KAUR DHAMI (p. 82)

After staying in Europe for some time, he (Bhai Ratan Singh) went towards countries like Brazil, Panama, Argentina and China. Members of Gadar Party were present in these countries. Pandit Jawaharlal Nehru and Bhai Ratan Singh represented the Congress and Gadar Party respectively. Bhai Ji (Ratan Singh) was in France itself when flames of the current (Second World War) war spread. France also joined the war. The French government arrested him in 1939 itself. There was no information about him; thereafter possibly, he may be passing his time in some jail in France.

FROM *NIRBHAI YODHA GADRI BABE GURMUKH SINGH DI JIWANI* BY BHAGAT SINGH BILGA, Chapter 7, pp. 65–7, February 1926

Ratan Singh (one of the members of Gadar Party), in consultation with Gurmukh, reached Mexico with a view to collect funds. However, he was unsuccessful in proceeding further to America. Gadar Party sent Ratan Singh on a tour of the branches of Gadar Party at Panama, Brazil and Argentina. Panama branch collected a huge amount and sent it to the 'Workers Newspaper'. He met Sardar Ajit Singh in Brazil. Discussions with him continued for many days. Even at that time Sardar Ajit Singh was all set to launch a movement for the complete independence of India, though Ajit Singh did not subscribe to the communist views of Ratan Singh, yet he was not against them either. Ratan Singh wished to motivate Sardar Ajit Singh towards Communist ideology (for more information refer the book, *Gadar Lehar de Anfole Varke*). Proceeding further from here, Ratan Singh reached the Rosario (Argentina) branch of the Gadar Party. At that time, Ratan Singh was travelling on an Afghan passport. This passport had expired. The British government had no inkling whatsoever of this tour of Ratan Singh. Rosario branch of Gadar Party took advantage of this and obtained a passport in the name of Labh Singh Jamsher from the British Council by declaring him an umemployed Indian labourer. A lot of Punjabi immigrants had reached Argentina after trying their luck all over. They were spread all over Argentina. Ratan Singh took Bhagat Singh along with him and toured Northern Argentina. He was accompanied by Boojha Singh Chack Maidas during his tour of South Argentina. Bhai Ratan Singh used to propagate the ideology of Soviet Russia. He used to openly proclaim, 'Get educated about revolution from Moscow University and reach India to fight for the freedom of India. The Gadar Party is once again geared up to fight against the British'. He used to raise the slogan openly, 'Now the way to freedom is to attack Delhi, via Moscow'.

Even though neither he was a good orator nor an expert in teaching maxims, yet the people were greatly impressed by his propaganda in simple language. They contributed towards the fund for *Kirti* (Workers) newspaper. The Argentina dollar was almost equivalent to one rupee. Due to the impact of his propaganda only, about seven Gadarites (members of the Gadar Party) reached Moscow University from Argentina and thereafter established workers and peasants' organizations in India when they reached there.

Teja Singh Sutantar, after getting his rank of a military officer, reached America on a Turkish passport. He annihilated the syndicate opposed to the Gadar Party in America and reorganized the Gadar Party on democratic lines and imparted training in guerrilla warfare to the units of the Gadar Party. He collected a huge amount by way of donation and dispatched the same to India through the Kabul Centre. The British government pressurized the American government, who directed Teja Singh to leave America. Thereafter, Teja Singh reached Panama where Bhai Ratan Singh was already present. At that time, the Panama Branch contributed the maximum towards funding the Gadar Party. After meeting Sardar Ajit Singh in Brazil, Teja Singh reached Argentina. Sardar Ajit Singh also reached Argentina. Both of them drew a plan to reach India and start a revolution against the British rule. British Intelligence agents were tracing the movements of Teja Singh. They approached the Government of Argentina and got the police to conduct searches in the office of the Gadar Party. During his stay of about one year in Argentina, Teja Singh selected the jungles of the hilly area of northern Argentina to impart practical training in guerrilla warfare. He gave training in the manufacture of gun cotton, sealing it in an iron case and blowing up hills and bridges. At night, he got gun cotton placed in a tunnel of a hill and demonstrated the blasting of a portion of the hill. Use of compass was also taught to find the direction of specific places so that one could reach there with the help of a map. Practical training in map reading was also imparted. A guerrilla must have the knowledge of all these things.

Political upheavals are a common occurrence in South America. Teja Singh had a narrow escape during one such upheaval. During his stay in Argentina, Teja Singh had even readied a guerrilla squad to be sent to India. Ajit Singh and Teja Singh were in favour of reaching India directly, whereas Bhai Ratan Singh was for receiving education at Moscow and then proceeding to India. The Gadar Party gave the green signal to the proposal of Bhai Ratan Singh. Accordingly, all the Gadarites, numbering about one hundred, including Teja Singh, Bhagat Singh and other students from New Zealand, Fiji, Kenya and India, reached Moscow.

APPENDIX 5

Economic Times, Sunday 12 July 1998

The real Dan Singh

...and all his namesakes are standing tall in Argentina.
Arthur J Pais ***speaks to the patriarch***

ARGENTINA has many Dhan Singhs. One is a successful fleet owner who came some six decades ago along with hundreds of fellow Sikhs and hardly any savings from India. They've created a tiny, vibrant community here of just about 1,000 people of Sikh origin and many of them are products of marriage between Sikhs and Argentinians.

There is also Dhan Singh, who at 81, is sprightly and mentally alert -the dean of the Indian community in Argentina.

And there is Dhan Singh, father of Virginia — a successful lawyer who has made an impressive but unsuccessful bid for more than six years to win an election to the national Parliament.

From time to time, the Argentina mainstream media seeks Dhan Singh's counsel. When Mother Teresa was ailing he was asked to comment. And when she died, his views were sought.

About two dozen Indians had arrived in Argentina in the first quarter of the century. Though they were bound for America, they were dumped on the way on various Caribbean islands. It was largely by accident that they were able to make it to Argentina. They hoped to reach America through the land route after working in Argentina for several years. But most, like Dhan Singh, married the local women and stayed put.

This Dhan Singh's story is little different. Born in Bhatinda district of Punjab and raised in Calcutta, he had no explicit desire to go to America. "One day I read in a Calcutta newspaper of the possibility of migrating to Argentina," he says. The news story mentioned Argentina was looking for hundreds of workers for its farms. "I also heard from some people in government who had visited Argentina that it was very much like India, very green and beautiful."

He did not hesitate to use up his meagre savings and sail for the New World, along with four of his friends. After a journey that took nearly a year, they reached Argentina in 1937. Dhan Singh was barely 20.

"I did not want to work for the British in India," he says -one of the strongest reasons for leaving. Naturally, he did not want to work for the British-run Argentinian Railway unlike two dozen Indians

ENCOUNTER

STANDING TALL: Dan Singh

who had come to Argentina about a decade before his arrival.

In some ways, his entry could never have been as traumatic as the few dozen Sikh soldiers of the British Army who at the end of the Boer War sought to go to America and Canada in search of better job opportunities. Many of them were dumped by the greedy and conscienceless agents at various ports in the Caribbean or the coasts of South America. These men knew little English -only Punjabi.

So when Dhan Singh arrived in Argentina, the few Punjabis in Buenos Aires helped him find a simple and inexpensive place to live and cook Indian food. Singh believes that given his cosmopolitan and pragmatic outlook, he did not expect problems in Argentina. Besides, he explains, he was much younger than the men who had preceded him. And being young meant that he could learn to read and write fluent Spanish.

"I blended with Argentina easily," he says. "It was the human warmth that influenced my decision to settle."

Though many Argentinians had misconceptions about Sikhs, once understood the Sikh religion and culture, their doubts and fear disappeared.

After doing odd jobs for nearly a year he became a truck driver. When he reminisces his truck driver days, Dhan Singh laughs saying it was a given thing in many towns and villages that if you can't make a decent living through education, you should at least drive a truck and earn some money.

It took him over two decades to find real success. He bought a number of grocery stores and began purchasing land. Marrying an Argentinian woman certainly helped. Together, they raised seven children.

Despite his preoccupation with business, Dhan Singh still found time to establish Hindustanica Association of Salta. Soon he would raise money to construct a small gurudwara in Rosario de la Frontera in Salta province, which was converted into an imposing but compact gurudwara about a decade ago.

Attached to it is a community centre. Dhan Singh has also reserved a part of his estate for the cremation rites of Hindus and Sikhs.

The gentleman now leads a semi-retired life but says he cannot really retire. For he has been working even before he became a teenager and since he has seen his hard work yield fruit, he says he is superstitious about surrendering himself to full-time retirement.

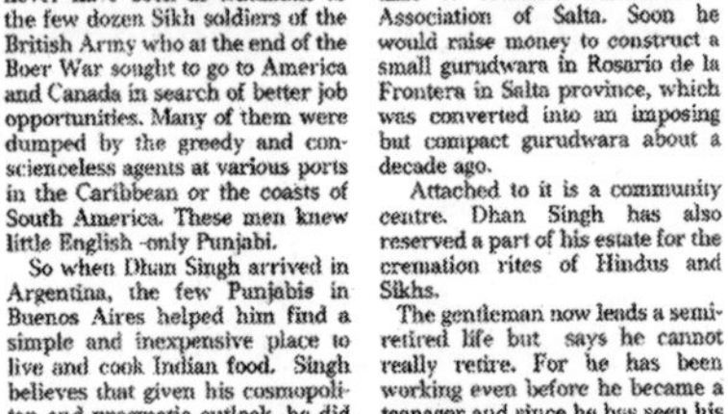

WARM WELCOME: Dan Singh greets Giani Zail Singh in 1884

APPENDIX 6

My Twenty Years in the Fiji Islands and the Story of the Haunted Line*

In my 21 years the story is told of a confrontation between a group of Punjabis and a European lawyer named Berkeley—but the account there makes several critical mistakes. The barrister Humphrey Berkeley did in 1912 take £25 each from 46 Punjabis who wanted to go to the Argentine Republic. He was brought to court and ordered to make a refund. The Punjabis were definitely cheated of their money by legal devices and connivances. But the rest of the facts as recorded in the court notebook and the *Fiji Times* (March to June 1912) do not match the details cited in my 21 years. According to those records and accounts, what happened was as follows.

In 1911 some Punjabi men set-off from the Punjab for 'the Argentine'. Said their leader, Armah Singh, in court: 'I heard about the Argentine in my own country. I came to Fiji because I thought it was the same as the Argentine, I don't know where the Argentine is.' When they learned that Fiji was not the Argentine they determined to go on. They were not indentured and had some money, and were advised to go to see Humphrey Berkeley. Berkeley was a leading barrister, who was brought to the Supreme Court six times as a defendant in civil cases from 1901 to 1912, five times for non-payment of debt, and once for fraudulent misrepresentation. He was never a plaintiff there, and almost always a loser. He lost all his debt cases (perhaps simply forcing court actions in order to delay payments) and settled the fraud case with a series of payments before the court case reached a final determination. He was also, in 1912, a very sick man, who was hospitalized before his legal

*By Totaram Sandhya, tr. & ed. John Dunham Kelly and Uttra Kumari Singh, Fiji Museum 1991.

battle with the Punjabis was complete, and who died long before matters were resolved for them.

What Berkeley did or did not promise the Punjabis was in dispute in the court testimony. It was likely that in part there was failure to communicate between Berkeley and the Punjabis. In many other court cases of the time there were complaints about the inability of the professional court translators to comprehend the testimony of Punjabi policeman, and barrister simply relied on their own clerks or whoever they could find to do their translating for them? But beyond the language barriers there were many profound divergences of claim. Most importantly, the Punjabis asserted that they always had intended to go to the Argentine, and had been promised passage there by Berkeley. Berkeley and his translators swore that they made it clear to the Punjabis that going to the Argentine was impossible, and that they were trying to arrange some other kind of voyage for the Punjabis, to San Francisco, Portland, Panama, Tonga or the New Hebrides—'any free country' that would have them.

What is clear is that in January 1912 Berkeley began accepting £25 each from the Punjabis. He had a plan—would use the money to buy and refit an old ship, the 'Clansman', which was for sale in the harbour, a boat now unwanted with the end of Polynesian labour recruiting. He would give the boat to captain, crew, and ship's doctor in lieu of wages at the end of the voyage, and thus keep as profit for himself whatever was left after outfitting the boat. Berkeley further decided on an arbitrary £3 3s fee for himself for each passage, did his mathematics, and told the Punjabis to pay him the £25 each, and that he required there to be fifty of them in order for passage to be arranged.

Armah Singh was the first to pay his £25, and then he and others recruited among local Punjabis for the extra men needed to reach the total of fifty. Ten men were recruited in Ba, and Punjabi money and Punjabis began to fill Berkeley's office. When he had gathered enough money, Berkeley bought the ship for £400 and had the refitting begun. He claimed in court that the Punjabis knew all about the plan; they claimed simply to have paid for passage. Once a total of £1110 was in Berkeley's hands, a leaving date was set. Said one of the Punjabis in court:

On the 20th I went to Mr. Berkeley's house with all my belongings, but went on board no ship. I know that Armah Singh got another piece of paper from Mr. Berkeley. It stated that it promised to take us on board on the 15th, I don't know of what month. No vessel was ready on that day. (From FT)

Berkeley's side of the story was that the Punjabis were crowding his office, and then when he got sick, pestering him at home. Finally he promised them a sailing date of 15 March. He said, 'The letter stating the date and sailing was written to get rid of the Punjabis when I was ill—(an aide) supplied the date. I wrote that if the ship did not sail on or about 15 March the money would be returned.'

What Berkeley had not reckoned on was that the ship inspection of the Harbour Master was much stricter for ships going on longer voyages. What was acceptable for an old ship making runs to the Solomons was not acceptable for ship intending to cross the entire Pacific. The ship was in such pathetic shape that each inspection found expensive new problems, and things reached a point where Berkeley would have to spend some of his £3 3s a head profit (which he had calculated and extracted from £1110 on the basis of 50 paid fares although there were only 46 to travel) in order to make the ship ready. There work stopped and 15 March soon passed.

The Punjabis complained to the Agent-General for immigration and to the Colonial Secretary—they later, after Berkeley's death, even raised money to send Armah Singh to argue their case before the Secretary of State for the Colonies in London. On 29 March Berkeley was again a defendant in court, not the Supreme Court but Suva Police Court, sued by W.H. Brabant, Chief Inspector of customs at Suva, on behalf of 'one Armah Singh, a Punjabi', for £25 and £10 compensation. Intense battles followed over jurisdiction, wording of the complaint and the interpretation of Section 328 of Merchant's Shipping Act, the last being the license for Brabant to bring suit, on instructions from the government. Berkeley and his lawyers used every device they could to dodge proceedings. However, at the end of the trial the Judge found against Berkeley, and ordered the £25 refunded and an additional £5 to be paid as compensation.

Unfortunately for the Punjabis, Berkeley appealed. On 21 May Berkeley entered the hospital, on 29 May an appeal on ten grounds was heard on his behalf by the Supreme Court, and on 12 June he died. But before he died he won. On 1 June, for the only time this century, Berkeley won as a defendant in the Fiji Supreme Court. The Chief Justice ruled that the Punjabi Armah Singh, and by implication all the Punjabis were not owed a refund because they had no specific contract with Berkeley, in particular no contract for a voyage to the Argentine. The Judge ruled that Berkeley had simply promised to do his best to find them a passage, but was not a 'passage broker, or as it might be termed, an emigration runner' (from FT). Critical to this decision was the way the judge resolved the conflict in testimony about planned and promised destinations, and leaving dates. He resolved it with reference to a document, not to the letter Berkeley wrote while sick, but the receipt given by Berkeley to the Punjabi. The receipt noted that Berkeley was paid £25 (not, as Sandhya and Chaturvedi asserted, only £16) but it did not state that Berkeley promised to provide passage to the Argentine. Thus, the judge ruled, there was no contract for this specific performance, and thus Berkeley had not broken any contract. The decision of the lower court was reversed with costs.

The Punjabis did, finally, reach the Argentine. On 6 June 1912 the government was already considering a plan to sell liabilities on the vessel. By 13 December the Punjabis had received this money amounting to 5 shillings per pound originally spent (i.e. 25 per cent), and they left that day for the Argentine via Wellington. Prior to their departure a warning was given to them, and to Indians generally, that according to the Secretary of State for India, who had made inquiries, there was little hope for employment in the Argentine. But Punjabis were apparently willing to take the risk. On 23 January 1913, Mr. J.J. Davies returned from having escorted the Punjabis as far as Wellington. He reported the amount of their savings, which he had held for them until they sailed for Buenos Aires—£2,700 in gold. Supporting these savings to be earnings made in Fiji, the *Fiji Times* of that day noted, 'what possibilities there seem to be in this country for Indians'. Davies added that 'the men went without giving any trouble whatever'.

The case of Humphrey Berkeley and the Punjabis, or as it was known at the time, 'the Clansman affair', well illustrates two general themes to Indians' problems in civil courts in 1912. The first, here in extreme form, was ignorance—ignorance of the legal forms and formulae necessary to protect one's self in contractual arrangements, and ignorance of the forms of Western culture in general. The Punjabis, with not know the names of the months, or even where the Argentine was. Legal documents were all 'pieces of paper', with promises written on them that the Punjabis could not read, but remembered from translated verbal explanations. Indian testimony in Civil cases in general abounded in references to 'pieces of paper', which could be contracts, leases, wills, warrants, simple letters, or nothing relevant to their business at all. The promises remembered in connection with them only occasionally matched their 'written content'.

THE FINAL RECKONING OF THE CLANSMAN CASE

It was described in the Appendix essay how Berkeley manipulated accounting procedures to secure his own profit mortgage and mortgage registration fees totalling £6.6.0 and a further interest charge of £3.5.10. Further, they charged a 5 per cent commission on the sale, i.e. £2315.0 and advance his own interests. However, government records of the sale of the Clansman reveal that many others also took a generous share of the Punjabis' money. To get a fuller picture of the number of individuals and public and private institutions who, on solid legal grounds, took full recompense for themselves before the Punjabis received their meagre returns, we need only consider the accounts of the final sale of the Clansman, prepared by Morris Hedstrom Limited, and the legal firm of Crompton and Muspratt, which is still on file in the Fiji National Archives, in Colonial Secretary's Office minute paper #4816 of 1912.

The Clansman was sold on July 31 to the Union Steamship Company of New Zealand for £475. If this amount in full had been returned to the Punjabis, they would have had close to half their original money back. Instead, however, Cromptons and Morris Hedstrom made several deductions and gave the government only £283.1.2 for the Punjabis' benefit. The largest single deduction was an advance of £140 given on 7 May against the eventual sale. This advance was not for the Punjabis, but rather for the European crew that had been hired to undertake the journey of the Clansman to anywhere, and even though this crew never sailed the Clansman anywhere, and even though the Punjabis were told that the money tied up in the Clansman was unavailable until the boat was sold, these Europeans were able to arrange a tidy settlement for themselves that included passages for all to Sydney. Another set of deductions from the sale sum were for expense connected with the boat: £2.10.0 for towing, £10.1.0 for a watchman, 2/6 for 'goods'. Finally, Morris Hedstrom Limited made deductions for their own financial benefit. Connected with the advance, which they considered a mortgage, were a mortgage and mortgage registration fees totalling £6.6.0, and further interest charge of £3.5.10. Further they charged a 5 per cent commission on the sale, i.e. £23.15.0.

Crompton and Muspratt took the £288.19.8 remaining from Morris Hedstrom Limited and then made deductions of their own: £55.0 for the probate of Humphrey Berkeley's over the remainder, £283.1.2, to the government for distribution to the Punjabis.

In all these proceedings, everyone except the Punjabis got full value for every claim they made. The Punjabis alone of those involved were without legal skills, standing and leverage, and they alone bore all costs and losses for the entire affair. The only exception to this generalization is that the government did not charge them for the case brought on their behalf. This was considered but was found to be both inappropriate and impossible anyway, since technically the case was brought by a government officer.

The same CSO minute paper, #4816 of 1912, also includes the petition from the Punjabis asking the government to take court action on their behalf. All forty-six Punjabis marked the petition, but only sixteen of them could sign their names, and of these, fifteen out of sixteen signatures were in Devanagari, unreadable to untrained Europeans. Only one could sign with Roman letters; thirty simply marked with an 'x'. The petition itself was written in English. However, it was not prepared by the Punjabis, but instead by an interpreter, Abdul Aziz Khan, who notes at its end that he has 'interpreted and explained the contents to the persons who signed this before me'.

APPENDIX 7

Travel Notes

Inderjit Singh Jaijee

Mr. Jaijee, used to work for Dunlop and was my neighbour in Calcutta in the early 1970s. Later on he settled in Chandigarh and became an MLA from Punjab. He is connected to the Patiala family. These notes are based on his expedition to South America (1979). When the author was in Belize, Philip Singh, a local resident, recollected having met a Sikh while he was passing through Belize.

ARGENTINA—Notes

Names of the people met:

Karam Singh Giani,	Granthi
S. Gurdial Singh	San Pedro de Jujuey
S. Piara Singh	"
Kamar Singh	"
Dhan Singh	Rosario de Salto
Surjit Singh	San Pedro de Jujuey
Rakha Singh	"
Chanan Singh	"
Jiva Singh	Rosario de Salto
S. Tara Singh	"
S. Chanan Singh	San Sarvdor de Jujuey
S. Achar Singh	Buenous Aires
Maj. Gen. Satinder Singh	"
Dr. Bali	"
S. Gurdial Singh Transporter	Tukman
Nama Singh	"
Thakur Singh	"
Kuldeep Singh	Gomez (oldest inhabitant)

They use national colours on their trucks Indian flag flown prominently. Old copy of *Guru Granth Sahib* 1923. Very few people can read it. Would like to have it exchanged with printed version. SGPC to be approached in this regard. Very large helping of prashad. Marriage with only ardas. Ardas without covering head. Sit down on chairs with having parshad in plates. Trouble over shifting of *Guru Granth Sahib Bir* to Rosario or another suitable place.

The earlier settler came during First World War and settled initially in Gumes, Province Salta. There are still 16 persons there. A large number of our Indians have married locally and their offspring speak only Spanish. Do not know the mother-tongue. All the Indians talk among themselves in Spanish. Punjabi is used only occasionally, particularly when they have to vent out annoyance. Not a single Indian understands English. A few people have taken university education. Amongst them is S. Gurdial Singh's daughter who is a psychologist. Two daughters of S. Harbans Singh, one daughter of S. Rakha Singh and one or two others. All university educated Indians are girls. Boys generally join the family business at an early age. A number of girls study up to school level and become teachers. Only one Indian boy is now studying at the university. Sports is regarded more as a professional activity. People who attend university and college are keener on watching it than in actual participation. Argentineans, as a rule, are very fond of sports. Main sporting activities being football, hockey, boxing, basketball, polo, horse racing. Indians are not keen on joining these sports. Nor are the Indians keen on joining government service for two reasons. (1) They are not keen on higher studies, (2) Government jobs do not pay well. It appears in Argentina, rich people take university education more for prestige purpose. For the school at San Pedro, Indians have donated three rooms. The rooms have been dedicated to Tagore, Gandhi and Nehru. The school celebrates the day of Indian Independence, 15th August by hoisting the Indian flag. The flag is also hoisted at Plaza de la Nations. Each year, the Indian community makes a donation to the school in the form of books, uniform, etc. Most of the settlers are Gills, Sidhus, Dhariwals, Grewals, etc. Almost all the settlers are Jat Sikhs.

South America in general has a joint family system. There is relatively less tension in mother-in-law and daughter-in-law relations. There are a few cases of divorce or desertion amongst the Sikhs. This is highly appreciated by the local society where marital ties are stronger than in the USA and Europe. Sikhs easily pick up local partners, as they are regarded as stable marriage partners. Most of the Sikhs still retain their Indian passports. A Punjabi is regarded as a hard worker and is respected by financial institutions where he is given preference to other communities, including the Argentineans.

Punjabis are farmers as well as wholesale dealers in essential commodities and are backed by large resources. They buy from the factories and sell to retailers. The margin of profit is 10 per cent but due to competition, it invariably comes down to 3–4 per cent on fast moving items like wheat, sugar, oil, rice, etc. On slow moving items the margin is higher. Inflation, however, is worrying the distributors. The retail seller is allowed a higher margin of profit. The check on the prices is the prevailing market rate. For example, wheat, rice, sugar, etc., do not fetch more than 2–3 per cent in the retail market. Both retailers and distributors generally then drop prices of fast moving items to attract the customers and make margin on the slow moving items.

1. Indian Publicity Department has done very little towards projecting the image of the country.
2. The general standard of living in Argentina is the same as in north India.
3. The Punjabis work as distributors of general merchandise, farmers, and transporters and take up jobs as mill workers and shop assistants.
4. Along with their own ceremonies, the Punjabis have adopted the ceremonies of the Christians of Argentina like baptism of children, adopting godfathers, etc. This happens in the cases where the children of these Punjabi settlers have married locally.
5. In case they marry locally, then the person after death is buried according to the local customs. The Indians are trusted and in case of loan by banks or credit by companies, they are given preference over locals or other communities.

6. In most cases, the women who get married to Indians in Argentina do not work as wages given to women in Argentina are not attractive enough.
7. The Indians have objected to the use of the word 'Indu'. They feel that Indian news regarding them should mention the word Indian instead of using the word 'Indu' as this reduces them to the level of the local Indians who in point of development are still far behind.
8. Indians do not, however, earn enough to go back to Argentina as wages and earnings are not attractive enough due to frequent inflation.
9. Great similarity between Punjabis and Argentineans specially in northern province where the percentage of local Indians is very large. This, however, tends to drown our people's cultural superiority due to being confused with the local Indians.
10. In Buenos Aires, respect for Indians is very great. A road, and a club have been named after India. Tagore is held in very high regard. So is Gandhi, Nehru and Mrs. Gandhi. Argentina had tried to follow the policy of neutrality earlier. But not now. Victoria Ocampo, a highly respected poetess of Argentina, was a disciple of Tagore and popularized Indian culture in Argentina.
11. Baba Teja Singh Swatantar came to Argentina to raise funds for the Indian revolutionary movement and also lived in Argentina for a while.

They think of Indians as very poor people, a country of perpetual famine but culturally advanced. Indian yoga has been well popularized. Our philosophy, music and dance are held in high esteem.

In North Argentina, land and climate, vegetables and fruits are almost the same as found in Punjab. The land is more fertile as it is a virgin land. The landholdings are very large but area under active cultivation is small. For instance, an Indian might hold 6,000 hectares out of which only about 2 hectares would be under actual cultivation. Only a few Indians have holdings above 25,000 acres but cultivate only 4,000–6,000 acres. Land price of a developed land ranges between 2,000 and 4,000 rupees per acre but they take only one crop per year except in case of vegetables where they take up to two crops. Due to lack of irrigation, they depend more on rain. Farm machinery is very expensive. Government loans to farmers are not popular due to inflation. Loans are given in dollars at 12 per cent interest but they have to be returned in dollars taking into account the depreciated value of the peso. Most Indians have retained their Indian passports. They do not interfere in local politics.

AUTHOR'S COMMENTS

Interesting observations on education of immigrants, professions adopted, financial status, marriages, joint family living, image of Indians, farming, farm and commercial loans, image of Sikhs and India, their philanthropy, etc. It is heartening to see their attachment to India and liberal outlook by naming donations under names of Tagore, Nehru and Gandhi. Their support of the Ghadar movement in early part of the twentieth century is commendable. Similarities between Punjab and North Argentina are significant. The immigrants interest in *SGGS* despite there being no gurdwara is to be noted. Gurdwara has since been established.

A Brazillian Sikh

LLANY

CHANDIGARH TRIBUNE, MONDAY, JANUARY 16, 2006

Sikh who runs only gurdwara in Brazil

TRIBUNE NEWS SERVICE

CHANDIGARH, JANUARY 15

Sohbag Kaur Khalsa, an American Sikh settled in Brazil, is running the only gurdwara in the country. Carrying the legacy of her late husband forward Sohbag, a yoga teacher, says there are no Sikhs but the gurdwara in San Paulo still runs packed with Brazilians who are regular visitors.

Relating the story of how she and her husband, a Brazilian who had become a Sikh while in the USA, laid the foundation stone of Guru Arjun Dev Gurdwara, Ms Khalsa said, "Nobody knew Sikhs in Brazil. We were the only two turbaned persons in ily dream and we broke ground in 2000. We made a a guesthouse for visitors and a clinic. On the second floor, the gurdwara is built."

It was a huge task for the couple to build the gurdwara since there was no other Sikh sangat in the city to support the project. So, they went to the USA and had stayed with their family and worked for eight months to earn money for the project.

They were able to save $10,000. During a vacation to the USA, she found out that her husband was suffering from cancer which was now in its terminal stage. So, they decided to start the gurdwara so that her husband could see it happening

On June 6, 2004, the gurdwara was inaugurated. Sohbag's husband, performed the ardas, his last public appearance. And then he died.

Born in Pennysylvania, Sohbag holds a degree in social work and started yoga while living in Maine. Then, she quit her job and moved to Boston where she began research on yoga and met Yogi Harbhajan Singh and became a Sikh.

Now, Ms Khalsa has come to admit two of her three children at the Miri Piri Academy. "I have come after 25 years to India. A lot has changed. Inflation is going up and cleanliness and purity is going down. I had a keen desire to see Harmander Sahib. So, I flew into Amritsar. My two sons, Ajit and Gobind, have been admitted to the Miri Piri Academy at Cheharta near Amritsar while my daughter is a web designer," she adds.

Sohbag Kaur Khalsa

APPENDIX 9

Peanut King

IN ARGENTINA, TURBANS = MAHARAJAS?

If you want royal treatment at nightclubs in Argentina, maybe you should consider investing in a turban! While playing golf in Buenos Aires recently, R. Viswanathan, the Indian ambassador to Argentina, Uruguay and Paraguay, had an interesting experience: the Argentinean players asked him where they could buy a turban and how to wear it. When the ambassador probed the reason for their interest, they pointed to a home within the country club complex and said:

'Here lives an Indian maharaja. He looks handsome with his turban. When he goes to the night clubs, he gets premium service and gets it free because they think he is a maharaja.'

When Viswanathan tried to explain that turbans do not equal maharaja status, the Argentineans asked him to shut up and not reveal this secret at the night clubs.

Turns out the 'maharaja' in question was Simmar Pal Singh, the 'peanut prince of Argentina', an employee of Olam, a 5.6 billion dollar NRI company and a leading global supply chain manager of agricultural products and food ingredients!

Simmar Pal Singh cultivates 12,000 hectares of peanut farms and another 5,000 hectares of soya and corn in Rio Cuarto area in Cordoba province, about 1,000 km from Buenos Aires. His target is to take his company Olam among Argentina's top three peanut players in the next few years. When he came to Argentina in 2005, his company was 28th in ranking in peanuts and he has already made it sixth this year. Argentina is the second largest exporter of peanuts after China, accounting for 25 per cent of the world trade in kernels. Rio Cuarto region produces high-quality peanuts with its ideal soil and agroclimatic conditions.

Simmar Pal came to Argentina in 2005 to buy peanuts for the company. When he found that the farmers preferred to sell their products to established companies and were hesitant to deal with new buyers, he proposed to his company that they should go into farming themselves. This was something new for the company which had been operating only in the field of trading and processing.

Seeing the fire in Simmar Pal's belly and the shine in his eyes, they wanted to give him a chance. He started off with leasing 700 hectares of land and grew peanuts.

It was a success. The company let him lease additional acreage. This year he has cultivated 17,000 hectares including 2,000 hectares in the province of Salta, about 700 km from Rio Cuarto. He has plans to continue the increase in acreage and grow other crops such as wheat, soya and pulses. Some of these and especially pulses could be exported.

In India, we have irrigation canals, dams, ground water pumps and issues of water table going down and free electricity for farmers. Argentines are free from these issues since their agriculture is almost entirely rain-fed. The rain gods take care of the rest!

Argentina could be a long-term source of supply of grains, oil seeds and pulses to India. Already India is importing from Argentina soya and sunflower oil for about $700 million a year. There are occasional imports of wheat. Sikhs/Punjabis and other Indians could go beyond imports and invest in agribusiness in Argentina. There is no restriction on foreign investment in agriculture. A number of foreign companies and individuals own land here. Cost of the most productive land is $15,000, which, I am told is cheaper than in Punjab. The Argentine yield per hectare is about three times higher than that of India in soya, peanuts and some other crops.

I hope other Sikh/Punjabi and Indian entrepreneurs will come to invest in Argentina, inspired by the successful example of Peanut Prince Simmar Pal Singh!

But, they should not forget the turbans.

(Courtesy: IANS)
Article by R. Vishwanathan, 3 June 2009

(*Author's note*: Mr. Vishwanathan is known for his 'Being Passionate about Latin America' theme. His website is worth visiting. He is promoting India to the South American countries—culturally, commercially and of course golf wise.)

APPENDIX 10

HLC Report: Estimated Size of Overseas Indian Community: Country-wise

(December 2001)

Country	PIOs	Indian citizens	Stateless	Total
Argentina	500			500
Algeria	5	40		45
Andorra		200		200
Angola	45	250		295
Argentina	1,200	400		1,600
Armenia		200		200
Australia	160,000	30,000		190,000
Austria	3,005	8,940		11,945
Azerbaijan		250		250
Bahrain	Nil	130,000		130,000
Barbados	2,100	100		2,200
Belarus		70		70
Belgium	Nil	7,000		7,000
Belize	500			500
Benin	450			450
Bhutan		1,500		1,500
Botswana	3,000	6,000		9,000
Brazil	1,500	400		1,900
Brunei	500	7,000	100	7,600
Bulgaria		20		20
Burundi	300			300
Cambodia	150	150		300
Cameroon	250			250
Canada	700,000	150,000	1,000	851,000
Cape Verde	4			4
Chad	125			125
Chile	39	611		650
China	5	300		305
Colombia	1	19		20
Comorons	50			50
Costa Rica	1	15		16

Country	PIOs	Indian citizens	Stateless	Total
Cote d'Ivoire	30	270		300
Croatia	10			10
Cyprus		300		300
Czech Republic	20	400		420
Denmark	900	1,252		2,152
Djibouti	280			280
Dominica		20		20
Ecuador		5		5
Egypt	40	1,350		1,390
Eritrea	30	1,723		1,753
Ethiopia	34	700		734
Fiji	336,579	250		336,829
Finland	410	750	10	1,170
France	55,000	10,000		65,000
G. Bissau	25			25
Gambia	135			135
Germany	10,000	25,000		35,000
Ghana	2,000	1,800		3,800
Greece		7,000		7,000
Guadeloupe	40,000			40,000
Guatemala	22			22
Guyana	395,250	100		395,350
Hong Kong	28,500	22,000		50,500
Indonesia	50,000	5,000		55,000
Iran		800		800
Iraq	50	60		110
Ireland	600	1,000		1,600
Israel	45,000	300		45,300
Italy	36,000	35,500		71,500
Jamaica	60,000	1,500		61,500
Japan	1,000	9,000		10,000
Jordan	30	900		930
Kazakhstan		1,127		1,127
Kenya	85,000	15,000	2,500	102,500
Korea (DPRK)		5		5
Korea (ROK)	200	2,500		2,700
Kuwait	1,000	294,000		295,000
Kyrgyzstan	100			100
Laos	18	107		125
Lebanon	25	11,000		11,025
Libya	400	12,000		12,400

Country	PIOs	Indian citizens	Stateless	Total
Lithuania		5		5
Madagascar	25,000	3,000	1,000	29,000
Malaysia	1,600,000	15,000	50,000	1,665,000
Maldives	1	9,000		9,001
Mali	20			20
Mauritius	704,640	11,116		715,756
Mexico	400			400
Mongolia		35		35
Morocco	25	350		375
Mozambique	20,000	870		20,870
Myanmar	2,500,000	2,000	400,000	2,902,000
Namibia	32	78		110
Netherlands	200,000	15,000	2,000	217,000
New Zealand	50,000	5,000		55,000
Nigeria	8,000	17,000		25,000
Norway		5,630		5,630
Oman	1,000	311,000		312,000
P.N. Guinea		1,000		1,000
Panama	211	1,953		2,164
Peru	10	135		145
Philippines	24,000	2,000	12,000	38,000
Poland	75	750		825
Portugal	65,000	5,000		70,000
Qatar	1,000	130,000		131,000
Reunion Islands	220,000	55		220,055
Romania	2	489		491
Russia	44	16,000		16,044
Saudi Arabi		1,500,000		1,500,000
Senegal	13	8		21
Seychelles	2,000	3.000		5,000
Singapore	217,000	90,000		307,000
Slovakia		100		100
Solomon Islands		20		20
South Africa				1,000,000
Spain	16,000	13,000		29,000
St. Lucia		200		200
St. Vincent & The Grenadines		160		160
Sudan	300	1,200		1,500
Surinam	150,306	150		150,456
Sweden	9,000	2,000		11,000

Country	PIOs	Indian citizens	Stateless	Total
Switzerland	8,400	4,800	300	13,500
Syria	1,800			1,800
Taiwan	1,800			1,800
Tajikistan	nil	400		400
Tanzania	85,000	5,000		90,000
Thailand	70,000	15,000		85,000
Trinidad & Tobago	500,000	600		500,600
Tunisia		70		70
Turkey		300		300
UAE	50,000	900,000		950,000
Uganda	7,000	5,000		12,000
UK				1,200,000
Ukraine		3,400		3,400
USA				1,678,760
Uzbekistan	40	650		690
Vanuatu		50		50
Venezuela	400	280	10	690
Vietnam		320		320
Yemen	100,000	900		100,900
Zambia	10,00	3,000		13,000
Zimbabwe	15,500	1,200		16,700

Index